Praise for
HOW TO SAY IT: GRANTWRITING

"Above all, Koch is aware of the importance of using language well. If the proposals that come from her readers are as clear, lively, and readable as the book itself, funders may even come to enjoy reviewing proposals."

—Benjamin R. Shute Jr., Program Director of Democratic Practice and
Corporate Secretary Emeritus of Rockefeller Brothers Fund

"Ms. Koch outlines in clear, simple English the strategies for writing a great proposal. Nothing will guarantee funding but a well-crafted, strategic, and well-researched grant proposal is certainly the first critical step."

—Ali Webb, Deputy Director of W. K. Kellogg Foundation

"Much of the success between funders and grantees rests on successful communication. Following Koch's proposal guidance would put this important relationship on a solid footing from the very beginning."

—Len Finocchio, Senior Program Officer of
California HealthCare Foundation

"Like a good proposal, Deborah Koch's book is well constructed and written in a way that speaks to its audience. It completely demystifies the proposal-writing process and deconstructs it in an easy to understand way. This book is an excellent resource that guides writers through the process of composing a proposal so that it clearly and persuasively conveys the importance of the project and the organization's ability to carry it out. Even as a seasoned grantwriter I found this book to be fresh, insightful, and very useful."

—Margaret Arthurs, Director of Corporate, Foundation, and
Government Relations of Hartwick College

"This is the most helpful and logical guide on grantwriting that I have seen in my long career of doing biomedical research. Ms. Koch has clearly 'been there and done that,' and knows how to convey her superb skills to others in a truly captivating manner. This book can lead grant aspirants out of the confusion generated by a thicket of grantwriting manuals on the bookshelves and toward a new state of clarity. Her straightforward advice will help readers get their good ideas funded and make a positive difference in their field."

—Ronald Newbower, PhD, Co-founder and CTO of the Center for
Integration of Medicine and Innovative Technology (CIMIT) and Former Senior
Vice President for Research at Massachusetts General Hospital

continued . . .

HOW TO SAY IT
Grantwriting

Write Proposals That
Grantmakers *Want* to Fund

DEBORAH S. KOCH

Prentice Hall Press

PRENTICE HALL PRESS
Published by the Penguin Group
Penguin Group (USA) Inc.
375 Hudson Street, New York, New York 10014, USA
Penguin Group (Canada), 90 Eglinton Avenue East, Suite 700, Toronto, Ontario M4P 2Y3, Canada
(a division of Pearson Penguin Canada Inc.)
Penguin Books Ltd., 80 Strand, London WC2R 0RL, England
Penguin Group Ireland, 25 St. Stephen's Green, Dublin 2, Ireland (a division of Penguin Books Ltd.)
Penguin Group (Australia), 250 Camberwell Road, Camberwell, Victoria 3124, Australia
(a division of Pearson Australia Group Pty. Ltd.)
Penguin Books India Pvt. Ltd., 11 Community Centre, Panchsheel Park, New Delhi—110 017, India
Penguin Group (NZ), 67 Apollo Drive, Rosedale, North Shore 0632, New Zealand
(a division of Pearson New Zealand Ltd.)
Penguin Books (South Africa) (Pty.) Ltd., 24 Sturdee Avenue, Rosebank, Johannesburg 2196,
South Africa

Penguin Books Ltd., Registered Offices: 80 Strand, London WC2R 0RL, England

While the author has made every effort to provide accurate telephone numbers and Internet addresses at the time of publication, neither the publisher nor the author assumes any responsibility for errors, or for changes that occur after publication. Further, the publisher does not have any control over and does not assume any responsibility for author or third-party websites or their content.

Copyright © 2009 by Deborah S. Koch
Cover design by Charles Bjorklund
Text design by Tiffany Estreicher

First edition: October 2009

Library of Congress Cataloging-in-Publication Data

Koch, Deborah.
    How to say it—grantwriting : write proposals that grantmakers want to fund / Deborah S. Koch.— 1st ed.
      p.   cm.
    Includes index.
    ISBN 978-0-7352-0445-4
    1. Proposal writing for grants.   2. Fund raising.   3. Nonprofit organizations—Finance.   I. Title.
    HG177.K63 2009
    658.15'224—dc22   2009023420

PRINTED IN THE UNITED STATES OF AMERICA

10   9   8   7   6   5   4   3   2

Most Prentice Hall Press books are available at special quantity discounts for bulk purchases for sales promotions, premiums, fund-raising, or educational use. Special books, or book excerpts, can also be created to fit specific needs. For details, write: Special Markets, Penguin Group (USA) Inc., 375 Hudson Street, New York, New York 10014.

To my delightful husband, Charlie, who successfully convinced me one night that I'm not a fraud.

ACKNOWLEDGMENTS

I offer my sincere thanks to . . .

Kathy Crawley, for recommending me to my agent and thus starting this whole exciting endeavor. Marilyn Allen, my agent, for always being encouraging and for cheerfully and patiently dealing with a new author. Maria Gagliano, my editor, for careful reading, good suggestions, and teaching me that a preposition is an okay thing to end a sentence with.

My mother, Audrey Koch, for being so attentive to the quality of my writing early on that I now cannot pass a "Drive Slow" sign without mentally adding an "ly." My late father, Reinhart Koch, who instilled in me the ever-useful question, "How do you know that?" and who would have happily debated each of my book's assertions. Irene Koch, for her big-sister pride in this accomplishment. Nina Koch, my younger sister, for eternal support, laughter, and reminding me repeatedly to save my manuscript to more than one place.

The Springfield Technical Community College community, in particular President Ira Rubenzahl and Vice President for Development/CFO Janet Wanczyk, for their constant appreciation of my work and encouragement of this book. Staff members Megan Ballard and Keith Bailey, for their creativity, high-quality writing, sparking of good ideas, and enthusiastic participation in the Sassy Acronym Society.

Enlace de Familias of Holyoke, MA, especially Executive Director Betty Medina Lichtenstein, who gave me the best description of a grantwriter's role when she presented me with a hurriedly written series of thoughts and told me she needed me "to dress it up." The Stavros Center for Independent Living, especially grantwriter Denise Karuth, who has generously shared her work.

The CFRNet (a corporate and foundation relations email list) and National Council of University Research Administrators (NCURA) communities, for always being a source of information and insights and for convincing me that government grantwriting isn't the horrid task I had imagined.

All my friends and family, who have been saying for years that I should write a book. (Of course, they meant about my life and travel escapades, but you'll have to wait for that one!) To each of you who has given your support and encouragement, known when not to ask "how's the book going," and participated in the name-the-book contest,

I give my joyful gratitude. To all who offered engaging conversations, shared clever thoughts, and let me bounce ideas off of them, a warm smile of appreciation. Particular thanks to Dee Royster, for loaning me her cottage as a writing retreat and her insights into book writing and peer reviews, and to Len Finocchio and Ali Webb, for an insider's perspective on grantmaking.

Everyone who has had a great idea that I could sell; without that, I couldn't have been a successful fundraiser.

Special thanks to the following organizations for permission to reprint their work: Arnold and Mabel Beckman Foundation (www.beckman-foundation.com); Smith Richardson Foundation (www.srf.org); Compton Foundation Inc. (www.comptonfoundation.org); Z. Smith Reynolds Foundation (www.zsr.org); Jessie Smith Noyes Foundation (www.noyes.org); Lynde and Harry Bradley Foundation (www.bradleyfdn.org); Ben & Jerry's Foundation Inc. (www.benjerry.com/company/foundation); JM Foundation (www.foundationcenter.org/grantmaker/jm); Springfield Technical Community College (www.stcc.edu); Groundwork Springfield (www.groundworkspringfield.org); Stavros Center for Independent Living (www.stavros.org); Enlace de Familias (www.enlacedefamilias.org); W. K. Kellogg Foundation (www.wkkf.org); and United Way of the Bay Area (www.uwba.org).

And my special thanks to all who allowed me to use proposal pieces and website material in this book.

CONTENTS

An Introduction: Getting Started..1

Words Matter   **1** / Why This Book Matters   **2** / Grantseeking and the Economic Downturn   **3** / How to Use This Book   **4** / Beginners FAQs   **6** / Grant Proposal Writing Process   **8** / Basic Components of a Proposal   **10** / Yes, You *Can* Write   **13** / Glossary   **14**

Part One: It's About More Than Content

Chapter 1: Make Sure Your Project Is Fundable 21

So What? Identify the Goal of Your Project   **22** / How Will You Know That You Have Achieved Your Goal?   **25** / Who Will Benefit from Your Project?   **26** / Is Your Project Doable?   **27** / Bonus Points for Project Design   **27**

Chapter 2: Is It a Good Match?
Show That You've Done Your Homework 30

Understanding the Grantmaker   **30** / Conducting the Research   **31** / Look at Grants Made   **32** / Good Match Criteria   **34** / Be Alert to Trends   **40** / Foundation Considerations   **42**

Chapter 3: Find Your Hook... 45

Writing Persuasively   **46** / The Hook   **46** / Determining Point of View   **47** / Preferred Problem-Solving Approach   **48** / Political Ideology   **57** / Use Buzzwords   **62** / Applying the Grantmaker's Words   **62**

Chapter 4: Say It to the Right Audience with the Right Style 64

Know Your Audience   64 / Operate from the Reader's World   66 /
Foundations   67 / Corporations   70 / Government   72 /
Learn from Your Rejections   76 / Overall Style Advice   79

Chapter 5: Creating a Well-Organized and Well-Structured Proposal 81

Proposal Organization Brainstorming   82 / Proposal Mapping   82 /
Formatting   83 / Make It Easy to Read   84 / Make It Easy to Follow   85 /
Make It Easy to Find Information   86 / Use a Proposal Introduction   86 /
Timesavers   87

Chapter 6: Make Your Case with Clarity, Logic, and Passion 90

Assume Nothing: Strive for Clarity   91 / Logic   94 / Passion   95 /
Examples of Using Clarity, Logic, and Passion in Your Proposal Presentation   96 /
Project Titles   105

Chapter 7: Overcoming Writer's Block 109

Techniques   109

Part Two: But Content Is What You're Selling

Chapter 8: Say It Effectively: The Letter of Inquiry 119

Procedure   120 / Technique   121 / Online Letter of Inquiry   121 /
Contents of a Letter of Inquiry   122 / Writing a Short Proposal   130 /
Example of a Short Proposal   131

Chapter 9: Say It with Substance: Organizational Description 137

Formatting   138 / Introduce the Organization   139 / Establish Capacity   144

Chapter 10: Say It with Conviction: The Statement of Need 150

Clarify Your Issue   151 / Demonstrate Knowledge of the Field   152 /
Present Your Problem-Solving Approach   153 / Talk About the

Beneficiaries   154 / Establish Organizational Capacity to Meet
the Need   154 / Examples of the Statement of Need   155

Chapter 11: Say It with Vision and Solutions: Goals, Objectives, Activities, and Outcomes 166

What Is a Goal?   166 / What Is an Objective?   167 / What Is an Activity?   168 /
What Is an Outcome?   168 / Guiding Questions   169 / Goals and Objectives
Technique   170 / Activities and Outcomes Technique   172 / Examples of Goal,
Objectives, and Activities Statements   182 / Make It Measurable: Outcomes   186

Chapter 12: Say It with Proof: Evaluation 187

Reasons for Evaluation   188 / Evaluation Considerations   190 /
Evaluation Methodology and Techniques   193

Chapter 13: Say It Expansively: Project Dissemination 201

Purpose and Value of Dissemination   202 / Dissemination Activities   204 /
Examples of Dissemination   205

Chapter 14: Say It Richly: Budget and Budget Narrative, Project Sustainability 209

Relationship of Budget to Project Activities   211 / How Much Money Should
I Ask For?   211 / Format   212 / Government Budgets   215 / Foundation
Budgets   215 / Budget Narrative   216 / Project Sustainability   218

Chapter 15: Say It Succinctly: Proposal Abstract/Executive Summary 222

Technique   223 / Example of a Proposal Abstract   225

Chapter 16: Say It with Flair: The Cover Letter....................................228

Purpose   229 / Technique   231 / Examples of Cover Letters   232

Appendix: Proposal Samples 235

1. Sample Letter of Inquiry to a Major Foundation   235 / 2. Sample Proposal
to a Community Foundation   239 / 3. Sample Proposal Narrative
to a Federal Agency   243

Index..263

Getting Started

Words Matter

In grantseeking, words can go where you can't—a government program officer's desk, a foundation boardroom, a corporation's headquarters—so you want to use them as the strategic, powerful tools that they are. Certainly when you are selling something—and with a grant proposal you are selling your vision, your solution, and your capacity to make it happen—you need to use words that grab the listener's attention. Your words need to be factual, but they also need to pop; they need punch. You want them to stand out so that *you* can stand out. Words matter, and that's what this book is about—using your words effectively to win grants.

How to Say It: Grantwriting is about how to find the words, frame the words, present the words, and use the words to effectively make the case for your organization and its projects. It is about writing winning grant proposals through the careful and purposeful choosing of words, and the careful and purposeful arrangement of them.

You probably make deliberate choices about which words to use in everyday situations and don't think consciously about it. But pause for a moment and assess your day today. Did you persuasively sway your coworkers to adopt your approach to a task? Did you artfully get your child to do his or her homework with a minimum of whining (from either of you)? Did you cleverly convince a fellow committee member to take on an unwanted chore? In each of those situations, you likely assessed your audience, determined what motivates them, and spoke accordingly.

Or maybe you've had the opposite experience, the times you've rebuked yourself with, "Oh! I should have said . . . !" or worse, "I should *not* have said that!" You lost an opportunity or you caused displeasure because you didn't have the right words.

Upon reflection, it's easy to understand the importance of how words are used. Now consider that in a grant proposal you don't have the advantage of adding emphasis, emotion, and meaning to your case through your facial expressions, body language, and intonations. All that you must convey must be done simply with written words; they are your proxy, they are your voice. They must express all the excitement, all the conviction, all the wisdom, all the compelling arguments you would deliver in person if you had the chance to do so.

Why This Book Matters

The *choice* of your words can be very important to the actions that follow. And for that reason, this book is focused not on the full spectrum of tasks that involve a grant proposal submission—there are many books that cover that—but specifically on the *writing* of the proposal. *How to Say It: Grantwriting* differs from other grantwriting books in three significant ways:

- It places great emphasis on understanding the supply side of the granting equation—the grantmaker. It explains how to recognize and grasp the importance of the individuality of each potential funder and shows you how to employ that distinction to your advantage.

- It gives you the tools to closely examine the project you are seeking to have funded and shows you how to shape it and present it in the most funder-appealing way.

- It teaches you how to write your proposal—tell your story—in a clear, cogent, accessible, and gripping way that will resonate with the well-chosen grantmaker to whom you are sending it.

Most of the samples of proposal components presented in this book are taken from winning grant proposals. In some instances, the grant proposal successfully brought in under $10,000; in other instances, it brought in well over $1 million. The principles of good grantwriting remain the same regardless of the size of the grant award. In two cases, I include before and after proposals: The before version had been submitted to a grantmaker but had not been funded; the reworked after version, however, did receive funding. In each case, the proposed project and the grantmaker did not change, but when I applied new structural arrangements and new words, the outcome did—the proposals got the attention and the funding they deserved.

Grantseeking and the Economic Downturn

As I write this book, our nation is facing a vastly changed and dire economic climate. As more and more people find themselves in positions of need, the nonprofit organizations that serve them are being tasked with increased responsibility and thus with increased need for financial support. In addition, organizations that rely on government funding for some portion of their budgets may be finding their allocations reduced, if not cut altogether. Therefore, for many organizations, receiving grant monies has become all the more important to their survival.

While a hurting stock market does affect the amount of money that private foundations can pay out in the form of grants, it doesn't stop the grantmaking process completely. As long as a foundation has investment assets, by law it must pay out 5% of those assets. But clearly if the assets have diminished in value, so will the overall grant awards. Whether a foundation chooses to make fewer grants of their standard dollar amount or the same number of grants with smaller amounts, the foundation is still making grants. The Foundation Center has collected and compiled information, which it is continually updating, from many national foundations about how the economic downturn will affect their grantmaking. A chart detailing this information, titled "2009 Foundation Giving Forecast," can be found at http://foundationcenter.org/focus/economy/forecast.html.

There will still be government grants available. The economic stimulus package passed into law in February 2009 offers many grantseeking opportunities because of increased funding to many federal government departments and agencies as well as to state governments. These current circumstances are likely to increase the competition for that source of revenue—all the more reason that you should learn to write a compelling grant proposal and all the more reason to carefully read this book to learn how. All of these circumstances suggest increased competition; the material presented in this book is intended to give you an edge in that competition.

How to Use This Book

This book is designed for both the beginning and the experienced grantwriter. For the beginning grantwriter, I offer step-by-step writing guidance and tell you what you need to think about as you write. For the experienced grantwriter, I offer a different way of looking at the purpose of each proposal section and share my grantwriting strategy secrets. No doubt you could offer me some good advice based on your experiences—and many of you have—but I hope that my words spark some new thoughts and approaches. If you are a brand-new grant-seeker, be sure to refer to the Glossary (on page 14) as you read.

This book will be helpful whether you are looking for funds as an organization or as an individual. I will use the words *you* and *your organization* interchangeably throughout the book to mean both types of grantseekers. As long as you meet the eligibility requirements of the grantmaker, your approach to writing as an organization or as an individual will not differ very much. What matters more is to whom you are writing; that is what will determine both your style and your content.

Related to that, this book does not address fundraising from individuals because that calls for a radically different style of writing. This book is specifically about getting competitive grants from both public and private sources.

When referring to the entities with the money, I will use the terms *grant-maker* and *funder* to mean the same thing. When referring to the people reading your proposal, I will use the terms *reader* and *reviewer* to mean the same thing.

A particularly useful maxim that I coined for thinking about grantwriting is this: *Who* is making the decisions from *what point of view* with *what knowledge*? This book is divided into two parts to help you answer this question: "Part One: It's About More Than Content" and "Part Two: But Content Is What You're Selling."

Part One will help you answer the "*who* is making the decisions" and "from *what point of view*" parts of the question. These are things that you can't change to suit your needs but that you must know to be successful in grantseeking. You are not in a position to tell the grantmaker who should be reading your proposal nor are you in a position to tell the grantmaker what its set of beliefs ought to be. But what you are in a position to do—and where you derive your power in the grantseeking process—is to arm yourself with the knowledge about the *who* and the *what*.

You may be tempted to skip the opening chapters of Part One because at first glance they do not appear to be directly about writing. The truth is, what they cover may be the most important parts of writing a winning grant proposal.

Chapter 1 tells you what makes a good idea a fundable project, identifying what criteria indicate fundability. For example, you can have a fabulous, creative idea that is exciting and dynamic. But if you aren't clear about what it is you're ultimately trying to achieve or you don't have specific measurable objectives detailed on how you will achieve it, then you don't have a fundable project.

You can write the most articulate proposal about a very well-designed project, but if you send it to the wrong grantmaker, you will not get funded. Chapter 2 discusses how to determine whether a particular funder is a good match for you. Given that most proposals are rejected because they are not good matches for the funder's stated interests and problem-solving approach, you should pay particular attention to this chapter.

Chapter 3 is what most sets this book apart from other grantwriting guides. It reveals how to find the hook—the story that will capture the reader's attention, the connection that will resonate with the funder.

Even if you are submitting your proposal to a funder who *is* a good match, if you do not write the proposal in a way that is accessible to the reader, your good ideas and plans may be lost. Thus Chapter 4 is equally important because it discusses how to determine who your audience is—who will be reading and assessing your proposal—and how to write to them.

Part Two is all about the last part of the question: "with *what knowledge?*" This part of the question is where you, as a writer, have control. Unless you've been a previous grantee, the funder is not likely to know much about your organization except what you tell it. You are the one who will give the reader the information he or she needs to properly assess your proposal. You are the one who will tell the reader about your organization, about your mission, about your goals, about your capacity, and about your intended project and what it will accomplish. That gives you both power and responsibility. Part Two will equip you to meet that responsibility.

Beginners FAQs

Some of the readers of this book have already had experience with the grant-seeking process and are looking to expand and refine their technique. But many of you are new to the process and picked up this book to unravel the mystery of grantwriting. This section speaks specifically to those of you who are beginners. Anticipating some of your questions, I first offer this FAQs.

1. *What is a grant?* A grant is the transfer of money given for a specific purpose—without the expectation of repayment—from a foundation, corporation, or government agency to an individual or organization to conduct research or activities that will contribute to the public good.

2. *How do I get a grant?* You ask for one by submitting a grant proposal, which is reviewed and evaluated in a competitive process by the grantmaker or its assignees. Some grantmakers prefer that you start the grantseeking process by first submitting a letter of inquiry (see Question 5).

3. *What is a grant proposal?* A grant proposal is a written form of communication between you as the entity that seeks grant money and the

grantmaker as the entity that has it. A grant proposal makes the request for funds and explains how those funds will be used. The full grant proposal can consist of many parts, such as an abstract, a proposal narrative, a timeline, a budget, a budget narrative, and numerous addenda and attachments. The basic contents of a grant proposal are itemized on page 11.

4. *What is a proposal narrative?* The proposal narrative is the most important part of a full grant proposal. It is the part that explains what you want to do, why this activity is important to do, how you will do it, and what positive outcomes will happen as a result. It is what most people think of when they use the term *grant proposal.*

5. *What is a letter of inquiry? How is it different from a grant proposal?* A letter of inquiry is a brief summary of your project in letter format; a proposal is the full description of your project. In a couple of pages you are telling the grantmaker for what purpose you would like to receive a grant and are requesting permission to submit a full proposal detailing your need and the proposed work to answer that need. Chapter 8 offers more information about a letter of inquiry, along with detailed instructions on its content.

6. *How long should a proposal be?* Most grantmakers will specify how many pages you have in which to describe your project and what you hope to achieve. Do *not* go one word over that limit or your proposal will be rejected for that reason alone! Proposal length can be as little as two pages or as high as a hundred, mostly related to the type of grantmaker and the complexity of the request. More and more grantmakers are using online applications and will be very specific, not just about page length but about the number of words you have in which to describe your project. If there is nothing in the instructions to indicate the expectations of the grantmaker, call to clarify what that funder thinks is an appropriate proposal length.

Grant Proposal Writing Process

Each chapter in this book, while it can stand alone, is part of a progression designed to lead you through the grantwriting process. But first it would be useful to have this progression—the basics of the grant proposal writing process—outlined at a glance.

Grantmakers have their own proposal requirements or preferences, so not all proposals will follow the exact same steps in preparation or require the same degree of effort and complexity. However, this section offers you a quick view of what has to happen to get a proposal written. Each of the activities mentioned in the following list is described in detail in the chapters to come.

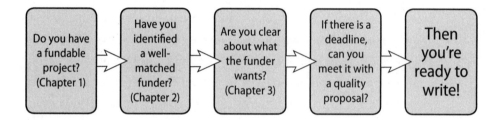

Steps for Grant Proposal Writing

1. Read the request for proposals (RFP) and any other grantmaker material thoroughly.

2. As you read the written materials, make a list of the grantmaker's buzzwords and make sure they are always in front of you as you write.

3. Be sure that you understand and can articulate the grantmaker's point of view.

4. Determine how the grantmaker wants the first point of contact to be: a phone call, an online intake form, a letter of inquiry, or a full proposal. Full proposals follow steps 5–20. Guidance on letters of inquiry can be found in Chapter 8.

5. Make a list of all documents and attachments that are required to be submitted as part of the proposal packet.

6. If available, examine the review criteria, and if a point system is used, make note of the points allotted for each criterion.

7. If there is a page limit, map out your proposal to determine how many pages or portions of pages to assign to each section. If a point system is used in the grantmaker's review process, be mindful that each section length should correspond to each review criterion's point value. The higher the point value, the longer that section should be.

8. Consider what information is best presented in chart form. For example, objectives, activities, and outcomes are frequently presented in a chart so that the reader can see how each relates to the other. Charts also can be valuable space savers.

9. If your project requires partners and involves outside people or organizations, engage these outsiders in the process immediately. Call a partnership meeting as soon as possible, determine who will do what project activity, and get letters of support moving.

10. If you'll be using an outside evaluator, contact that person as soon as possible, especially because that person may be willing to write the evaluation section of your proposal.

11. Following the grantmaker's instructions and answering all of its specific questions, write your proposal narrative.

12. Develop a visual representation of your timeline.

13. Develop a budget and budget narrative, also known as a *budget justification*.

14. Make sure that anything that is in the proposal narrative is reflected in the budget and that anything in the budget is reflected in the proposal narrative.

15. Fill in whatever forms the grantmaker requests.

16. If they are permitted, prepare attachments.

17. If requested, write a proposal abstract/executive summary.

18. If allowed for, write a cover letter.

19. Double-check your list of required documents and attachments to make sure you have everything.

20. Have at least one other person review and edit your proposal and make sure that everything that should be in it *is* there.

Basic Components of a Proposal

For some grantmakers, a letter of inquiry is preferred or required before a full proposal can be submitted. Detailed guidance and component descriptions for letters of inquiry can be found in Chapter 8. If your letter of inquiry has resulted in an invitation to submit a full proposal, this section outlines the basic components of that proposal, and Chapters 9–16 cover each component of the proposal in more detail.

Generally, the grantmaker will give you a precise application form or an indication of what questions it wants answered; this should be your first point of reference in structuring your proposal. However, if there are no fixed or defined requirements, the following provides a good guide for laying out a proposal.

Except for organizational description, which may be embedded throughout the document, each of these components is presented in the order in which it is likely to be in your proposal. With the exception of the abstract and the budget and budget narrative, the components listed here are known as the *proposal narrative*. Each component is discussed in the chapter indicated. Although the abstract would go on top of your proposal packet, it is not discussed until Chapter 15 for two reasons: (1) not every grantmaker requests this component, and (2) generally, you would write the abstract after you have written all of the narrative, drawing from it to do so.

Abstract/Summary (Chapter 15)

- In a very succinct fashion, answer the following: What will be done? Why, how, by whom, and for what purpose? For how long and at what cost? What are the outcomes, and who will benefit?

Introduction (Chapter 5)

- An introduction won't be necessary if you have an abstract/summary because the content is similar.

- In a paragraph or two, present your proposed project and what you expect the beneficial outcomes to be.

- These brief initial remarks are the first thing that you say to the grant-maker and should create a strong, positive declaration about what you will do and allow the proposal to flow into why these actions are necessary, which is your statement of need.

Organization Description (Chapter 9)

- Briefly state your mission, history, leadership, and programs and how these things relate to the work you propose to do.

- Indicate how your organization has the capacity to undertake the work that you propose.

Statement of Need (Chapter 10)

- What is the issue you are addressing?

- Why does this matter? How do you know this?

- Why is what you propose necessary?

- Who benefits? Make sure you can indicate the public good achieved.

Goals and Objectives (Chapter 11)

- What do you hope to achieve?

- What are the measurable and time-specific steps that must happen to reach your goal?

- Why do you choose to address the issue in the manner that you have?

Project Activities and Outcomes (Chapter 11)

- What are the specific activities involved? Who will do them? How?

- Present a timeline of activities.

- What specific outcomes will be achieved?

- Why is your organization the best one to do what you propose to do?

Evaluation (Chapter 12)

- How will you know that you did what you said you would do?

- For an evaluation, you will need to have already written project goals and objectives that are truly measurable so that you can actually determine if they have been met. Enumerated goals and objectives—without the detail given earlier in the proposal—are listed alongside the accompanying evaluation steps to be taken to measure each one.

- Describe your evaluation methodology precisely.

- It is a good idea to build in evaluation throughout the life of the project so that you can have good information for making midcourse corrections if necessary.

Dissemination (Chapter 13)

- Many grantmakers want the rewards of the projects they support to be shared with other people or organizations that might benefit from this knowledge. Therefore, a plan for dissemination of lessons learned is of interest to them.

- State the purpose for dissemination.

- Link dissemination activities to your project goals and objectives.

- Be varied and creative in the ways you choose to share your findings.

Budget and Continuation Funding (Chapter 14)

- Show your budget in table form and use a budget narrative to explain each item.

- Include other sources of funding, both cash and in-kind. Do not overlook the value of all in-kind contributions, including those of your collaborators.

- Indicate how the project will be funded after the grant has run out.

Yes, You *Can* Write

You may think you don't know how to write well and are discouraged by the grantwriting task before you. It's more likely that you don't know how to approach writing, how to arrange your writing, how to *think* about writing. With the guidance, examples, and exercises offered here, I hope to give you the tools to acquire those skills and then, perhaps, to acquire the necessary self-confidence to accompany them. Armed with this knowledge and vision, you are likely to be more successful in securing the necessary funds for your cause.

And if you are successful with future grant proposals, then I will know my words to you have been well chosen—they have done their job—and I can rest with satisfaction.

Glossary

Cost Sharing: Cost sharing means that the grantmaker expects that the individual or organization receiving grant monies will also be contributing dollars, effort, goods, or services to the cost of the project. A funder requiring cost sharing does not expect to pay for the full cost of the project. Other terms that may be used to indicate the same thing are *match* and *challenge*.

Indirect Costs: Indirect costs are what is commonly referred to as *overhead*. These are costs not directly associated with conducting your project but those that your organization incurs as a result of project activity. These may include salaries of staff who assist in the functioning of the organization—such as fiscal, technological, administrative, clerical, or facility personnel—and may include costs associated with your facilities, such as rent, electric, and phone. Indirect costs are more commonly associated with governmental grant budgets, but some foundations will allow a small percentage of overall grant costs to be charged for indirect costs.

In-kind: An in-kind contribution is a noncash contribution to the project by you or your organization. It's related to cost sharing. Things such as the value of non-grant-funded staff time spent on executing grant-funded activities or the value of organizational materials used in performance of grant-funded activities could count as in-kind contributions.

Letter of Inquiry: A letter of inquiry is a very condensed version of a proposal and is sent to a potential funder for the express purpose of gaining permission to submit a full proposal. It may also be called a query letter, pre-proposal, concept paper, or letter of intent.

Measurable Objectives/Measurable Outcomes: These terms are generally used when discussing the evaluation of the grant-funded project. It is not enough to state what it is you expect to happen as a result of your project activities (outcomes); you must state these things in a way that can be measured so that it can be determined whether each objective was realized.

Mission Statement: Reference made to a mission statement in this book refers to the carefully crafted document that forms the basis of why your organization exists—your organization's stated vision, values, and goals. It is not something that is written just for the purposes of a grant proposal, but it is something that may be included in your proposal.

Over-the-Transom Proposals: An over-the-transom proposal is one that is not responding to a specific request for proposals (RFP) and is usually sent to a private grantmaker who indicates an ongoing interest in a particular topic and does not specify deadlines for receipt of proposals.

Principal Investigator (PI): This term is primarily used for government proposals, especially those emanating from academia. A PI refers to the person who will be the leader of a grant-funded project.

Review Criteria: Review criteria are a series of things by which your proposal will be graded. Review criteria may include need for the project, project design, project implementation, organizational capacity, project evaluation, range of collaboration or partnerships, and reasonableness of the budget. All federal government proposals will indicate what these criteria will be, and most departments or agencies will indicate how many points will be assigned to each item.

RFP (Request for Proposals): This is a document prepared, produced, and distributed by a grantmaker, either public or private, which is actively seeking grant proposals to address a specific concern. The RFP will specify very clearly who is eligible to apply, what types of projects the grantmaker is seeking to fund, and a deadline for receipt of proposals. RFPs may also be called requests for responses (RFR) or solicitation of applications (SOA).

PART ONE

It's About More Than Content

It is natural to think that grantwriting is just about *writing*, and without question what you write and how you write it are of high importance. Many might argue that a proposal's content is what matters most, and it would seem ridiculous to refute that. But I make the case that a winning proposal is about more than its content because the depth of its content depends on knowing fully what you are writing about, why it matters, and why the reader should care. To meet those conditions, you must first take several preliminary steps involving research, analysis, and awareness. A large part of writing the best proposal that you can write happens before you actually start writing. Your organization may have a remarkable idea about how to solve global warming, but if you don't present this idea in an accessible way to the right people, in the right manner, it will not get the attention it deserves.

You need three things before you can start writing a grant proposal effectively:

- A well-thought-out project worth writing a proposal about (Chapter 1)

- The identification of a well-matched grantmaker to receive that proposal (Chapter 2)

- In-depth knowledge about that grantmaker's history, world outlook, subject matter interests, preferred applicants, grant award patterns, and application procedures, which will give you the information you need to write to the grantmaker in a way that can be heard (Chapters 3 and 4)

Once you have done this initial background work, it is time to focus on the writing. Chapters 5–7 walk you through overall writing strategies and techniques that will be useful before you embark on tackling the specific components of the grant proposal. The chapters in Part One explore issues that are true regardless of the subject matter about which you are writing. They offer instruction on how to write with clarity, logic, passion, and organization.

CHAPTER 1

Make Sure Your Project Is Fundable

There are two sides to a good funding match: the grantmaker and the project. Chapter 2 addresses whether the grantmaker you're approaching is a good match for your project. But before you explore any grantmaker as a potential funder, you need to be clear that the project you are proposing is indeed a fundable project. Writing a winning proposal depends on having a winning project to sell. If your project is not well thought through or well designed, it doesn't matter how eloquent your proposal is—funders will see its weaknesses and decline to fund it. It is up to you to demonstrate to the grantmaker that your good ideas are also solid plans and that, if funded, you are ready to undertake the work described in your proposal.

This chapter covers what makes a project fundable and whether your project in its current design meets those criteria. If your project doesn't meet those criteria, I'll show you how to find the fundable project in a good idea. To aid you in this task, I will ask you a series of questions to consider about the project for which you are seeking funding. Some of the questions may initially be a challenge to you, but if you put effort into answering them, you will be one step closer to a fundable project.

So What? Identify the Goal of Your Project

If I were to ask you what you need a grant for, you would likely cite a certain activity that you want to undertake or particular resources that you need to continue your work. If I then asked, "Why is that important? Why does it matter? What will that do? Who does that help?" could you answer those questions? Could you find an adequate reply to the implied question, So what?

This is perhaps the most important question that you can ask about the project you hope to get funded. And many people will find this the most difficult question to answer. This is because people frequently confuse *means* and *ends* when thinking about what they are trying to promote in a grant proposal.

When I say *means* I'm referring to the way in which you go about your organization's work. Means are the tools that you use to get the work done, the actions that have to happen in order for you to achieve your goals, the *how*. While means are important to achieving your goal, *they are not the sole reason you are seeking the grant.*

Ends are the reason your organization exists, its purpose, its goals, its mission. Ends are what you are trying to achieve, the *why*. Ends are what a potential funder cares most about, the ultimate purpose for any actions you might take. To determine what your ends are, focus on the main purpose or accomplishment you want to achieve, not the tools or activities you need to achieve it. Grantmakers are not as interested in buying specific goods or services as they are in addressing the larger issue.

When trying to decide if something is the means or the ends, think about whether it is an activity or a goal. For example, maybe you need a new computer for your organization, but the computer is not the end point; it is the means by which you're trying to achieve another purpose. Maybe the computer is needed so that you can do client intake. Maybe the computer is needed to help children become proficient in a task. Maybe the computer is needed to design a public awareness campaign. In each of these cases, the computer is the tool that is needed to achieve a particular goal; it is not *the* goal. And in each of these cases, the computer is a line item in the budget and the intake, proficiency, and public awareness campaign are activities that the proposal should address. But even then, the intake, proficiency, and public awareness campaign are not the ultimate goal of the project; they, too, are the means to an end.

To arrive at these projects' goals—the ends—you need to ask, So what? once again and carry the inquiry forward. Why do you need to do client intake? Why is children's proficiency important? Why is a public awareness campaign vital?

Let's use that last question to go a few So what? steps further. Maybe the reason you need a public awareness campaign is because your organization wants people to be aware of the importance of recycling. Well, So what? Why should people care about recycling? Because then there will be less waste going into landfills. So what? Because then there will be fewer landfills. So what? Because then the government can find a better public purpose use of those funds, it can find a better public purpose use of that space, and there will be less of a threat to public health. Ahh, that's what you're selling—government efficiency, environmental caretaking, and public health. That's the So what?

In answering this question repeatedly, you are distilling your thoughts to the essence of your organizational or personal mission. The project you propose should affirm this mission. It is not that describing the project's specific activities and resource needs is unimportant—it's very important—but it's ultimately not your main point. If your proposed project does not have some part of your organizational mission underpinning it, then it's not a fundable project.

Let me present you with a more complex example of the So what? challenge. Many years ago, when I was working at a university as the director of foundation relations, a scientist asked for my assistance in working on a grant proposal. He was conducting research on very particular bacteria and was very excited about this research. Not being a scientist, I was having a hard time sharing his enthusiasm about bacteria and also knew that, unlike governmental programs, there would be limited foundation interest for supporting basic research. I had not discovered the So what? question yet so I peppered him with questions, trying to understand his urgency about this research. Why is this important? What will it yield? But to myself I was thinking, "Why would someone care about this?" Finally during the course of my questioning, the professor told me that these particular bacteria could eat up a toxic spill in water without leaving a toxic residue. "Aha," I responded, "I'm not selling research on bacteria; I'm selling clean water!"

This brings us to another part of the So what? exercise. To help you answer this question, think about the policy implications of the work you are proposing to do. Policy implications are the considerations about an idea or an action that affect the public good. Some private foundations were initially established because their founders saw it as a way to affect public policy without having to rely on legislator agreement. And as I discuss in Chapter 3, many grantmakers have a very specific policy point of view. If you can't identify the policy implications of your work, then you will be hard-pressed to make an argument that your project is in alignment with the grantmaker's vision.

SO WHAT? PRACTICE 1

Imagine that I've told you that I work in a nonprofit senior center and that I need to raise money to equip a weightlifting gym there. Your first reaction might be, "Yes, that would be nice; wouldn't we all like to have a personal gym?" Here's how our conversation might unfold after that:

"No, it's really important. Our seniors need to lift weights."

"Why does that matter?"

"It not only strengthens their muscles but also loosens their joints and gives them more energy."

"Okay, that's nice for them as individuals, but if we have to make choices about how to use our limited money, I'm not sure why that is important."

"Because that activity gives them better mobility, and if they have better mobility then they're more likely to move around."

"So what?"

"Well, if they move around more, it is better for their overall health, and they will need fewer assists. And not only is better health good for our clientele but it lowers health care costs."

"Oh, I see, you want to improve senior health and lower health care costs in the process. The weights are one means by which you can achieve that goal."

Let's say you're a photographer and you are looking for money.

"What do you need money for?" I query.

"To buy six cameras and tons of film," you tell me.

"Yes, I know you're a photographer, but six cameras? Why does one person need six cameras?"

"Because I'm going to the Middle East to a children's peace camp and will be teaching them photography."

"Why do you need to teach them photography?"

"So they can take pictures of what happens around them."

"Why does that matter?"

"That way they can tell their stories through pictures."

"So what?"

"If children from opposite sides can't talk with each other but can tell each other their stories through pictures, it might build an awareness of each other's realities and advance cultural understanding between them."

"That's nice for them, but what will that do?"

"If we're lucky, this awareness and understanding at a young age will promote coexistence and peace as they grow older."

"Ah, you need money not just for cameras but to promote peace."

How Will You Know That You Have Achieved Your Goal?

Once you've completed the So what? exercise, your project should have a focused goal. The next step is to make sure that goal has measurable objectives associated with it. Having clearly defined, well-articulated goals and objectives is crucial to having a fundable project as well as having specific activities designed to meet those goals and objectives. (More information about how to write goals, objectives, and activities can be found in Chapter 11.) Being able to state expected outcomes and how you will know when you've met your goal is essential.

Using the So what? example of weight equipment for the senior center, the goal of that project is to encourage better health among the seniors through weight training. One of the measurable objectives to ensure that that goal is achieved would be to establish and conduct six sessions of four weightlifting classes each throughout the year. Among the activities necessary to make sure these classes are held would be to purchase the weight equipment, train staff on how to use the equipment, design the classes, and recruit seniors to enroll in the classes. Another measurable objective of equal importance to achieving the goal of better health would be to establish a follow-up mechanism to ensure that the seniors are using the equipment regularly and correctly. Activities related to this objective might include developing a buddy system for exercising or a tracking mechanism of how many seniors use the weights each week. Another measurable objective would involve establishing and monitoring indicators of good health. All of these objectives and activities are measurable. For example, at the end of the grant period, you could indicate whether you met the objective of holding six sessions of four weightlifting classes each throughout the year.

Who Will Benefit from Your Project?

An important part of policy considerations for your proposed project is who will benefit from the work your organization will do. Just as having clarity about the project's goal is vital, this is an equally important concern when designing a project.

Who benefits? Is this an appropriate population to benefit? How many people will benefit? If you cannot clearly answer these questions, you don't have a fundable project yet. Most funders will have identified a very particular population that they hope will be served through their grants. If you draw out the So what? exercise long enough, you ultimately end up with people and how their lives are affected by the project. The answer to, Who benefits? is crucial.

Is Your Project Doable?

Many of us can get excited about an idea and overreach. Just as it is difficult to narrow down a topic when writing a paper for school, so is it difficult when conceiving and designing a fundable project. Be careful of ideas larger than your organization can possibly manage.

To give you an idea of the difference between a good idea and a good project, I offer this example. World hunger is something that we all care about, that we all would like to see eradicated. But is it possible for a single project to do that? No. However, is it possible to address hunger within your own community? Yes. Operating a food bank, running a soup kitchen, and setting up a way to bring meals to shut-ins are examples of fundable projects. And getting even more specific within these activities, such as conceiving of a clever way to deliver your anti-hunger program in a rural area, makes it even more of a precisely envisioned fundable project.

There are other things to consider about scale. Does your organization have enough staff to do the work? Does it have sufficient skill and knowledge to do the work? Can a project of the size you envision be effectively managed? Could you really hope to effect the desired change with the resources you have? Is it, in fact, doable?

Make sure that your project has a definitive beginning, middle, and end. This is one of the ways in which you indicate that you have thought through your project, that you know what it will take to achieve your goal, and that you know in what order activities need to happen. This thought process is another way of double-checking whether or not your project is in fact doable.

Bonus Points for Project Design

Once you have determined that you have a fundable project, you want to strive toward having a highly fundable project. The following elements will elevate your project's appeal to funders:

- Funding your project will **benefit many** people who are in need. Funders want to change the world for the better but do not have the resources to meet all needs. Show them how far their investment will go with your project.

- Your work will be done **collaboratively** with other parts of your organization or with community partners, such as schools, local government, nonprofit and community groups, or businesses. Related to the far-reaching investment point above, funders believe that collaborations are more likely to serve large numbers of people in an efficient and effective manner.

- Your project is **inclusive** of those you seek to help, in planning, directing, or execution. This demonstrates that the thinking behind your project design is grounded in reality. For example, when you developed your project plan, did you consult with the people your activities will most affect? If you have a project advisory board, does it include members of the community that you seek to help?

- Your organization has made its own **investment** in the project. This shows the value your organization places on a project by the degree to which it tries to make it happen. Investment is not only cash, it can also be personnel, equipment, space, or volunteer resources.

- Your project will **leverage** other investments in your project. This is very appealing to funders; it indicates that your organization is well regarded by others and that you've made efforts to garner support from other sources. Leveraging is sometimes specifically required by the grantmaker as an indication of related institutions' commitment to the project. It is also a way for the grantmaker to feel that its money triggers investment in the community. A handful of private foundations may request that their grant monies be used to specifically challenge the organization's supporters to increase their contributions.

- What you propose is **novel**, is a new way of looking at things, shows exciting promise. This is especially important with foundations, who want to be associated with new, cutting-edge work, particularly if it becomes a standard by which others operate or if it changes policy in a way that supports their targeted constituencies and issues. Foundations have often been thought of as the laboratory for government because they can take more risks in seeking a solution to community or societal problems, and if the approach is found to be sound and effective, sometimes government will adopt it.

- The outcomes of your work are **replicable**, so other organizations may adopt your approach and methodology. Again, funders want their investments to go as far as possible; replicability allows more people to benefit.

- You can demonstrate that the **work will be continued** after the grant has ended. This is not always a realistic expectation, but it is one that will enhance your project's appeal if it's true.

I hope this chapter has caused you to pause and reflect on the quality of the project for which you seek funding and to examine it closely to see if it truly is a fundable project—not just a good idea—and that you have fully thought through what it would take to make that good idea happen. If you have followed the suggestions in this chapter, you are now equipped with a fundable project to propose and ready to proceed to the next step: finding a well-matched funder.

CHAPTER 2

Is It a Good Match?

Show That You've Done Your Homework

If you were applying for a job smartly, you would find out as much as you could about the organization or company before sending your résumé and cover letter. You would make great effort to demonstrate that you know all about its mission and operations and would be sure to make connections between your knowledge and skills and the company's needs. Similarly, if you were crafting a romantic letter intended to convince a potential sweetheart that you *are* the person your desired one needs, you'd be very careful to show that you understand who he or she is, that you are in agreement with his or her worldview, and that you alone can make that person's dreams come true.

Now, do you put the same effort into understanding a potential funder before you write and send a grant proposal?

Understanding the Grantmaker

You are reading this book because you want to be successful in getting grants. There are two necessary components to a grant award: a funder willing to bestow a grant, and a fundable project eligible to receive it. To be a successful grantseeker, you need to put equal effort into understanding both. Chapter 1 addresses what makes a project fundable; this chapter advises you on how to understand the motivations and operating basics of grantmakers. Your goal—once you have smartly framed your project and gathered all your information about a potential funder—is to be able to answer this question: Who is making the decisions from what point of view and with what knowledge? This chapter discusses the *who*.

Grantmakers consistently report that the primary reason they reject proposals is that what is being proposed isn't a good match with their stated goals, preferences, and limitations. Making sure that both you and your proposed project are a good match with the grantmaker is essential for any grant proposal. To make that determination, you will have to conduct research on each potential funder you are considering. Grantmaker research is a vital first step to writing an effective proposal. It is the step that will answer the question, *Who is making the decisions?*

Conducting the Research

Thorough prospect research can be an elaborate process; the basics in this chapter will help you get started. The Research Roadmap on page 33 gives you a visual overview of the process.

However, you may wish to investigate the topic beyond what I tell you here. The Foundation Center (www.foundationcenter.org) is a valuable nonprofit resource for learning about and conducting all the steps in grantseeking and has an especially useful tool for research called the Foundation Directory Online. You can get access to this research database either through subscription or by going to an established Foundation Center Cooperating Collection—usually a public library—to use it for free. These cooperating collections exist in every state and are listed on the Foundation Center's website. There are other grants research databases available for purchase. The Foundation Directory Online is the database that I prefer not only because it is fruitful and easy to use but also because it is produced by a nonprofit entity that makes sure that it is accessible to all who wish to use it.

Your initial assessment about a potential grantmaker can be made from information posted in a grants research database, such as the Foundation Directory Online. However, once you identify a potential funder, I recommend that you review that funder's material directly. Not only is it likely to be more up to date but it removes another person's unintended biases, so you alone determine what information is and isn't valuable. Check first to see if the grantmaker has a website. If a foundation does not have a website, call and request the most recent annual report, grant guidelines, and list of grants made (which may be posted in the annual report). Government programs will post all information online, and you can sometimes request to receive copies of successful proposals. Generally, unless they have a separate foundation, corporate funders provide less extensive information. Read everything fully. The funder is telling you who it is; you need to listen carefully because you will use this information as you craft your proposal. Developing a persuasive argument depends on understanding what will resonate with the proposal reader. Chapter 3 covers this in depth.

SOURCES OF INFORMATION ABOUT FOUNDATIONS

1. Read information from a foundation database (such as the Foundation Center's Foundation Directory Online) profiles.

2. Look at the foundation's website or printed materials.

3. If not available from the website or other sources, look at the foundation's tax return (called a 990-PF) to see a list of grants made and a list of the board of directors. You can look at 990s on the Foundation Directory Online or on a website called GuideStar (www.guidestar.org), which is a free resource; you just need to register.

4. Gather information about the foundation from general news articles, philanthropic media, and electronic mailing lists where your peers who have had an interaction with this foundation may post findings.

Look at Grants Made

Grantmaker research includes looking at what a grantmaker says and, more important, looking at what it does. Grants made are a good indicator of what

Research Roadmap

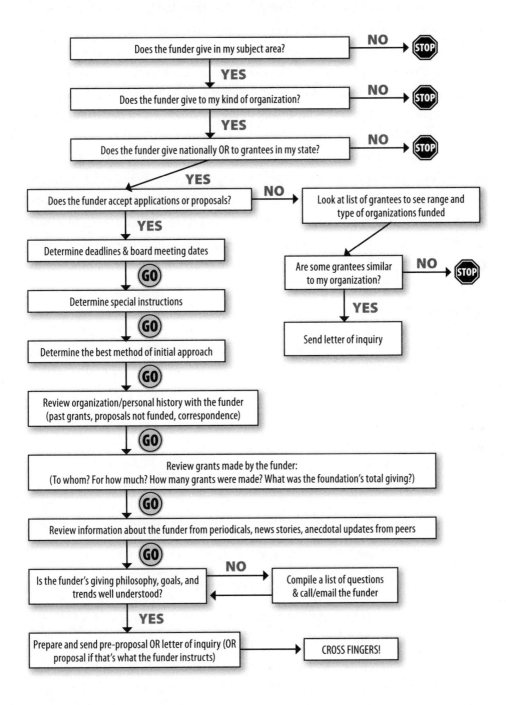

Does the funder give in my subject area? **NO** → STOP

YES

Does the funder give to my kind of organization? **NO** → STOP

YES

Does the funder give nationally OR to grantees in my state? **NO** → STOP

YES

Does the funder accept applications or proposals? **NO** → Look at list of grantees to see range and type of organizations funded

YES

Determine deadlines & board meeting dates **GO**

Determine special instructions **GO**

Determine the best method of initial approach **GO**

Review organization/personal history with the funder (past grants, proposals not funded, correspondence) **GO**

Review grants made by the funder: (To whom? For how much? How many grants were made? What was the foundation's total giving?) **GO**

Review information about the funder from periodicals, news stories, anecdotal updates from peers **GO**

Is the funder's giving philosophy, goals, and trends well understood? **NO** → Compile a list of questions & call/email the funder

YES

Prepare and send pre-proposal OR letter of inquiry (OR proposal if that's what the funder instructs) → CROSS FINGERS!

Are some grantees similar to my organization? **NO** → STOP

YES

Send letter of inquiry

the funder values. As you examine the list of grants awarded, ask yourself these questions: Does the grantmaker demonstrate that it funds what it says it does? Does the grantmaker fund organizations like mine? Does it fund a lot of activities like those in my project? Does it correspond in method to my project or organization's approach? As you scan a grants list, look for patterns in organization name and type, and patterns in grant size and frequency. Looking at grants made by a funder you are eyeing is a very good way of determining who they are.

For small and local family foundations, look to see if they give their money to the same grantees each year and if they give money to mainstream grantees, such as the American Cancer Society, the YMCA, or the local symphony orchestra. If they give to the same grantees every year, then they're not very open to new grantees. And if they give only to mainstream organizations, then they're serving more as a vehicle for individual giving rather than as an entity seeking to work with a variety of previously unknown nonprofit organizations presenting new ideas.

Another way to zero in on good match funders is to investigate where organizations like yours are getting their funding from. Plug the names of your organizational associates into a grants database and see what funder names come up. This is a very quick way to determine grantmaker preferences and to assure yourself that your activities would be appealing to them.

Good Match Criteria

There are many ways in which the proposed project, your organization, and the grantmaker need to match:

- Is your organization an **eligible** applicant?

- Is your organization within the funder's preferred or restricted **geographic area**?

- Is your work in alignment with the funder's stated **subject matter** interests?

- If you are applying under a particular **request for proposals (RFP)**, does the project you propose respond to the specific issue the RFP seeks to address?

- Is the **amount of money** you are requesting appropriate for that funder?

- Does your organization's **problem-solving approach** and point of view match the funder's? (See Chapter 3 for more information.)

Eligibility

Most grantmakers make it clear in their materials what types of organizations or individuals they will and will not fund. This should be the first thing you check, because if you or your organization is not eligible, there is little point in going any further. I say little point rather than no point because in some instances, you can arrive at eligibility through other means. For example, some funders will not make grants to public entities, but will accept a proposal on behalf of a public entity from a "friends of" type of organization, as long as that organization has its nonprofit status, usually referred to by the tax code designation 501(c)(3).

When you are checking the grantmaker's stated limitations, know that some are indisputable. However, you should not be deterred by others. For example, if you see the words *unsolicited proposals not accepted*, this often means that you may send a letter of inquiry (see Chapter 8) as a first step, and if they are sufficiently impressed or intrigued, you might be invited to send a full proposal.

Another delicate matter is that some grantmakers will say that the only eligible applicants are those that are "preselected." Generally you will not get past this hurdle, especially if the funder is a very small family foundation. However, there are two things you can try: (1) review the list of the board of directors and see if you know anyone, and (2) call and ask how one becomes preselected. Or, if you live in a sparsely populated region, you could adopt the attitude of a woman I once met while conducting foundation research for a client. When I decried the eternal preselected limitations I kept seeing, she replied, "Oh, I'm not worried about that. In Vermont, where I'm from, everyone knows everyone." I have every confidence that she always found her "in."

Geography

Geography is an extended part of eligibility. Some funders—often corporate or smaller family foundations—keep grantmaking to a confined geographic area. Corporations generally have a preference for funding in communities where they have their headquarters and operations. Small family foundations may wish to spend funds only in the community in which they reside. Some funders will state their geographic boundaries in very precise, "only" terms; others will use the word *preferred*, which gives you some leeway. It is not impossible to persuade a potential private-sector grantmaker to expand its geographic horizons, but it is highly unlikely, so I would not spend much time pursuing that option unless you have a 100% match of goals, subject matter, and problem-solving approach that makes your project just too delicious to ignore.

If that is the case and you wish to pursue this possibility, first look at the grants made by the funder you are eyeing. If you see *any* grants made outside of the stated geographic area, then it is possible to convince the funder to do so again. Chances are, however, that these grants are the result of one person's personal preferences and associations. For example, if you see a grant made outside of the stated geographic area that has been made to a secondary or postsecondary school, you can be pretty sure that somebody on the board of directors of that grantmaker went to that school or has children who are going to that school. Another possible way to overcome the geography barrier is if you are located out of the grantmaker's geographic area but are doing work within that area or are serving citizens of that geographic area in a different location. And finally—and this is generally a strategy that will work only with smaller foundations—use or try to establish personal connections with a member of the board of directors.

Subject Matter

Once you pass the eligibility and geography tests, the subject matter match measure is the most important one to pay attention to.

With foundations, money is set aside for grantmaking because the founders believe that there are specific societal problems that need additional help and attention, and they want to play a role in addressing those problems. Maybe they lost a loved one to a particular disease, maybe they've always loved the outdoors, maybe they are concerned with the role of government, maybe they want to encourage entrepreneurialism, or maybe they believe that education is the most reliable route out of poverty.

In most cases, the established priorities of the grantmaker are based in strongly held beliefs, and if you want to be successful with that funder, you should honor those stated priorities. If a friend told you he was vegetarian, would you serve him meat? Would you insist that he would really like the meat if he would just try it? No, not if you truly respect that friend's choices. If your supervisor asked you to produce a report on office energy-saving alternatives, would you instead submit a report on office personnel matters, saying that was a more important matter on which she should focus? No, not if you wanted a good evaluation. In both instances, a strong preference has been stated, and if you want to be well regarded by either person, you honor that preference. So it is with grantmakers. If you want to be taken seriously in your funding request, demonstrate that you take their subject matter choices with equal seriousness.

Grantmakers will state their subject matter interests in their material. They will be listed on their websites, in paper documents, or in grantseeking databases. Some will state broad categories, such as arts, education, or health; others will be more precise within those categories. Some will have more than one area of interest, which may or may not be related to one another. Some may make sweeping statements about wanting to help a specific community or population. These choices have been determined long before you arrived on the scene. Pay attention to what you are being told and honor it.

Pay attention, too, to the grantmaker's history, mission statement, and vision statement. All of this is useful information when you are trying to make a connection with a funder. In most cases, if you read all of its materials, you will be given insight into the grantmaker's subject matter choices. The founding set of beliefs will tell you a lot about how to frame your proposal. This is covered in more depth in "Problem-Solving Approach," later in this chapter, and expanded on in Chapter 3.

Once you are clear on what the subject matter interests of the potential grantmaker are, examine the nature of your organization's work to be certain that they coincide.

Request for Proposals (RFP)

Requests for proposals are regularly issued by grantmakers, particularly government ones. The federal government posts all RFPs on Grants.gov (www.grants.gov), a searchable website where you can sign up to receive daily notices of these opportunities based on your preferences. If you are trying to keep your email inbox uncluttered, you may visit this website and do detailed searches whenever you wish.

Philanthropy News Digest (http://foundationcenter.org/pnd), a web-based newsletter of the Foundation Center, also regularly posts RFPs and will email you RFP alerts by subjects you determine. In some instances, you can sign up to receive notices of RFPs on individual grantmakers' websites or you can sign up to receive regular newsletters that, in addition to general information about their grantmaking, may include RFPs (if the foundation operates in that manner).

Finally, check with member organizations that represent the subject areas in which you are seeking funding. Frequently these organizations will have someone who is keeping track of granting opportunities and will regularly share this information with their members. This is useful because the RFPs will be very specific to your subject area.

You have a greater chance of getting funded from a foundation by responding to an RFP than by sending an unsolicited proposal—the proposal equivalent of cold calling. The reason for this is that the foundation is announcing its intention to give grants for a specific purpose, and it spells out very clearly what it is looking to fund. Government grants are awarded from a similar process; agencies have an interest in particular issues and distribute RFPs to see those issues addressed. This specificity makes it easier to write a proposal because you know exactly what the funder is looking for, but it also means the realm of proposed projects is more limited. To be successful, your project must address precisely what is being requested. For example, if the RFP is about education, but explicitly about K–12 education, do not submit a proposal geared to post-secondary issues. When reviewing an RFP for its funding potential, if you don't meet the expressed focus, it's not a good match.

Size of Grants

You don't ask the Ford Foundation for $5,000, and you don't ask a community foundation for $500,000. An important part of good match grantseeking is making your ask appropriate to the funder's ability and tradition. When you are sizing up a potential funder, there are several pieces of financial information that should be of interest to you:

- How much money does the grantmaker give overall?

- How many grants are funded?

- What is the range of grant amounts?

- What is the average size of grants? Was there one grant that was particularly big that might skew that average?

- Is there a financial pattern to the giving? For example, you notice that most of the funder's grant awards are between $10,000 and $20,000.

In issuing an RFP, federal government grant programs will usually tell you how much money is available overall, how many grants they expect to make within that round, and either an approximate grant award amount or grant floor and ceiling amounts. If this information isn't outwardly offered by the grantmaker you are pursuing (and with private funders, it's unlikely to be as precise), the best way to determine the appropriate grant size request is to look at the grants made in recent years within a program or on the grantmaker's total grant list. Generally, I recommend that when a grantmaker's materials are not clear about something, call the grantmaker. However, calling to ask how much money you should ask for is not your best approach. The assumption is that you know how much your project is going to cost and can see the size of grants that are being made and therefore can tell whether or not the two things match on your own. That said, it is not unusual to approach more than one grantmaker to fund the same project, and you could call to ask a grantmaker which of the pieces of your project it would be most interested in funding. For example, if your project activity includes a single event, you could ask a particular grantmaker to fund just that event; or if your project includes producing a publication, you could ask a particular grantmaker to fund that publication.

Problem-Solving Approach

One good match criterion that many people miss is the problem-solving approach. In fact, it's such an important point that I've devoted much of Chapter 3 to exploring it. Most funders will have very particular notions about how societal and community problems are solved. One grantmaker may believe that to solve a particular problem, research is what is needed most of all; another grantmaker may believe that the problem can only be solved through direct service delivery; and another may be convinced that only through advocacy and public policy can the problem be solved. Even government grant programs are rooted in a fixed mind-set, designed by either legislative action or administrative directive. Determining which problem-solving approach defines the grantmaking of a given funder is a very important research step to take. To be a good match, you want your problem-solving approach and the funder's to align.

In addition to problem-solving approach beliefs, many foundations have a set ideology and some have a definitive political viewpoint. If that is the case, it is crucial that you assess whether your project fits in with the funder's ideology. If it does not, it is definitely not a good match. Some grantmakers will state their preferences overtly, but for others you may have to read between the lines of their history, mission statement, program descriptions, and grants made to fully grasp their leanings. I teach you how to do this in Chapter 3.

Be Alert to Trends

In the grants world, as in every other niche, there are things that are in vogue, both in topic and in approach. Trends will be evident in response to current events, such as natural disasters, energy crises, or health epidemics. Topical trends can be broad subjects that have the nation's attention, such as obesity, homeland security, or going green. Or the trends can be found within a broader topic and reflect a new viewpoint about how a particular issue should be addressed, such as the focus on learning communities within the broader category of education. In addition to paying attention to current news stories, track topical trends by checking websites, newsletters, and magazines that deal with your subject matter. Another way to determine the giving trends of a particular grantmaker is to look at its recent grants made.

Trends can also reflect different approaches to problem solving. For example, as I write this, many grantmakers are placing a heavy emphasis on funding projects that are guided by what is called evidence-based intervention. This means that the proposal activities you choose, as well as the underlying policy that directs those choices, are grounded in research or data that demonstrate that those choices are effective.

There are trends in grant administration and management. The emphasis on evaluation—a formal assessment of how well you performed your project activities—is an example of this. In recent years, accountability in any scenario has become of prime importance, and grant-funded projects are no exception. Funders want to know if you in fact did do what you said you were going to do. Unlike many years ago, not only will today's grantmakers give you money to conduct an evaluation of your project activities but the evaluation section is often weighted quite heavily during proposal assessment. Many grantmakers, certainly government sources, are in tune with evaluation methodology and expect to see a sophisticated use of it. See Chapter 12 for more information about evaluation.

Most proposal reviewers today have an expectation of seeing these evidence-based interventions and evaluation as part of the proposal. Usually grantmakers will indicate problem-solving or grant administration and management trends such as these in the application instructions.

Topical, problem-solving, and grant administration and management trends can be found by scanning philanthropic media and organizational websites, such as the *Chronicle of Philanthropy* (www.philanthropy.com), Giving USA (www.givingusa.org), the Foundation Center (www.foundationcenter.org), Independent Sector (www.independentsector.org), and the Center on Philanthropy at Indiana University (www.philanthropy.iupui.edu). It is to your advantage to pay attention to what is hot in the grantmaking world. For trends in government grantmaking, follow the words and actions of legislative and executive bodies.

Foundation Considerations

To get a full picture of a given foundation, you want to learn about its history, its founding, its staff, and its trustees. Look at the chart on page 43 for some of the questions you should seek to answer to become well informed about a potential grantmaker.

For example, information about a foundation's founding and longevity is important because you need to know if original beliefs are still the operating beliefs. If the founder is still involved in the foundation, likely that is the case. If a foundation is new, it is probably still working out its grantmaking behavior, and you need to pay frequent attention to it to see if there are relevant changes being made.

Learning about staffing is equally important because it affects how you will interact with the foundation. If the foundation is so small that it has no staff or only a part-time person, it is best that you avoid calling with your questions. This also tells you that the board of directors will be important in the review process; likely any staff is going to be administrative only. If a foundation is large enough to have several program officers, you should put some effort into knowing about the program officer who would be reviewing your proposal. For example, if you know that the program officer used to be a professor in the subject matter of his or her portfolio, this will affect how you present your proposal. You know that, among other things, a professor is likely to care about supporting data and citations, so you would make sure to include those. Conversely, if you know that your program officer used to work in an organization similar to yours, your writing would seek to remind him or her of the challenges facing such an organization.

Also be sure to look at a foundation president's or executive director's annual report or website letters for any indication of the direction that they intend their foundation to go; sometimes you can learn things this way that you might not otherwise know. For example, one year the Beldon Fund's executive director made a surprising announcement in his annual report letter: The foundation had decided that rather than making grants in perpetuity (as most grantmakers do), because of the urgency of addressing environmental issues, it was going to spend down all of its assets within a specified number of years.

FOUNDATION CONSIDERATIONS

Consider the Type of Foundation

- Is it national, regional, or local?
- Is it a private foundation, family foundation, public foundation, corporate foundation, operating foundation, or vehicle for individual giving?

Consider the Foundation's History and Current Frame of Mind

- Read historical accounts to understand the basis for the institution's founding.
- Learn from president's or executive director's letters in annual reports; this is often where new directions are indicated.
- Does it have a perpetuity or spend-down mind-set?
- Are there distinct political leanings?

Consider the Age of the Foundation

- Is the founder still alive?
- How old is the foundation?
- How far removed from its original intent/ mission is it?
- How many years has it had staff?

Consider Staffing

- Is there any? How many are full-time professionals?
- What do program officers do?
- Has the head of the foundation always been the same?
- Don't overlook personal history of prominent staff.

Consider All Sources of Information

- Pay attention not just to what they say but to what they *do*.

Consider the Foundation's Grantmaking Approach

- How does it think problems are best solved?
  - Direct service?
  - Research?
  - Educating policymakers?
  - Advocacy and activism?
  - A mixture?
- Does it run its own programs?
- Does it use RFPs or have an open solicitation policy?
- How many funding rounds a year does it have?
- Is it accessible or tightly controlled?
- Does it make site visits?
- Does it use peer reviews?
- Who makes decisions?
  - Program staff?
  - Leadership staff?
  - Board?
  - Family members?

Consider Your Organization's History with the Foundation

- Have you applied before?
- Have you received a grant: when, for how much, to do what?
- Has there been any other contact?

Consider That the Foundation May Evolve

- Even when you think you know the answers to these questions, they may change soon thereafter! Always double-check the foundation's materials or website before submitting a proposal.

News like this can make a big difference if this is a targeted prospect for your organization. In this case, it meant that a lot more money would be available from this funder, albeit for a limited time.

You also need to have information about when and how you should be contacting the foundation. Find out when the funding cycles and deadlines are; if those are not specifically stated, determine how often the board meets. Clarify the foundation's preferred mode of applying—that is, does it want to talk to you first, does it want a letter of inquiry, or does it want a full proposal as the first point of contact? Gathering this information and acting accordingly will better position you in your grant pursuit.

"Foundation Considerations" on page 43 provides you with an at-a-glance reminder of some of the things you should be thinking about as you are getting to know the grantmaker you are pursuing. (Some of these considerations will be more fully explored in the next chapter.) The foundation will be able to tell whether you have taken the time to understand who it is.

With each proposal submission, demonstrate that you've done your research and know that your organization and project fit with the funder's view of the world. You should be able to demonstrate that you are sending your proposal to the right place, that the potential funder is a good match, and that you can identify what you and this funder have in common.

If you are sending a letter of inquiry (see Chapter 8), be sure to say in the first or second paragraph the ways in which the project you are submitting coincides with the funder's vision and preferences. If you are submitting a full proposal, you can use your cover letter to point out this connection; or if it fits in another section in the proposal, point out shared beliefs, values, and approaches to problem solving.

Making sure your project is a good match to a grantmaker's interests and viewpoints is crucial to its success.

CHAPTER 3

Find Your Hook

Throughout this book I ask you to consider, *Who* is making the decisions from *what point of view* and with *what knowledge*? because I believe if you can answer this question fully informed, you are greatly improving your chances of writing a winning proposal.

Chapter 2 discusses how to learn about a grantmaker and addresses the first part of that question: *Who* is making the decisions? This chapter delves into the *what-point-of-view* part of the question. Point of view has two parts: the preferred problem-solving approach of the grantmaker and the political ideology of the grantmaker. (These parts are explained further on pages 48–62.)

When you are writing a proposal, it is not enough simply to state needs and the work proposed to address those needs. You must find the hook—the words that will resonate with meaning, purpose, and connection to the proposal reviewer. You find the hook by first identifying the underlying beliefs and principles of the prospective grantor. Once you identify the funder's guiding philosophy, you can craft your message to speak to those perspectives.

In this chapter, I show you how to identify a grantmaker's point of view and how to write *to* that point of view. You will learn how to read the grantmaker's materials to find the clues about its point of view, and when the grantmaker doesn't make its point of view obvious, you will learn how to read between the lines to understand who the grantmaker is and what it believes.

In the previous chapter, you learned what basic criteria you must meet to be a good match with a grantmaker. But to beat out the competition of other good matches, you need to take it a step further. After determining a grantmaker's point of view, it is to your advantage to write your proposal in such a way that demonstrates that you understand this point of view and that you and the work you propose to do are in complete alignment with it. Once you have done that—once you have found your hook—you will not only be a good match but be a *great* match.

Writing Persuasively

You may have a marvelous idea on how to address a particular community problem and have carefully thought through the steps needed to turn your vision into reality. But if you don't make an unquestionable link between your work and the funder's goals, if you don't demonstrate through your words that you get it, you will not be successful in receiving a grant.

How you talk about your work matters. You need to write in a way that is not only absorbing and attention grabbing but also forceful and irrefutably cogent, without being perceived as harsh or scolding. In other words, you need to write persuasively.

You want to bring the reader to the point where he or she can't do anything but agree with you. Yet persuasion in grantwriting should not be about trying to trick somebody into believing what is not true; it should be about presenting your case in such a way that the reader not only concedes that your proposed work is on target with the funder's mission and viewpoints, but also finds that what you propose to do is so gripping, so necessary, so undeniably possible that if he or she did not act in your favor it would be sinful. And then, if this person is on a review committee, he or she should be motivated to convince the rest of the committee that this is so!

The Hook

A large part of being persuasive is finding your hook. The hook is the unshakable connection between you and the grantmaker. You can picture the hook—

you can see it reaching out to the reader, latching on, and not letting go. It is the proof that you see the world in a shared vision, that the work you propose to do is in tandem with the work that the grantmaker wants done, that all of the policy planets are in perfect alignment, and that your organization is fully equipped to accomplish what you propose to do.

You may have had the experience of finding the hook as you're preparing a grant proposal. It's the Aha! moment when suddenly you see what it is about your proposed work that will resonate in multiple ways with the funder. For example, it's the moment when you not only note that the funder shares your interest in homelessness but also see that, based on the funder's past grantmaking, you both are very focused on the need for affordable housing and, more than that, believe action should begin with the private sector. Other would-be grantees may also work on homelessness projects, but if the majority of the funder's grants are related to affordable housing, and those would-be grantees are focused on homeless shelters, they are not as good a match. Or if those would-be grantees *are* focused on affordable housing but approach it from a governmental action point of view, again, they're not as good a match.

Determining Point of View

Grantmakers, predominantly foundations, have distinct personalities. As with humans, they have set beliefs about how the world is and a precise vision for how they wish it to be. They know what issues they care about, what isn't working well in that field, and what they are hoping their monies will change for the better. They have an established approach to how they think problems should be solved. And sometimes, they have strong political views.

Just as people do not want to be treated as if they were exactly the same as the next person, a grantmaker wants to be recognized for its individual characteristics. Yet one of the biggest mistakes that grantseekers make is to blanket a slew of potential funders with the same proposal.

Either directly or indirectly, funders are telling you who they are, what they care about, how they think about things, and what they want to know about you and your work. Are you listening? Do you get what they need? Can you feel it?

Could you answer Freud's paraphrased question, "What does this grantmaker want?"

For each grantmaker you wish to approach, you will need to put in the time and effort to answer these questions. But it is an investment worth the undertaking, because having a clear picture of the *nature* of the funder is a critical step in grantwriting. Your writing must demonstrate that you get who the grantmaker is. You let the funder know this through what you propose to do and the language that you use to describe it.

Some things you can learn directly from the grantmakers' materials. Many funders tend to be very forthcoming about who they are and what they care about and go to considerable ends to share this information with grantseekers. However, some grantmakers are shyer about telling you who they are, sometimes simply because they don't have the staff to prepare the materials, but other times because they intend to be a bit mysterious. This is where learning to read between the lines comes into play.

As you examine each grantmaker's preferred problem-solving approach and political ideology, its point of view will become clearer and clearer and, accordingly, your hook will become clearer and clearer, too.

Preferred Problem-Solving Approach

What does the grantmaker want? A funder's approach to problem solving is instrumental in answering this question. Not all grantmakers approach philanthropy in the same way. You could have five funders who all care about the same topic but have five different beliefs about how best to tackle problems in that field. Let me tell you a fairy tale that will illustrate this.

Once upon a time a very unusual thing happened—three directors of nonprofit organizations decided that work was under control enough that they were going to go have a picnic by the river. (Yes, it would be unusual for that to happen, wouldn't it? I told you this was a fairy tale!) They spread out the blanket, pulled out their lunches, and enjoyed the beauty of the day. All of a sudden, one of them noticed a bunch of children flailing about in the river.

He ran to the river, jumped in, and began to grab as many children as he could and put them safely on shore. He yelled to the other two directors to help him.

The second director also had jumped into the river, but instead of pulling the children out of the water, she began to teach them how to swim. Both of these directors felt such urgency about the situation and couldn't understand why the third director wasn't in the river next to them. They called to her as she was running upstream, "Where are you going? Why aren't you helping us?"

The third director yelled back over her shoulder, "I *am* helping you; I'm going upriver to see why these children are in the river and to stop it!"

All three directors wanted to do something to handle the problem of children who can't swim being in the river. And in each of these instances, each director *did* do something that addressed the problem. The first director felt he needed to tackle the immediacy of the situation. The second director thought she could give the children the tools they needed to help themselves out of the problem. And the third director believed that the source of the problem is where she needed to direct her attention. Each acted importantly, but each acted differently.

And so it is with grantmakers. Each will have a belief about how best to deal with the problems that it seeks to alleviate. Most problems need to be addressed by a variety of approaches for effective solutions, and even though some grantmakers will entertain more than one approach, they generally have very specific preferences.

Problem-solving approaches include the following:

- Direct service

- Research

- Research for policy purposes

- Research for activism purposes

- Educating the public or policymakers

- Activism

A funder's problem-solving approach is not just about whether it thinks research or advocacy will solve the problem but about what it thinks the nature of the problem is or who the population is that it wishes to benefit. For example, the goal of ensuring a trained workforce to meet industry needs is different from the goal of making sure that people have sufficient training to get a job. Yes, perhaps the outcome is the same—people who need it will have jobs—but the steps you take and the rationale for those steps will be different. In a proposal that I worked on, it was clear that the grantmaker's focus was on industry, not the workers. This made a difference in how the statement of need was structured and how goals and objectives were framed.

Problem-solving approaches may also involve a belief about the proper level at which you tackle a problem. For example, some grantmakers may prefer to focus their efforts locally, others statewide, others regionally, others nationally. And yes, in some cases these choices may relate more to the size of the grantmaking organization, but there are grantmakers who give nationally who state that they prefer local and regional approaches to problem solving.

Grantmaker beliefs will also affect preferences in terms of who are the appropriate players in addressing a particular problem. For example, when considering the issue of illiteracy, one grantmaker may believe that parents are the best point of intervention and will fund only those programs that engage parents in reading regularly to their children at an early age. Another grantmaker may believe that libraries are best equipped to help people achieve literacy and will fund only those programs focused on those sites. Yet another grantmaker may believe that illiteracy is best tackled by adult volunteers and will fund only those programs that engage that populace. In each case, the grantmaker cares about increasing literacy but has a definitive idea about how that should be done, and its grantmaking reflects that.

A grantmaker's preferred problem-solving approach will affect not only to which grantmaker you submit a proposal but also how you write that proposal. For example, for a grantmaker who is focused on research, you will spend a good portion of your proposal explaining the design of your research, the methodologies you will use, and the credentials of your proposed researchers. For a grantmaker with an expressed interest in activism, you will spend a lot of time demonstrating that your activities are inclusive and supportive of intended beneficiaries, that you are regarded as an authentic voice for them, and that you have a successful track record in securing the desired changes.

The next sections define each of the problem-solving approaches listed on page 49 and present examples. Using grantmakers' words from their websites, I demonstrate how foundations can have very specific notions about which problem-solving approach they are hoping their grantees will use. I'll show you how to find the words that will help you understand a grantmaker's preferred approach.

Direct Service

Direct service is exactly what the term states; it refers to services that are provided directly to the intended beneficiaries. The activity of a direct service organization immediately addresses the outcomes of a larger community or societal problem but does not necessarily seek to address the underlying root causes. For example, if the issue is hunger, a direct service organization might run a food bank or a soup kitchen rather than conduct research on food scarcity or try to affect public policy regarding hunger. Generally, nonprofit organizations that provide direct services are ones with a local focus dealing with the local populace.

Here is an example of a direct service foundation's description:

THE JOHN DOE CHARITABLE FOUNDATION

The foundation focuses its funding to those organizations that provide assistance in the following areas:

1. Organizations dedicated to helping children with life-threatening illnesses through direct services.
2. Child abuse organizations providing direct services and prevention education.
3. Missing children's organizations providing assistance through direct services and prevention education.

This local grantmaker makes it clear, by using the phrase three times in three numbered points, that direct services is what it funds. The only other problem-solving approach that this grantmaker acknowledges is "prevention education." Even if your organization works with children who have life-threatening illnesses, you would not approach this grantmaker with a proposal to conduct research on the causes of those illnesses. If your organization works with children who are victims of child abuse, you would not approach this grantmaker with a proposal to rehabilitate the abusers. While you and the grantmaker may share beliefs about the importance of protecting children, you would not be offering that grantmaker a project that meets with its preferred problem-solving approach.

Research

Some grantmakers will award grants only to support research. They are focused on the pursuit of knowledge, on finding answers to societal problems, on discovering cures, on inventing things, or on designing things that will improve the quality of life for all. Again, using the example of hunger, the grantmaker interested in using research to address societal problems might be interested in funding investigations into agricultural methodology or crop planting choices and techniques. Grants of this nature frequently go to academia but are not limited to such.

Here is an example of a foundation's stated interest in research:

ARNOLD AND MABEL BECKMAN FOUNDATION
The Arnold and Mabel Beckman Foundation makes grants to program-related, nonprofit research institutions to promote research in chemistry and the life sciences, broadly interpreted, and particularly to foster the invention of methods, instruments, and materials that will open up new avenues of research in science. The Foundation does not consider proposals that fall outside of these programs.

This foundation is very clear about what it will and won't fund. When you read its materials, you'll see that it highly values research as a tool and wants to ensure that the world always has people interested in being highly trained researchers, particularly in chemistry and the life sciences. You'll learn that the founder was a highly successful inventor. Even though you both might share a belief in the importance of research to our society's well-being, you would not approach this funder with a project that, through active protests, seeks to convince the federal government to put more money into research.

Research for Policy Purposes

Some grantmakers specifically want their research to be used to affect public policy decision making. They believe that public policy should be rooted in facts, information, and knowledge and seek to provide funding that acquires that necessary information. Using the topic of hunger, an example of research for policy purposes would be an investigation into why people are hungry in the first place. There would be a difference in how you would choose to mitigate hunger if it is a result of low wages and joblessness or if it is a matter of a food distribution system failure.

Here is an example of a foundation with a focus on research for policy purposes:

SMITH RICHARDSON FOUNDATION

The mission of the Smith Richardson Foundation is to contribute to important public debates and to help address serious public policy challenges facing the United States. The Foundation seeks to help ensure the vitality of our social, economic, and governmental institutions. It also seeks to assist with the development of effective policies to compete internationally and to advance U.S. interests and values abroad. This mission is embodied in our international and domestic grant programs.

The Domestic Public Policy Program supports projects that will help the public and policymakers understand and address critical challenges facing the United States. An overarching goal of the Foundation's grant making is to support projects that help stimulate and inform important public policy debates. To that end, the Foundation supports research on and evaluation of existing public policies and programs, as well as projects that inject new ideas into public debates.

The phrase that most describes what this foundation seeks is to "help stimulate and inform important public policy debates." Obviously, this funder believes very strongly that good policymaking is rooted in good information. While further examination of its website cites a few topics that the foundation is currently interested in, such as school reform, the topic may change over time, but the preferred approach does not; informed public policy debates are what matter. Therefore, even if your organization shared an interest in school reform, you would not approach this funder to fund a charter school; however, might be interested in research about the effectiveness of one.

Research for Activism Purposes

Research for activism purposes is related to research for policy purposes because activism generally seeks to sustain or change a specific public policy. The grantmaker that chooses to fund this approach to problem solving wants to ensure that activism is based on knowledge and solid information. Continuing with the example of hunger, consider a river on the West Coast that has provided salmon as a steady staple in the local Native American tribes' diets for years and years. Imagine that electricity providers erected a dam on this river, thereby impeding the natural migratory progress of salmon. For those who object to this dam and plan to be vocal about it, research for activism purposes might involve determining the number of salmon currently migrating in the river and how that relates to pre-dam salmon numbers and what is needed by the tribes for sustenance. The reason for collecting this information would be to have ammunition to argue a point.

The following is an example of a foundation that, among other grantmaking approaches, believes research is most useful if it is connected to activism:

COMPTON FOUNDATION INC.

We believe that research and activism should inform each other, and that both perspectives are necessary for productive public debate and effective policy change. The Foundation actively encourages creative collaboration between agencies, institutions and/or foundations, and projects that advance human knowledge by connecting theory with practice.

This foundation explains its problem-solving approach quite eloquently with the final phrase of the ending sentence, "connecting theory with practice." Its words indicate that both the fields of research and activism have something to learn from each other, as might organizations representing these two approaches. While the foundation focuses its grants on specific subject areas, it is clear that how you go about work in any of those subject areas also matters. For example, even if you shared an interest with the foundation in peace and security, you would not submit a proposal to study effective peacekeeping techniques unless that proposal also included activities designed to use the results of that study.

Educating the Public or Policymakers

Many foundations are supporters of advocacy, although they may not use that word. They may fund activities that directly lead to some change, but they believe that the greatest changes are likely to happen at the public policymaking level and encourage that engagement. Returning to our example of combating hunger, a grantmaker may wish to fund efforts that will inform the public about the prevalence of hunger in their own communities or that will inform federal policymakers about the nuances of food stamp provisions in the Farm Bill.

Here is an example of a foundation that spotlights education for public policy purposes:

Z. SMITH REYNOLDS FOUNDATION INC.

The Foundation seeks to foster a government that is accountable to the needs of the people; a media that provides fair and substantial information on issues facing the state and its people; a citizenry that is engaged, well-informed and participates in the life of the state; and sound public policy that is built upon comprehensive and balanced research. The Foundation invests in organizations and projects that achieve the following:

- Increase educational opportunities for local and state policymakers . . .
- Create credible, timely, policy-relevant research on pressing issues (particularly those within the areas of focus of the Foundation)

- A populace that is educated about and participates in civic affairs
- Increase knowledge of, participation in and discourse about state and local government policies and politics . . .

By its stated approach, this foundation demonstrates that it clearly understands three pivotal agents of change—the government, the people, and the media—and that it wants grant activity directed toward these entities. Among other stated fundable strategies, it is clear that education on the issues is a preferred strategy of this grantmaker; thus, any proposal that you submit should reflect that. The foundation seeks to make grants in the following subject areas: Community Economic Development, Democracy and Civic Engagement, Environment, Pre-Collegiate Education, and Social Justice and Equity. A well-matched community economic development project, such as organizing a small business incubator, would focus on educating the public and policymakers about the ramifications of such a project and seek public input, in addition to the actual creation of said incubator.

Activism

Several grantmakers believe that the shrewdest form of activity to fund is that which brings immediate attention and action to the needs of a particular populace or problem. Activity that engages people directly in their own fates, that pushes for change, and that does not accept quiet acquiescence is what is most appealing to these grantmakers. An activist approach to the issue of hunger might be to protest rising food costs or to give people the tools to grow their own food.

Here is an example of a grantmaker with a strong interest in activism:

JESSIE SMITH NOYES FOUNDATION

The Jessie Smith Noyes Foundation promotes a sustainable and just social and natural system by supporting grassroots organizations and movements committed to this goal.

Our funding priorities are shaped by a view of the Earth as one community, an interconnected web of life in which human society is an integral part. . . . In our view, social change movements require that all people have the opportunities and resources to actively participate in civic life. Therefore, we actively seek out organizations led by people of color and/or working in low income communities that foster such activism. We define people of color organizations as those where people of color are the primary decision-makers and constituents and whose mission and work are based on a race/ethnic consciousness.

Whenever I see the word *grassroots* I know that that grantmaker is open to, if not preferring, an activist approach to community problem solving. In addition to outwardly using the word *activism*, there are other words in this foundation's materials that indicate this bent: "environmental justice, social change movements, actively participate in civic life, and bring together organizations and activists from diverse movements." If you shared the foundation's interest in protecting the environment and wanted to be funded by this grantmaker, your proposal would be very action oriented, engage and be led by the people living in that environment, and involve collaboration with other organizations.

Political Ideology

Just as the grantmaker's approach to problem solving affects what you submit, so does its political ideology. Government grant programs are first envisioned and goals specified by a legislative body, which operates from a political perspective. Many foundations were founded by people with definitive public policy beliefs. In fact, one might argue (and we could, at length) that affecting public policy was the reason foundations were started in the first place. Whether it is from a government or a private grantmaker, the offering of money to address a particular community or societal problem is rooted in an acknowledgment that a problem exists in the first place. And while there may be universal agreement that this problem exists, there are likely to be many opinions as to *why* it exists, what the desired outcome should be, and the steps needed to be taken to get to that outcome. All of these beliefs spring from one's core convictions and principles. Political ideology informs a lot of grantmaking.

Drawing further on the employment example in the previous section, if the issue is unemployment, there is a philosophical difference among programs that promote worker cooperatives, job training, postsecondary education, apprenticeships, micro-lending, or welfare-to-work initiatives. Each of these approaches to unemployment is based on a specific belief as to why the unemployment exists and a specific belief about what it will take to tackle it. That is why you want to know if the grantmaker you're approaching has a very definitive political ideology, because even if you agree that a particular problem exists, you may be in opposition with each other on why it exists, and that will affect how you think the problem is best solved. For example, if you believe the person is unemployed because of discriminatory practices in hiring and the grantmaker believes the person is unemployed because of a lack of personal incentive, your focus on providing legal assistance is not going to be of high interest to that grantmaker, whose focus is on building initiative, even though you both state that you care about unemployment.

As with grantmakers' preferred problem-solving approaches, political ideology takes into consideration at what level of geography or organization the grantmaker believes actions should take place. Likewise, political ideology can also be concerned with who the appropriate actors are in a problem-solving action. There can be very strong beliefs about who has responsibility for undertaking and overseeing a project.

The first step in identifying a grantmaker's political ideology is to key in on buzzwords found in its materials (see page 62 for more information on buzzwords). What language does it use to describe what its trying to achieve? What language does it use to describe how it approaches grantmaking?

As you'll see from the following examples, some of the words grantmakers use make their beliefs quite clear. But many grantmakers will not overtly state what their political ideology is; often, you have to read between the lines to determine what it is, even if they believe it strongly.

If you can't identify the grantmaker's approach and ideology from its mission statement, you can sometimes tell from its grantmaking. Look at the grants made. Pay attention to the names and types of organizations that it funds. Are there any patterns? Are there concentrations in the type of grantee? Does it fund any grantees with known ideologies? If possible, check for what the grants were made; what types of activities were consistently funded? Answers to all of these questions will tell you a lot about who that grantmaker is.

At times, everything will not be so cut and dry or so obviously one way or the other, even with digging. Although most grantmakers will express a preference in a problem-solving approach, not all funders will have very strong political beliefs that will affect their grantmaking. But you need to pause and consider what you hear their words saying before arriving at this conclusion.

Identifying the Ideology

Let me demonstrate how to identify a political ideology with examples taken from grantmaker websites. First I will give you the grantmaker's words, and then I'll provide my interpretation of those words. Initially, I have purposely chosen grantmakers that have strong beliefs so that you can easily see the indicative words. I will follow those examples with a more complex one.

THE LYNDE AND HARRY BRADLEY FOUNDATION

The Bradley brothers were committed to preserving and defending the tradition of free representative government and private enterprise that has enabled the American nation and, in a larger sense, the entire Western world to flourish intellectually and economically. The Bradleys believed that the good society is a free society. The Lynde and Harry Bradley Foundation is likewise devoted to strengthening American democratic capitalism and the institutions, principles, and values that sustain and nurture it. Its programs support limited, competent government; a dynamic marketplace for economic, intellectual, and cultural activity; and a vigorous defense, at home and abroad, of American ideas and institutions. In addition, recognizing that responsible self-government depends on enlightened citizens and informed public opinion, the Foundation supports scholarly studies and academic achievement.

No doubt after reading that paragraph you were able to identify several words or phrases that tell you who this funder is: "the tradition of free representative government and private enterprise"; "strengthening American democratic capitalism"; "limited, competent government"; and "responsible self-government." From these words I see founders who probably align themselves with a libertarian viewpoint. They believe government should be limited, and the role of the market in a functioning society is important to them.

Diving deeper, I pick out words such as "preserving and defending," "dynamic marketplace," and "vigorous defense." Even though these words were not specifically being used to talk about armed defense and the marketplace, the choice of them to describe other things tells me something about the writer's outlook. Yes, you could also pick out phrases that might be representative of other perspectives or be considered neutral, such as "flourish intellectually," "free society," "cultural activity," "enlightened citizens," and "scholarly studies and academic achievement." But overall as I read that paragraph and look at the words used to describe this foundation's underlying values, a clear picture of a conservative outlook is painted.

BEN & JERRY'S FOUNDATION

The Ben & Jerry's Foundation offers competitive grants to not-for-profit, grassroots organizations throughout the United States which facilitate progressive social change by addressing the underlying conditions of societal and environmental problems. All of the Foundation's funding decisions are made by a team of Ben & Jerry's employees that meets once a month to review proposals. . . . Although the Ben & Jerry's Foundation doesn't prioritize any particular issue area for funding, we do focus on the types of activities and strategies an organization uses for creating social change in any number of areas. The Foundation will only consider proposals from grassroots, constituent-led organizations that are organizing for systemic social change. We support programs and projects that are examples of creative problem-solving.

This foundation's words offer a stark contrast to the first example. Again, I'm certain you were able to pick out some key words that define the funder: "grassroots organizations," "progressive social change," and "organizing for systemic social change." These words signal a liberal viewpoint. And more than liberal, I am seeing that being inclusive is very important to this grantmaker; note these words: "facilitate," "funding decisions are made by a team of Ben & Jerry's employees," and "constituent-led organizations." In addition to the clue given by having company employees make the funding decisions, I also pick up by the following words that this grantmaker is concerned with process: "types of activities and strategies an organization uses." Finally, the foundation demonstrates a belief that one must address root causes of problems in order to be effective: "addressing the underlying conditions of societal and environmental problems."

JM FOUNDATION

Jeremiah Milbank created The JM Foundation in 1924 to help integrate people with disabilities into all aspects of American life. He was also an ardent champion of individual liberty and limited government. To realize his vision, The JM Foundation Directors support activities that foster self-sufficiency, personal responsibility, and private initiative. The Foundation's current philanthropic goals are to encourage market-oriented public policy solutions that enhance America's unique system of free enterprise, entrepreneurship, and voluntarism.

There is little mystery here as to what this foundation founder's beliefs were; they are well spelled out. The paragraph describes a man who shares the Bradleys' libertarian outlook: "ardent champion of individual liberty and limited government." A good deal of language promotes market-based remedies: "encourage market-oriented public policy solutions" and "enhance America's unique system of free enterprise, entrepreneurship."

Although these words are fairly obvious as to the foundation's vision, there are a couple of things that initially seem a bit out of place from that vision, but upon further reflection are understandable and match it: "help integrate people with disabilities into all aspects of American life," and "voluntarism." What I learned from reading more of the foundation's website is that Jeremiah Milbank's initial interest in people with disabilities had to do with helping returning World War I veterans. Also, looking at the words "foster self-sufficiency, personal responsibility, and private initiative," I suggest that Mr. Milbank wanted to aid veterans in becoming self-sufficient. An interest in personal responsibility in lieu of government responsibility accounts for the interest in voluntarism. Last, notice that those three phrases—"foster self-sufficiency," "personal responsibility," and "private initiative"—are about individuals as the primary actors, not government.

Use Buzzwords

Pay attention to the grantmakers' buzzwords, especially the ones that they use in an RFP. These are the words that will be used several times throughout the funder's materials. The funders are telling you what they care about. They are telling you what they want to see from you. In your response, you want to echo the grantmaker's language and style. You want to talk in a way that resonates with the funder.

As you read an RFP or the funder's materials, highlight the buzzwords in one color and highlight the action words—that is, the specific instructions on how to submit a proposal—in another color. Make a bulleted list of the buzzwords in large type, and as you are writing the proposal, keep that list where you can easily see it. This will be especially important if you are writing under deadline. As you write a particular section or answer a funder's question, keep your eyes on those buzzwords, for they will guide you. I know from experience how useful this advice can be; I've been so pressed against a deadline I could hardly breathe and those buzzwords kept me focused on what was important to the grantmaker, and I wrote accordingly.

Applying the Grantmaker's Words

Whenever you uncover a potential grantmaker, pay close attention to what it is saying to you; it is telling you who it is. And after you have investigated that potential funder, it is very important that you compare the fundamental values of the project you are proposing with the stated values of that grantmaker. If you are coming from two different points of view, it's not a good match; find another grantmaker—you're not going to change its mind.

But if after reading the grantmaker's materials, it is clear that not only do you match in topic but you match in approach and ideology, then it's a *great* match. And part of being a great match is to convince the potential funder that you *are* one—that you understand who it is, what it cares about, what it believes, and how it approaches problem solving. The words in your grant proposal should say, in essence, "I hear you, I agree with you, and I'm giving you something that will really resonate with your vision."

Before you begin to write your grant proposal to this grantmaker, immerse yourself in its personality. Remind yourself of how it sees the world and consider how it might react to what you propose. Think of the words that it might use to describe what you propose to do and use those words as you write. Give the grantmaker language that it can recognize.

CHAPTER 4

Say It to the Right Audience with the Right Style

The first steps on the path to grantseeking success are to examine your project to ensure that it is fundable (Chapter 1), to research potential grantmakers to assess whether or not they are a good match for that project (Chapter 2), and to explore the grantmaker's viewpoints to find your hook (Chapter 3). This chapter takes grantwriting preparation one step further—learning about your audience, about who will be reading your proposal, and then crafting your writing to speak to that audience and increase your likelihood of funding. You want to use your words to connect and be accessible.

Know Your Audience

Knowing your audience is fundamental to good proposal writing; in fact, it's essential in any good writing. This knowledge will affect your writing style, your vocabulary, what you emphasize, what information you include or don't include, and the order in which you present it all. Think about it: Do you talk to your child in the same way as you talk to your boss? Do you use the same voice in a job-seeking cover letter as in a personal letter? No, you don't. And you instinctively understand why. Take this same sensitivity to your audience and recognize that the funding world is not homogeneous; you will have a variety of audiences, each of which needs your astute attention.

Who will be reviewing your proposal? Will it be a government or foundation program officer, a peer review committee, a member of a foundation's family, a corporate marketing director, or a board of directors? Will the reader be so intimately familiar with your discipline that very academic or scientific language is not only okay but expected? Or should you write for the educated layperson? These are questions that you should answer before you begin writing because you want your writing to be accessible and to connect with the reader. Being mindful of your audience makes both of these things more likely. And writing to your audience is a way to show respect, because you are acknowledging who they are, how they are approaching their task, and what is important to them. You are confirming that you are *listening*.

If it is not immediately clear from the grantmaker's materials who will be reviewing your proposal, ask! This is not an unreasonable question to pose and will guide you in framing your proposal so that it is both useful and inviting to the reader. It is possible that more than one type of person will be reviewing your proposal—a staff person and the board of directors, for example, or a review committee and a program officer. But in those cases, focus on the first reader because that's who the proposal has to get past in order to get to the second reader. If you understand that a particular program officer will be the key reviewer of your proposal, then you want to find out as much as you can about that person. If that person works at a foundation, you may be able to find a biography on the foundation's website or check the archives of *Philanthropy News Digest* (http://foundationcenter.org/pnd) or the *Chronicle of Philanthropy* (http://philanthropy.com) for that person's name. There are also biographical databases you could investigate, such as Marquis "Who's Who on the Web" (www.marquiswhoswho.com). To gain an understanding of a person's outlook on the grantmaking subject matter and approach, research that person's writings, and inform yourself of his or her educational background and previous employment. This type of information will tell you a lot about who that person is, which could be useful to have as you write.

In addition to knowing who will be reading your proposal, you also want to clarify who is ultimately making funding decisions and who has the capacity to influence those decisions. Does a review committee or a panel advise or decide?

Remember that you should approach a grantmaker in the way it requests and write in a way that the reader will recognize. Grantmakers have reasons for requesting that we supply information in a certain way; it is not up to us to try to convince them to do it otherwise. It is our job as grantseekers to acknowledge that not one approach or style suits all grantmakers. Respond in a way that demonstrates this understanding and an awareness of to whom you are writing.

Operate from the Reader's World

Consider that your readers come to the table with a specific mind-set, background, and set of experiences that affect how they see the world and how they determine what is and isn't of value. They will grade your proposal with this perspective as their basis. That means you need to be mindful of how they measure success for themselves. Consider the things by which they are graded, by which they determine if they've produced something of worth, and make sure to have those things in your narrative.

For example, if the person who is reading your proposal works in academia, chances are that he or she values knowledge of related literature, research, and data. So if you don't use these measures in your narrative, it will be harder for that reader to be convinced of the validity of what you're proposing or of your competence and capacity to do the work. Or if the person who is reading your proposal works in the corporate sector, he or she is likely to value tangible outcomes. So if the proposal is about addressing unemployment, for example, that reader is more interested in seeing specific, spelled-out steps that will lead to the targeted beneficiaries getting a job rather than a lengthy discussion of structural problems in the economy.

Picture a reader saying to you, "Prove it to me in a way that I recognize." One way to do this is to cite well-known data sources for your field. If there is a national association affiliated with the type of work you do, see if it has literature or research that upholds your proposed choice of activity and cite it.

This tells the reader several things: (1) that you know enough about the field to know that this organization is highly respected within it, (2) that the course of action you have chosen is grounded in others' research and deliberations, and (3) that the facts and figures support your outlook. It gives you credibility.

Grant proposals have three primary funding audiences: foundations, corporations, and government. A different writing and presentation style is needed for proposals to each type of potential funder. This style is rooted in the funder's motivation for giving and in its way of operating. Let's review how this plays out for each group.

Foundations

Motivation for Giving

Foundation grants are intended to effect social change. As with governmental grantmaking, foundation grantmaking is about addressing specific needs, but foundations are often established because it is believed that government has not adequately or appropriately addressed those needs. Foundations are a vehicle by which an individual (the founder) can have a non-legislative impact on public policy.

Keep in mind that foundations also want to be associated with greatness—to be the entity that made the difference in solving a societal or community problem. Because of their independence, foundations have more freedom to be grantmaking risk takers than does government. As mentioned earlier, they are often thought to be the laboratory for government, funding innovative programs, which, if proven to be effective, may later be adopted and funded by government as one of its own established programs. Head Start is an example of this process.

Staffing

You will find a variety of audiences within the foundation world. Larger and midsize foundations will have program staff that receive, review, and recommend proposals to a decision-making board of directors. Although the board makes final funding decisions, program officers are generally the ones determining which proposals to submit for their approval. In smaller family foundations with little or no staff, it is the board—usually made up of family members—who decide which proposals to fund. More often than not, the staff's functions in these foundations are more administrative than programmatic. The way you present your idea will depend on which of these readers you need to convince.

For example, if you know the name of the program officer who reviews proposals in the program area you are applying to, you can learn something about that person's background—his education, experiences, interests, and history with the funder. If you find that she has extensive knowledge of the subject area that relates to your proposed work, then you can use a shared vocabulary that will resonate with an expert. However, if you know that the reader is someone who cares about the type of work your organization does but is not fully immersed in it, you will present your project differently, making sure not to use overly technical terminology, for example.

Some foundations post this background information on their websites. If you subscribe to any philanthropic media, such as the *Chronicle of Philanthropy*, search the archives. The Foundation Center's online newsletter, *Philanthropy News Digest*, has a regular section called "People in the News: Promotions and Appointments," which gives brief bios about new appointees and is searchable. If you belong to an email list, ask fellow readers for information about grantmaker staff. Sometimes convention programs have bios on grantmaker speakers. And then there is the ubiquitous research tool, the Google search engine.

Review Committees

Some foundations, such as those dealing with research, will have peer review committees, much like those in government. As in government, these reviewers are chosen for their experience and expertise with the subject. They will be given a set of criteria by which to judge your proposal, but you might not have access to those measures as you would with a government grant. That's why it's all the more important to educate yourself about the foundation. You increase your likelihood of getting a grant if you understand where a foundation is coming from—its founding, its history, its mind-set, its values—and recognize how this affects giving practices. I devote a large part of Chapter 3 to a more in-depth exploration of how to read a foundation's operating principles and frame your message accordingly.

Community foundations and other public charities frequently use review committees, sometimes referred to as distribution committees. Review committees may also be used to determine how to allocate scholarships. Unlike research-specific review committees that primarily draw from academia, these are more likely to be made up of a group of community leaders who will have varied subject matter expertise. Your writing style should take this into consideration.

Style

Generally, writing to a foundation calls for a different style from writing to a government, corporate, or individual prospect. Your proposal will read more like a paper you've written for a class, as you are building a case based on proven need and innovative solution.

But unlike government proposals, there is no assurance that your proposal will be read in full. Therefore, your writing must be particularly engaging; your first paragraph must be so compelling that the reviewer wants to read the second one. You must demonstrate immediately that the work you propose to do is in perfect alignment with the foundation's goals and objectives and then prove that you have the capacity to do it well.

Whether you are responding to an RFP or are sending in an unsolicited proposal will affect your writing style. As noted previously, it is easier to get funded when responding to an RFP because the foundation is saying it will be funding proposals in a specific area; you don't have that assurance in an over-the-transom scenario in which the foundation may or may not fund proposals in one of its stated areas of interest. Moreover, in an RFP, the foundation has made it very clear what problems it seeks to address, the approach or approaches it most favors in doing so, how much money is available, and what questions—either roughly or precisely—it expects you to answer. Because of this specificity by the grantmaker, your language can be much more focused and precise; when writing an unsolicited proposal, you must figure out the funder's current direction and you don't have as much grantmaker-provided information.

You are more likely to have freedom in how you present your information in a foundation proposal than in a government proposal. This is not to say that foundations don't have specific questions they want you to answer; it's just that many tend to be more relaxed about the way in which you answer these questions.

But this doesn't mean that a proposal shouldn't have logic and structure to it. It means that you can write in such a way that each paragraph leads logically to the next, so that the reader is nodding and saying, "Yes, I see" and is hungry for each subsequent paragraph. However, this may eventually change, as more and more foundations are putting applications online that have a strictness and conciseness similar to government ones, sometimes even more so.

An important exception to the building-a-case foundation writing style is if the proposal is going to a small family foundation, where decisions are made only by family members. In these cases, you should write as if you were writing a fundraising request to an individual, because that is essentially what it is.

Corporations

Motivation for Giving

Corporate philanthropy is about corporate visibility; it's marketing. This is not to say that the people managing corporate philanthropy are lacking in genuine compassion, but grants are made with marketing and corporate benefits in mind. Unlike government and foundations, corporations are for-profit entities, and it's natural that they would behave in accordance with economic goals. This is a key distinction to keep in mind when writing corporate proposals.

Audience

The first thing you need to know is whether your proposal is going to a corporate foundation or to the corporation itself; this will affect your approach. If the corporate foundation is a separate entity with its own staff, it will behave much in the same way as a private foundation, and you should respond accordingly. There are also hybrid forms of corporate philanthropy, in which the foundation will be called a corporate foundation although it is not separately run and is managed by in-house staff. If it is not immediately apparent which of these approaches the corporation uses, it's okay to ask and get clarification about its grantmaking process.

If your request is going to the corporation directly and not a foundation, you might be dealing with a marketing person, a public relations person, or a plant manager, all of whom will likely have the same broad motivation for giving: visibility, marketing, community goodwill. However, each might have different trigger points according to his or her position. For example, the plant manager might specifically be interested in how the funded actions will affect her workforce. Will it make the city a nicer place to live? Will it train or positively affect future workers? On the other hand, the marketing person is focused on whether the company's name will be visible as a result of grant activity. These distinctions may affect what you choose to emphasize or deemphasize in your proposal.

Pay attention to who will be reading your proposal initially and who will be making the decisions; they may not be the same person or even at the same location. Are you sending your proposal to corporate headquarters, or are you dealing with a local plant or office? Does headquarters give the local person clearance on deciding what will and won't be funded, or does that local person just receive the request and pass it on to headquarters? The answers to these questions may make a difference in how you approach your proposal. If the corporation's materials don't make this clear, call to get clarity; start with the local office or plant first. It is okay to ask what the grant review procedure is.

Style

Generally, a proposal to a corporate entity will be short, use bullets, and make it clear what visibility or other benefits the corporation will enjoy as a result of funding your organization. The exception to this rule would be if you are approaching a corporate foundation, in which case you will be writing as you do to any private foundation, but keeping the corporation's high need for visibility in the forefront.

Brevity and conciseness are essential elements to a corporate proposal. The corporate world tends to be fast paced, eager to get to the point, and results oriented. Your proposal presentation should respect that. Likewise, consider that the corporate world likes winners and, therefore, will be more receptive to self-promoting language.

Government

Motivation for Giving

Government grant programs exist because the legislative body has identified a community or societal need that it chooses to address through non-governmental means. The executive body must carry out those wishes through grantmaking to outside entities. Thus, the core motivation for giving by government program staff is more likely related to doing a good job of grantmaking than it is to promoting a particular outlook, as might be the case for foundations.

Grants are often used as a policy tool to stimulate specific behavior and outcomes. For example, while all may agree that early education is vital to children's later success, there will be disagreement about the best way to deliver this education. Generally, government RFPs will reflect the prevailing political viewpoint in their program directives and evaluation criteria, and these may change when authority changes.

However, despite this connection to political policymaking, both federal and state government grant programs will have a high sensitivity to being seen as fair in their distribution and seek to have geographic and organizational diversity in the allocation of funds.

Review Committees

Federal government programs routinely have review committees or panels evaluate proposals. Proposal reviewers are often people outside of government who serve on a singular committee for a particular round of funding. However, at some federal agencies, such as the Department of Education, these committees can consist of federal employees in addition to outside reviewers. Although reviewers may serve on more than one review committee over time, the makeup of a review committee changes with each funding round.

Because they are federal employees, departmental program officers are a more constant presence than the ever-changing review committees and are open to chatting with would-be applicants about their programs. Thus, it is possible to establish a relationship with them. Not only can they give you useful feedback about what you are proposing to do but if your proposal is not successful, they can provide you with reviewers' comments or tell you why you were turned down.

When submitting a federal proposal, you will have three different audiences to address: a departmental program officer, the people on the review committee who fully read your proposal, and the people on the review committee who read only an abstract or selected parts of your proposal.

To varying degrees, reviewers are subject matter experts and likely work in your discipline. Reviewers are selected because they are established in their field. However, despite this commonality, some peer reviewers may not fully understand your work. Although there may be some who are intimately familiar with it—and perhaps know more than you do!—there will be some who, even though they work in the same field, will have different specialties. You need to write with both audiences in mind.

While precise steps will vary according to each department's rules, generally the full pool of proposals is initially reviewed by the program officer, and those found to meet the basic eligibility requirements are sent in subsets to teams of reviewers. Unlike in the private sector—where there is no guarantee of your proposal being read at all—your proposal will get a full reading and by more than one person. Keep in mind, however, that sometimes not all people who have a vote on your proposal are reading it in its entirety. Your proposal may be summarized by one person who will lead the discussion of it, outlining its strengths and weaknesses. Therefore, you'll want to make it easy for that person to capture your highlights and strengths.

Chapters 5 and 6 will walk you through the necessary steps for creating a proposal that is clear and easy to read and summarize. These qualities are especially important with the review committee structure. The most clearly written and persuasive proposals with unimpeachable methodology will receive the best ratings.

Review Criteria

The difference between government and private-sector grantmaking is that because government is "of the people, for the people, by the people," it must be open and accessible to all eligible grantseekers.

Part of the beauty of this transparency is that you will always know the review criteria on which your proposal is being graded. Review criteria are those things that the grantmaker has determined are indicators of good project design and capacity, such as project activities, organizational capacity, project evaluation, and reasonableness of the budget. All federal government proposals will indicate what these criteria will be, and most departments or agencies will designate how many points will be assigned to each item. Grant opportunity announcements and departmental websites will spell out precisely what the purpose of the grant program is, what they are looking to fund, and how your proposal will be evaluated.

The review criteria rule all; pay attention to them! Your review committee does. They are given strict instructions to follow the department's stated review criteria when judging proposals; they take this very seriously and will not veer from this assignment. Therefore, if you want to be successful, you need to write with the review criteria squarely in the forefront of your brain.

In addition to their subject matter expertise, reviewers apply a taxpayer's viewpoint during their evaluation, asking, Does the work being proposed have broad value? Do we, as citizens, really care if we have this information? Do we really care if this activity is done? This is our money; is this a good way to spend it?

Also consider that an audience drawn from among your subject matter peers will know the literature and what other work has been done in your field. Their knowledge and experiences will give them some sense of whether what you propose is overreaching or realistic. In addition to your proposal narrative, your timeline and your budget will provide clues for that analysis.

Government reviewers are also concerned with whether your organization has what it takes to implement the work you propose to do. Smaller or lesser-known organizations have to work harder to be convincing of their capacity to perform. The résumés or curricula vitae (CVs) of your project managers or principal investigators (PIs) tell a lot about the person's experience and abilities and will be critical in conferring that assurance. If you throw a well-known name into your proposal to impress, you'd best defend why that person is involved in your project and specify exactly what that person will contribute to it.

Style

Government proposals give you less room for imprinting your own style. The application process will require you to answer a series of questions in the order that they are asked, and you must keep within word or page limitations while doing so. There may be times when you think a question has been asked and answered already, but if an RFP asks it again, you must answer it again. This rigidity limits your ability to build your case as you wish to present it, but you must be vigilant in making sure that your essential points are inserted somewhere, somehow, much like a politician strives to stay on message. For example, let's say you're writing a proposal about providing self-defense training and you notice from the way the RFP is worded that the grantmaker cares a lot about making sure the training is provided quickly and efficiently. When describing the training you will deliver, you would make sure to use those two words—*quickly* and *efficiently*—throughout the proposal.

Your writing style will also be affected by the dominance of the review criteria, as discussed earlier. Make it easy for any reviewer to put a check mark next to each review criteria by using narrative headers that correspond to review criteria terms used in the RFP. If, because of space limitations, you need to make choices about what sentences or words stay in the proposal, ask yourself if they are necessary to be convincing that a particular review criterion has been met. If you are a full-time writer, you may have to let go of your pride in eloquence and focus instead on precision, brevity, and bare facts. Write to the review criteria.

Technical Assistance

Most federal government grantmaking is now done electronically, including proposal submission. Departmental websites have grant program information, tutorials on how to apply for a grant, information on how grants are reviewed and processed, and guidance on how to prepare a grant proposal. If you are new to government grantmaking, I urge you to make use of these resources. You should also avail yourself of the many technical assistance tools that agencies offer, such as conference calls, webinars, and meetings.

Learn from Your Rejections

If you're not successful the first time, especially with government grants, and want to resubmit a proposal for the same program, you can learn more about what your audience is looking for by requesting the reviewers' comments. Many government program officers will encourage you to do this and resubmit in the next round. Some foundations will provide you with feedback on unsuccessful proposals, but it is usually through conversation with a foundation staff person rather than receiving official reviewers' comments.

You have a gold mine of information in your reviewers' comments; scrutinize them and incorporate the lessons learned into your subsequent proposal. You will see not only the assessed point totals but the reasons the readers gave those scores. With government grants in particular, the point system is important to ensure that all proposals receive quantifiable assessment. The points allotted to each criterion will vary not only from department to department but also from RFP to RFP. But generally you will know these point allotments ahead of time and should be using them to guide your proposal preparation.

For those proposals for which you do get reviewers' comments back, I recommend making a chart similar to the one on page 77 in which you identify all of the criteria by which you were judged, with the total points allotted for each criterion, and list how each reader graded you by that criterion. If there are subcategories within each broader category, isolate the points of those subcategories so that you can really determine just where it was that you lost the readers, and thus lost points.

Total each reader and each subject area, and see in which area(s) you had the highest number of possible points and in which areas you had the lowest number of possible points. You will begin to see patterns of where you were strong and where you were not. Look to see if there was joint agreement about how you fared in each criterion or if one reader skewed the numbers.

But don't get mad at anonymous reviewers when you see that they've missed a point you feel you made quite clearly. Maybe you did tell them that piece of information they say is missing, but apparently you didn't tell them in a way that they could hear. As I noted earlier, that's your responsibility; you must communicate to your audience.

After you have tallied all the points, take a look at what the readers are telling you by virtue of how they allotted the points. Did you lose points because the project design itself wasn't good, or did you lose points because the presentation of that design was unclear? You can fix both things, but be clear about what it is that needs fixing. All the good writing in the world can't hide poor project design. And likewise, a fabulous project poorly presented cannot be known as a fabulous project.

Let's look at the chart below and see what we can learn from this example. The first thing that I notice is that there is not a wide variation among the three readers' assessments. Their reactions for each category are very similar, telling me that this assessment has validity.

	Significance 10	Need 15	Project Design 20	Partnerships 15	Org. Capacity 10	Budget 10	Evaluation 20	TOTAL POINTS 100
Reader 1	8	13	17	9	7	8	15	77
Reader 2	9	14	18	11	7	8	17	84
Reader 3	9	13	17	10	7	9	16	81
TOTALS	26	40	52	30	21	25	48	242
Avail. Pts.	30	45	60	45	30	30	60	300
Lost points	4	5	8	15	9	5	12	58

The next thing that pops out at me is how disappointed the readers were in the Partnerships category. Some grantmakers are fond of projects that involve multiple people or organizations—partnerships—because they believe that a unified approach to problem solving is smart. They may require that you approach your project in partnership with others and will grade how well you have done that. That the category Partnerships is where we lost the most points says that either we did not do a good job of finding partners or of using partners in the project design or we didn't do a good job of telling the grantmaker that we did. Are the partners we chose to work with of significance to the problem we wish to address? Did we have letters of commitment from our partners confirming their involvement? Are the activities in which the partners will be involved appropriate? Are partners expected to contribute to the project and ours did not? Clearly, if we want to be successful the second time we submit this proposal, we need to reexamine and fix the Partnerships category; we lost 15 points there.

The other area in which a bit of effort could gain points is Evaluation. Maybe they didn't like our chosen evaluation methodology. Maybe they thought the evaluation should be conducted by an outside entity, and we decided to do it in-house. Maybe the evaluation was not directly linked to stated outcomes. But if all those things are intact, then we need to look at how we presented the material. (See Chapter 12 for more information on evaluation.)

The reviewers' comments tell me a few more things of note. They believe we have reasonable capacity to do the work, but they're not wowed by us. We need to be more convincing of our abilities. With scores of 17 and 18 out of 20, it shows that our project design is quite acceptable to the readers, but again, it apparently lacks the power that a 19 or 20 would indicate; we would have to read their comments to understand what they see as missing. For each of the places where we only lost a point or two per reader, you might be swayed to think that's not so bad. But cumulatively these lost points can add up to a lost opportunity.

Use the reviewers' comments as the gift that they are to strengthen your proposal. Although you cannot know who will be serving on the next review committee, if the same comment or assessment comes up more than once among the original reviewers, then it is something you should pay attention to for the next round.

It is always worth asking for feedback after a proposal rejection; it's how you learn to prepare a better proposal. As mentioned earlier, most government offices will readily provide you with the reviewers' comments. Many foundation or governmental program officers make themselves accessible after an unsuccessful proposal review, and a conversation with them can be very valuable. A foundation program officer offered me this insight into proposal rejections, "If your proposal was denied it is okay to ask why. This is a time to understand why your proposal was denied, and listening carefully can assist you in shaping your next request. Remember, this is not the time to debate the merits of your request, as the funder's decision has already been made, but a time to foster or maintain that funder/applicant relationship."

I learned this many years ago while working at a university. We had submitted a proposal to the Hewlett Foundation, made it to the finals, but were not selected for funding. While at a conference we both attended, I arranged to meet with the program officer and asked him to tell me how we might strengthen the proposal for future submissions. I listened carefully and reported my findings back to the campus. We reworked the project design, submitted a refreshed proposal the following year, and received a grant! We wouldn't have been successful without that program officer's thoughtful and open assessment.

Another foundation program officer pointed out to me that "[i]f a proposal is rejected, you should respond with a 'thank you' to the program officers who reviewed it. They often spend a good deal of time with your proposal. If they make suggestions about where you might take it for funding, be especially appreciative."

Overall Style Advice

One of the ways to tell what style of writing will resonate with a potential funder is to look at its own style when describing its grantmaking areas of interest and grantmaking approaches. In what order does it discuss the issues it cares about? From what point of view does it approach the topic? Does it write in a manner that is more academic or more colloquial? If you pay attention to how it's using words, you will get some clues as to how to use yours.

Style relates not just to the words or how words are used but also to how they're visually presented. Do you notice that the funder uses bullet points a lot? Does it have frequent headers? Does it use a table of contents? If you are uncertain how to organize or present your material, and there are no guidelines, make note of the grantmaker's materials and how they look.

Do not presume that all readers share your use of language. Unless you know that your academic or subject matter peers will be reviewing your proposal, write it for the educated layperson. However, when you know that your proposal will be read by peer reviewers, you should be sure to use all the recognized terms within your field. When trying to make decisions about when to use technical or nontechnical language, your best bet is to put nontechnical language in the sections describing larger concepts, such as need and goals, and use technical language in the methodology sections.

Before you begin to write, be clear about who your audience will be and think about what writing and presentation style is needed for proposals to a foundation, to a corporation, or to a government entity.

CHAPTER 5

Creating a Well-Organized and Well-Structured Proposal

By teaching you how to think about your project and prospective grantmakers, Chapters 1–4 give you the groundwork on which to build your proposal. The next step in the grantwriting process is to think about the organization and structure of your proposal.

Imagine that your proposal is the last proposal a reviewer is reading on a Friday afternoon of a hellish week. Imagine how a reviewer might regard your proposal if it is disorganized, if the answers to the questions that have been posed by the grantmaker can't be found, or if the reviewer can't identify whether or not a particular passage is addressing a particular review criteria. A poorly arranged, incomplete proposal will earn low points, no matter how good the underlying idea of it is. Help your reader avoid further frustration and stay focused on the content of your proposed work by making the grant proposal *easy to read*, *easy to follow*, and *easy to find information*.

Keep in mind, too, that government peer reviewers often read proposals in addition to their regular jobs. With this audience, it is not only kind but smart to make your proposal visually and factually accessible. Presentation matters.

Proposal Organization Brainstorming

When you are first thinking of applying for a particular grant, I recommend that you pull together the team of people who will be involved in that grant for a brainstorming session. Although not everybody needs to be engaged in the actual writing of a proposal, they can all add to a conversation about how you will address each component of the proposal. This early-on consultation will serve many purposes. It will (1) tighten your project design, (2) ensure group consensus on what you envision doing, (3) provide opportunity for creative input, and (4) keep you, the writer, on track. After this session, draft an outline of the proposal for the group's review and reaction. Ideally, you would want the group to review and edit a full proposal, but that's often unrealistic given deadlines. However, an early outline review by others at least gives you the opportunity to have your proposal arrangement and logic checked before you undertake writing the full proposal. This organizational tool will serve you well and will later be appreciated by proposal reviewers.

If the grantmaker you are approaching does not have a set proposal application or group of questions you are to answer, refer to the "Basic Components of a Proposal" on page 10.

Proposal Mapping

In addition to having specific page limitations, many grantmakers will have specific questions they expect you to answer within that page limitation. Before you begin to write your proposal, roughly map out how much space you will use to respond to each question or each topic. In those instances in which points have been allotted to each question or topic, you should apportion your space accordingly. For example, if a statement of need gives you a maximum of 10 points, but project activity is worth 35 points, you want to give project activity more space. Mapping this out ahead of time will save you from overwriting a section.

Here is an example of how I distributed the number of allowed pages (which was further limited by the requirement that they be double spaced!) according to one grantmaker's evaluation criteria.

Evaluation Criterion	Point Value	Number of Pages
Statement of need	10	2
Partnerships	20	4
Project plan	25	5
Outcomes and impact	30	6
Organizational capacity	10	2
Integration with regional strategies	5	1/2
Bonus: Integration with federal program	5	1/2
Totals	105	20

This is also a time for making decisions about proposal structure, not just deciding on your header hierarchy but also determining how you will differentiate paragraphs and where you might use charts or tables.

Formatting

Many funders will specify the format of your proposal. In the interest of ensuring fairness among applicants, government agencies can be particularly precise and strict about basic formatting requirements. Before you begin to write, see if the agency has a set style guide. In addition to having set guides, some agencies, such as the National Institutes of Health and the National Science Foundation, have informative websites to guide you through the application process and to give proposal design and writing guidance.

Grantmakers will indicate the number of pages, margins, spacing, minimum font size, and sometimes even acceptable fonts. I know of one foundation that requests that all proposals be submitted on recycled paper. Whatever the funder's requirements are, follow them! Sometimes proposals are denied a review strictly because the applicant did not follow formatting instructions.

Do you want to explain to your board that the proposal was rejected because you used three-quarter-inch margins instead of one-inch? Pay attention; if the grantmaker has preferences, it will tell you what they are.

Answer all questions posed. Fill out all forms. If there is a legitimate reason you don't respond to a specific question or request for information, acknowledge the request and state why you can't respond to it.

In addition to page limitations, funders will sometimes designate a set number of words that may be used to answer a particular question. Do not go over that limit! You'll be saved from yourself if this is done online; generally, online applications won't let you type 251 words if it says it only wants 250. Your challenge, then, is in the editing.

If the grantmaker has not given you precise instruction on how your proposal should be laid out, look at that funder's materials and see how they are laid out. This will give you an idea of how they use space, how they use headers, and what is visually appealing to the people likely to be reading your proposal.

At the bottom of each page of your project narrative, insert a footer with not just the page number but also the name of your organization. There are two reasons to do this. One is pragmatic; if your proposal is one of a group of proposals and gets dropped while being copied, it will be easy to put it back together correctly. The other reason is more subliminal; the reader will continually see the name of your organization as he or she reviews the proposal.

Make the proposal easy to copy or scan. This means clips rather than staples, loose pages rather than bound.

Make It Easy to Read

You need to give your proposal every advantage that you can. You don't want the reader to be put off before he or she can even begin the review. People can make judgments from just a visual examination of your proposal. So take a look at it. Is there enough white space? Does the reader need a magnifying glass to read it? Will it lay flat while someone is trying to read it? A good standard to adopt when preparing proposals is to think about what annoys you and to avoid doing that.

Be attentive to the basics; reviewers can get unnecessarily distracted by typos and spelling, punctuation, and grammatical errors. And what does such sloppiness say about your organization?

Some applicants will attempt to cram as many words as they possibly can into a limited space, thinking that every one of those words is vital to making their case. They may reduce margins, they may write in an impossibly small font, or they may avoid paragraphing altogether. While the temptation to do these things may be great, a proposal that is difficult to read does not serve you. Fifty-year-old eyes don't do well with 10-point fonts, and aggravated readers don't award high points. Edit instead.

Make It Easy to Follow

One way to make a proposal easy to follow is to use a header hierarchy. A header hierarchy establishes a set format that indicates main sections and sub-sections of a proposal by consistent use of font size, heading positioning, capital letters, bold, underlining, and italics. The heading hierarchy makes materials easy to find, demonstrates the relative importance of each section, and makes it easy to see relationships among topics. If you use a consistent style throughout the proposal, you enable the reader to easily follow what is new material.

Each writer will have preferences, but certain things imply importance over others. For example, using all capital letters suggests a higher level of importance than upper and lowercase together. Using bold letters indicates a more encompassing topic than does using underlined ones. A centered heading is more pronounced than a flush left heading. Whatever format you decide to use, use it consistently. Here is an example of a heading hierarchy:

HEADING 1

Heading 2

Heading 3

Heading 4

Make It Easy to Find Information

Do simple things to enable the reader to stay with your message. Use headings that correspond to the information requested. This is particularly important with government proposals, for which readers take the review criteria and associated points very seriously. Competition for government funds is rigorous; funding decisions can be made on a difference of a point or two. Improve your chances for funding by making it very easy for proposal reviewers to find the section that relates to each criterion. One way to do this is to use the review criteria as the headers so that readers can easily assess whether you have addressed the question sufficiently. Don't make them dig for it; make it easy for them to award you points.

There are other simple things you can do to make it easy to find information. For example, if the proposal is longer than fifteen to twenty pages, use a table of contents. To allow readers to pick and choose what they will read, divide your material into distinct sections with obvious headers. In lieu of a table of contents, you could use tabs to mark sections. If your narrative references information in an appendix or an attachment—and you're not doing an electronic submission—make sure that a tab marks that appendix or attachment. If you reference another section in a proposal by page number, double-check that the page number is correct.

Use a Proposal Introduction

The grantmaker should be introduced to the basic tenets of your project on the first page of the proposal. This first page may be labeled "Proposal Abstract" or "Executive Summary," but not all grantmakers request or require one. In instances in which a separate section is not used, a one- to two-paragraph introduction is recommended; if you have the space, it could be slightly longer.

An introduction can take one of two approaches; in both cases, you are setting the stage for the following section. Sometimes the content of an introduction will be somewhat similar to the content of an abstract or summary (see Chapter 15), in that you are announcing what you intend to do and what you think will happen as a result. However, rather than seeking to condense the entire proposal's contents, as you would in an abstract/summary, in an introduction you are presenting a powerful and positive statement about the action you propose to take and the beneficial outcomes that will result, with little detail. These brief initial remarks make it so that the first thing you say to the grantmaker is a strong, affirmative declaration about what you will do, and allows the proposal to flow into why these actions are necessary, which—unless otherwise dictated by the grantmaker—will be covered in the immediately following section, the statement of need (Chapter 10).

In other cases, you can use the introduction to give the context for the project's focus, which can include current conditions, your interests and concerns, and a brief explanation of why you chose to go this route. Turn to page 96 for a before and after example of a proposal opening that uses this tack. Also peruse the introductions of the proposals in the Appendix.

Timesavers

Many people have grantwriting as a duty on top of other work and would be able to produce more if they had some timesaving solutions. I offer two such solutions below.

Language Library

If you must write a lot of proposals for your organization, it behooves you to have a language library. A language library is a collection of written material that will likely be needed in a proposal, such as an organizational description, a mission statement, and clientele demographics. Depending on the nature of your organization's work, other things that are useful in a language library might be census bureau and employment statistics, information about the geographic or demographic community you serve, and research findings that uphold your organization's approach to its work. The goal of the language library is that if you are asked to give your organization's history, it's there; you've already written it. If a description of your regular programs is required, it's there. If you suddenly need to know the high school dropout rate in your community, you aren't scrambling to find it; it's there.

The best source of this material is the proposals and reports you've already written. As you write each proposal, be mindful of what may later be useful. After the flurry of meeting a deadline and proposal submission has passed, intentionally pull out parts of the proposal that you may need to come back to for a future proposal and put them into a language library with topic headers or subject-specific files for easy retrieval. Another approach would be to keep a topical list of what material is contained in each proposal so that when you say, "Help! I need to write an evaluation plan!" you'll have one to use as a template.

Speaking of templates, save your budgets and budget narratives so that you don't need to spend time setting up a new spreadsheet or document format the next time you need to pull together a budget for a proposal. Timelines and charts are also useful to have in a language library. While the content may differ, an already formatted document can be a big timesaver. Charts can be created and reused for a wide variety of things, such as objectives and outcomes, logic models, and partner roles.

If you don't have the material already written, you should generate stock paragraphs for things that are not likely to change much, such as your organization's mission statement, history, description, and standard programs. You may even want to have several versions of these things to fit varying space restrictions that may arise.

Common Proposal Forms

Most states have a regional association of grantmakers that serves both grantmaking and grantseeking communities. These organizations provide information, resources, philanthropic educational programs, and networking. Some of them also provide a singular proposal form that can be used to submit proposals to their many foundation members. These forms may be called a "Common Proposal Form," "Common Grant Application Form," or "Universal Grant Application." These forms have an efficiency that serves both the grantmaker and potential grantees and are gaining more and more use. You have an advantage if the foundations in your state use this form because you can fill out parts of it once and use it for several proposal submissions. Go to the Forum of Regional Associations of Grantmakers' website (www.givingforum.org/s_forum/index .asp) and click on "Locate Your Regional Association" to find a regional association of grantmakers in your state. While you're there, nose around; the website has additional pages of interest to grantseekers.

*   *   *

Give your good ideas an opportunity to be heard by presenting them in an accessible way. If a reviewer can't easily find your responses to the criteria by which he or she must judge you, then you're likely to lose points. Taking the time to make your proposal easy to navigate and visually pleasing is worth the effort. Now let's talk about how to make it interesting to read, as well.

CHAPTER 6

Make Your Case with Clarity, Logic, and Passion

If you've read from the beginning of this book, you've gone through several grantwriting preparation steps—project design, research, strategizing—and now you are ready to write a proposal. Your goal in grantwriting is this: After reading your proposal, a stranger to your ideas should be able to convey to another person exactly what it is you're trying to accomplish, how you will go about doing it, and why that's necessary and important. To achieve that goal, you need to write in a way that is clearly understood, that builds a case, and that stirs the reader. Toward that end, this chapter will focus on writing with clarity, with logic, and with passion. Remember, your words are your ticket into the minds and hearts of your readers; they must be well chosen.

If you think you can't write and that just getting basic words down on paper is an accomplishment, don't be cowed by my call for clarity, logic, and passion. I am certain that you use these qualities in your daily conversations. In fact, one of the best writing techniques you can initially use is to write as if you were talking to a friend, trying to convince him or her of your project's worth. Because you are trying to be convincing, you will summon up your logic and passion. Don't worry about how polished the words sound at that time; you can dress them up later.

Think of your grant proposal not just as a vehicle for telling but also as a means of inspiring someone to action. And it all has to be done with words, *your* words. They need the power of clarity to make sure you are understood. They need the power of logic to erase doubt about the strength of the project. And they need the power of passion to rouse empathy and to assert your commitment.

Assume Nothing: Strive for Clarity

How many times in conversation have you noticed that somebody completely misunderstood what you said even though you thought it was abundantly clear when you said it? A misheard word, a momentary distraction, the use of an unfamiliar term—any of these things can result in miscommunication. Or maybe you weren't saying it as comprehensibly as you thought you were. And when the other person's reaction is not what you had expected, you're baffled. Didn't I make myself clear? Why didn't she understand me? What is his problem? No, *he* doesn't have a problem; if you have not adequately communicated and you are seeking money, it is *your* problem.

The problem of achieving unambiguous communication is compounded in writing because you are not able to see your reader's face. You do not have the advantage of seeing expressions that would indicate understanding or confusion. That's what happens with a grant proposal; you don't have a second chance to make your case, so you must write in a way that leaves no room for questions the first time. Therefore, it is essential that you pay attention to writing with precision and clarity.

Writing with clarity achieves three main grantseeking goals:

- It allows the reader to focus on the proposal content.

- It saves you space with proposals that have page limits.

- Most important, it enables you to be understood.

Focusing the Reader on Content

Each sentence has to make sense; a sentence should not raise a question that is not immediately answered. You don't want a reader's first reaction to your sentence to be, "Huh?" because then you run the risk of losing his or her focus on your main points.

If a reader understands what you are saying with a first pass through a paragraph—if she doesn't have to fight the words to get a clear picture—it keeps her focus on the proposal's content. Remember, content is what you're selling!

If your writing is easy to follow, more likely the reader will be quickly engaged, and you will be able to hold her attention. Avoid any distractions that keep the reader from absorbing the content easily. Have a person outside your field read your first draft and let you know what is and isn't understandable. If his response to any sentence is the dreaded "Huh?" then you have more precise and descriptive writing to do.

Saving Space

You want each word to count, so you need to use your words smartly. Many grantmakers will have page limitations, and there will be times when you don't see how you can adequately tell your story in that small of a space. Examine each sentence and determine whether each word is essential to making your point. You'll find that when you are revisiting each passage, your attempts to ensure clarity will often result in space-saving cuts.

Being Understood

In lieu of conversation, your grant proposal is the main tool for communication between you and the grantmaker. Therefore it is your responsibility to make sure that it adequately serves that role—that it truly communicates. Most of the time you will be writing with an educated layperson in mind, but it is important not to assume anything about what is known by that person.

Do not assume vocabulary is shared, that acronyms are known, or that the reader knows all about your town or organization. Do not assume that the barriers you face are well known, that your methodology is evident, or that budget expenditures are self-explanatory. In one concise rule, I urge you to

Assume nothing!

The first part of the assume nothing test is to make sure that your terms are defined. If the reader doesn't understand you because he or she doesn't grasp a particular term or concept, it's your job to make sure that all essential terms and concepts are defined. Chapter 4 asks you to consider the needs of your audience, and use of terminology is one way you do that. Even if you think that anybody in your field would know a term, unless you have seen it used in the grantmaker's literature, and when everything that follows in your proposal depends on an understanding of that term, define it the first time you use it. Be as specific as space allows. And do not use jargon or slang; do not use abbreviations or acronyms without spelling them out the first time.

Likewise, even when you think an activity, a relationship, or a principle is unmistakably obvious, spell it out. When you are deeply immersed in a particular topic, it becomes second nature to you, so it's easy to assume that others know what you know and you neglect to explain vital components. But to the uninitiated, not everything is obvious. If the reader doesn't understand everything you're saying, you run the risk not only of not making your points but of aggravating the reader. The only exception to the definition rule is if you are an academic writing to fellow academics, then you can use terms *basic* to your field. But keep in mind that not all of you are studying the same thing within your field, so define terms more particular to your work.

Have someone who is not intimate with the project read your first draft and make note of what questions he or she has while reading. This will be a helpful guide as you are writing. If he says he needs more information in certain places, and you've got the space to expand without going over the page limitation, then do so.

While reviewing another's proposal, I have had the experience of being more distracted by questions than I was engaged in reading it. And the more I got into a challenging mode, with thoughts of "How do you know that?" or "Why is that so?" the less focused I was on what was being presented to me.

That doesn't serve the grantseeker well. You don't want to leave any room for confusion or skepticism on the part of the reader.

Logic

Writing with logic serves many purposes. Logic enables you to build your case, point by point. It offers a direct route through the proposal, answering the who, what, when, where, why, and how questions. It helps the reader navigate from section to section with smooth transitions. Logic reduces confusion; it anticipates the questions of the reader as they would be likely to arise. Logic's most important role is to be so convincing that the only reaction to what is presented is not only that your approach is reasonable but that what you propose makes perfect sense.

If you write with logic and your presentation is clear, rational, and level-headed, you instill a reassurance in the reader that your organization has the capacity to do the work that you propose. A proposal that is disorganized, that jumps all over the place, and that makes claims without having first laid the groundwork for such claims would not inspire a reviewer to recommend you for funding, the subliminal thought being: If your organization can't manage a sharp grant proposal, how could it manage the work the grant would fund?

Answer Likely Questions

Approach your writing task as if you were the one who has the money to give away. What is it that you would want to know? You'll find that what you want to know is very similar to what the funder wants to know. Many funders will give you a precise order in which they want you to present your materials or will ask you to answer particular questions. If that is not the case, start with a basic outline that, in a logical order, answers questions a potential funder might have:

- What is the problem you seek to address?

- Why is that important?

- What do you propose to do about it?

- How will you accomplish that?

- Why have you chosen that method?

- Why are you the organization that should do this work?

- How will you or the funder know that you've accomplished what you set out to do?

These questions correspond with the "Basic Components of a Proposal" presented on page 10 and are further described in Part Two.

Rationale vs. Method

A common writing mistake that people make is mixing rationale with method. By rationale I mean *why* are you doing this work? What is the reason it's important? Method refers to *how* you will be doing this work, the activities you'll be undertaking. You should keep your discussion of why you are doing what you propose separate from how you will be doing it. Generally, rationale is explored in your statement of need (see Chapter 10), and method is discussed when explaining goals, objectives, and project activities (see Chapter 11).

Passion

You want your words to evoke emotion yet at the same time to confer confidence. Both goals can be met by allowing the passion of your organization's commitment to its mission come through. You want your commitment and desire for change for the good to be infectious.

Passion is a tricky yet necessary element to have in your writing. Whereas clarity and logic can hold readers' attention, passion can capture their attention. But when I say "passion," I don't mean words that you would expect to be accompanied by violins. I mean words that indicate how much you care about what you're doing and how much you care about what you want to be doing for the people whom your organization serves. You want your passion to be so convincing that it could move a person to your way of thinking. You want your passion to express urgency about the need for what you propose to do so as to inspire action.

Examples of Using Clarity, Logic, and Passion in Your Proposal Presentation

The goal of the first paragraph is to be so engaging that it makes people want to read the second paragraph. The same is true of a proposal's opening pages. This is where you either grab or lose a reader; you need to make it clear what your proposed project is about and generate sufficient enough interest to keep the reader with you.

Let me demonstrate the power of compelling opening paragraphs and pages with two proposals, using before and after examples. Both of these documents have the same origins. In the first two months of my current position at a community college, on two separate occasions I was asked by two different faculty members for assistance in submitting a grant proposal; each proposal had been submitted the year before and was declined. Both professors wanted to resubmit a proposal for that year's funding round. The purpose of the grants had not changed, and the funders to which each wanted to submit the proposal had not changed. What *did* change was how the proposals were written.

For each of the full proposals, I kept the bulk of the project description previously written, but I rearranged a lot of the narrative, deleted redundancies, made sure that terms were defined and that precise activities were delineated, and substantially changed the first page. In both cases, we resubmitted the proposal, and in both cases, they got funded. Because the project design did not change and the targeted grantmaker did not change, it was the presentation of the material and some editing that made the difference.

Example 1: Proposal to the National Science Foundation

OPENING PARAGRAPH: BEFORE

This four-year Advanced Technological Education (ATE) Resource Center proposal, submitted by Springfield Technical Community College, will create a structure for rapid development and refreshment of new Information and Communications Technologies (ICT) academic content, respond to new ICT and ICT-enabled technologies and more rapidly and broadly disseminate this content nationally. The National Center for Telecommunications Technologies (NCTT) will form (or formalize) an ICT Community of Practice (CoP), an expanding group of academic professionals and industry experts who share a common goal of insuring a quality and industry-relevant education for all students of Information and Communications Technologies.

OPENING PARAGRAPH: AFTER

From its inception, the National Center for Telecommunications Technologies' (NCTT) work has been grounded in one primary goal—*to create a comprehensive and sustainable national education system for the Information and Communications Technologies (ICT) industry* and that goal remains the core mission of NCTT's proposed work.

OPENING PARAGRAPH: ASSESSMENT

I knew fairly quickly that the first part of the old proposal had to be reworked because my reaction to the opening paragraph, no matter how many times I read it, was "Huh?" I think you would agree this is not the preferred reaction. This proposal needed a stronger, clearer, more concise statement with punch. In the succinct, revised opening paragraph, you know who the organization is and why it exists. You are set up to understand what the rest of the document is about, and you're ready to read it.

REMAINDER OF THE OPENING PAGES: BEFORE

The work accomplished by NCTT over the past ten years serves as the solid foundation for the proposed ICT Education Community of Practice. Today many community college ICT and ICT-enabled programs are challenged by the need to make extensive and fundamental changes with little support or direction. The proposed NCTT ICT CoP will provide program assistance, a forum for the dynamic exchange of ideas and content, an interactive workspace and a dynamic library where current and new content, subject matter experts and support are readily available and accessible.

This proposal will expand the regional capacity of NCTT and improve and build upon the popular NCTT hands-on technical conferences where faculty and industry professionals present on current and emerging technical topics and network amongst each other, sharing curriculum and program ideas and taking away classroom ready materials. Proposed activities will increase the number of the CoP's subject matter experts (SMEs), the amount and quality of content available for program improvement for both faculty and industry professionals, and insure that classroom-ready materials reflect current and emerging technologies.

This proposal will also create a national, extensive and rapid dissemination system that includes current industry trends and emerging technology information as well as usable content materials for faculty and business professionals. Leveraging the use of Web 2.0 technologies, NCTT's will create a rich and interactive workspace. These technologies include audio and video podcasts, blogs, micro-blogs, Webinars, Wiki's, Massively Multiplayer Online Role Playing Games (MMORPGs) including Second Life, etc. Activities will insure that any faculty or administrator, employed technician or industry engineer can readily access ICT content and information wherever they can sign on to a computer.

The heart of the CoP will continue to be the bi-annual NCTT conferences that serve as forums for the exchange of technical content, provide information on academic program changes in response to technology changes and growth, and facilitate the sharing of ideas regarding pedagogy, laboratory equipment needs, and curricular changes. These popular conferences are unique in that they are a contributory gathering in which participants actively engage in developing technical and program solutions. NCTT will continue to refine the call for presentations/papers that is circulated throughout the country using NCTT's listserve, website and other methods and select presentations according to relevance of content. Circulation will continue to grow with presentations reflecting technical content from research universities, four year colleges and community colleges. As circulation increases, so does the NCTT geographic coverage, the diversity of participants, the types and subjects of presentations and access to subject matter experts in these fields.

NCTT's goal for its next grant period is to create a Community of Practice (CoP) that will:

- Continue to expand the capacity of the organization,
- Continue to provide readily accessible and relevant content to academic and business professionals nationally,
- Direct the exchange of ideas and experience of the members into focused activity,
- Create and develop an interactive workspace and dynamic library of content, curriculum and skill standards,
- Provide focused business and industry participation involving regional and national companies,
- Provide greater resource support to CoP members and help identify funding sources for program improvement and development.

REMAINDER OF THE OPENING PAGES: AFTER

The ICT industry—driven by a demand for instantly accessible information—is profoundly transforming the world. Voice, data, and video communications across a worldwide network are creating opportunities that did not exist a decade ago. Preparing an appropriately skilled workforce is a major challenge for the ICT industry because of quickly changing technology. Anticipating constantly and rapidly evolving breakthroughs in technology, NCTT—an Advanced Technological Education Resource Center—believes education is the key to meeting this challenge. NCTT's response to these high-speed developments is founded in the answers to three important questions: (1) how can ICT pedagogy—both content and means of delivery—be kept current, (2) how can a group of highest quality subject matter experts be readily engaged, and (3) how can the best of this knowledge be shared and disseminated across the nation quickly?

For the past ten years, NCTT has demonstrated a creative and effective way of answering these questions and shaping ICT education. Through the continuous collection, examination, analysis, and synthesis of ICT scientific and pedagogical material and the use of innovative, up-to-the-minute dissemination methods to share best practices, NCTT constantly and consistently meets ICT academic and industry needs. And what NCTT has learned from this intensive effort is that the universal element in the equation is the ICT people involved. NCTT draws on the knowledge of subject matter experts, listens to the needs identified by industry professionals, and responds to faculty requests. People are the source, the tool, and the beneficiaries of NCTT's inventive program.

Therefore, it is not surprising that NCTT seeks to build on its program success by solidifying, formalizing, and expanding this network of ICT people into a Community of Practice (CoP), an expanding group of academic professionals and industry experts who share a common goal of ensuring a quality and industry-relevant education for all students of Information and Communications Technologies. NCTT believes that a strong ICT Community of Practice will assure the crux of its goal—a comprehensive and sustainable ICT educational system.

Community of Practice

Today many community college ICT and ICT-enabled programs are challenged by the need to make extensive and fundamental changes with little support or direction. The proposed ICT CoP will provide program assistance, a forum for the dynamic exchange of ideas, an interactive workspace, and a dynamic library where current and new content, subject matter experts, and support are readily available and accessible. For its next grant period, NCTT will create a Community of Practice (CoP) that will:

- provide readily accessible and relevant content to academic and business professionals nationally,
- ensure students receive and use classroom-ready materials that reflect current and emerging technologies,
- direct the exchange of ideas and experience of the members into focused activity,
- increase the number of NCTT's subject matter experts (SMEs),
- create an interactive workspace and dynamic library of content, curriculum, and skill standards,
- provide focused business and industry participation involving regional and national companies,

- reach out to underrepresented groups and encourage their participation in the field,
- continue to expand the capacity of the organization, and
- provide greater resource support to CoP members and help identify funding sources for program improvement and development.

REMAINDER OF THE OPENING PAGES: ASSESSMENT

After reworking the opening paragraph, I next determined that the proposed community of practice needed to be highlighted because this objective was the heart of the proposal. The first thing I did to establish its importance was to make sure the initial description of it appeared on page one; in fact, unlike the before proposal's opening, I made sure that everything in the introduction of the proposal fit on one page. To set the community of practice information out visually, I gave it a title. But because a community of practice is not necessarily a well-known concept, I had to set the stage for why you would want one or need one. And I had to make the transition from the initial goal statement of NCTT in the opening paragraph to the community of practice section to make the connection as to why NCTT would pursue this approach. I launched the education-to-workforce challenges (which likely would cause the peer reviewers to be nodding their heads in agreement) in paragraph two of the opening page, and by posing the questions found at the end of that paragraph, I laid the groundwork for the community of practice. I wanted readers to respond to the questions with an eager anticipation, "Yes! How can we do that?"

In paragraph three there is a very intentional key word designed to make you open to and accepting of the community of practice idea; can you find it? The word is *people*. Yes, whether you are from business or from academia, you want to have material that you can read, absorb, consider, challenge, and use to further your work. And you want easy and quick access to this material. But the material is not where the focal point should be. We lose sight that it is people who produce this material, people who design and operate the mechanisms by which it can be shared, and people who use it. Paragraph four expands on the importance of people to the process and purposefully connects people who do the work to the NCTT goal stated in paragraph one.

The foundation laid, I barely changed the paragraph from the former proposal that identified what the community of practice would do, although the bullet points that followed were very carefully put in a particular order. In addition, three extra points were added; mention of students had been missing, as had mention of the inclusion of underrepresented groups and of the expansion of subject matter experts, even though all were important to the work being proposed.

Example 2: Proposal to the National Collegiate Inventors and Innovators Alliance

OPENING PARAGRAPH: BEFORE

Historical Context

Since the inception of the Springfield Enterprise Center and the Entrepreneurial Institute in 1995, Springfield Technical Community College has been a leader in promoting entrepreneurship education and business incubation at the community college level. Our vision for community college entrepreneurship serves to complement the mission of the National Collegiate Inventors and Innovators Alliance by fostering innovation and entrepreneurship within the Community College segment of higher education. Community colleges now enroll almost half of all entering college freshmen and over 52% of all U.S undergraduates. Given this increasing enrollment demand, coupled with our historic role of supporting local and regional economic and business development, progressive community colleges now view entrepreneurship education as integral to achieving their mission.

OPENING PARAGRAPH: AFTER

<u>Introduction:</u> For a lot of people, engineering carries an undeserved stigma—they think it is not a creative endeavor, that it has no room for individual self-expression. As a result, many students who might thrive in and contribute to the field avoid it, lessening the available pool of potential engineers needed to meet workforce demands. In a July 2007 speech to Workforce Innovations 2007 in Kansas City, Missouri, U.S. Depart-

ment of Labor Secretary Elaine Chao noted that, "Over the decade ending 2014, our country will need over 900,000 engineers, including aerospace, biomedical, civil, computer software, and environmental engineers." Springfield Technical Community College's (STCC) focus and course-work strives to address this demand, but training just those expressing interest in engineering isn't enough, more students need to be recruited to the field. Therefore, recruiting from those groups typically uninterested and/or under-represented in engineering isn't just about opening doors of opportunity, it's also a sensible way to meet industry demand.

Yet meeting engineering demand isn't only about filling jobs. Because engineers are essential to design, it's also about ultimately improving the conditions under which all people live. STCC shares the Lemelson Foundation's and, thus, the National Collegiate Inventors and Innovators Alliance's (NCIIA) vision that "Invention, innovation and entrepreneurship are powerful forces that catalyze real and meaningful improvements in people's lives." For that reason, STCC not only seeks to turn out function-ally competent engineers, it seeks to produce engineers who can approach their tasks with open-minded, team-oriented imagination.

Toward this end, STCC proposes a first level, E-Team-based course, *Entrepreneurship: Where Art Meets Engineering*, which addresses the overall need for more engineers combined with the equal need to inspire a more creative approach to societal problem-solving through design.

OPENING PARAGRAPH: ASSESSMENT

The old narrative started out with historical context (which I put in a different location in the new narrative). As a consequence, you didn't know what the proposal was about until the second page. My guess is that the reader subcon-sciously would have been unenthused by this point. I wanted to grab the reader right up front. I was able to cut a sufficient number of unneeded words in the rest of the narrative so I could add a half-page introduction in the beginning and still meet the five-page limit.

Everything about the way the new introduction was written was quite inten-tional. For example, NCIIA's website notes that "The NCIIA places a high value on grant proposals that demonstrate concern for the earth and the health and welfare of humans." The funder is telling me something I need to pay attention to here; it even uses the words *high value*. It would be foolish to not address issues on which they said they place a high value. So, in the new second and third paragraphs I speak to this four times. Can you see those four occasions?

- It's also about ultimately improving the conditions under which all people live.

- STCC shares the Lemelson Foundation's and, thus, the National Collegiate Inventors and Innovators Alliance's (NCIIA) vision that "Invention, innovation and entrepreneurship are powerful forces that catalyze real and meaningful improvements in people's lives."

- It seeks to produce engineers who can approach their tasks with open-minded, team-oriented imagination.

- The overall need for more engineers combined with the equal need to inspire a more creative approach to societal problem-solving through design.

I also learned this from the NCIIA website: "NCIIA grant proposals are reviewed by panels of busy professionals who volunteer their time." I took a guess that these busy professionals who cared about entrepreneurship, innovation, and invention might be engineers, or at least were used to working with engineers. I figured that maybe they were sick of how engineers are regarded as being smart but staid and that they would care about having more people in the workforce who approached the world and their work with creative design. The first sentence was intended to draw in the reader by acknowledging what they already know and the unfairness of it. The next three sentences described the problem that was likely to ensue as a result of what was stated in the first sentence, intentionally using U.S. Department of Labor data and linking our school's efforts toward meeting this broad challenge. The reaction I hoped to elicit from the readers as a result of the last sentence of that first paragraph was a resounding "Yeah!" How could you not feel good about opening doors of opportunity and being sensible at the same time?

The short, final paragraph of the introduction tells the reader how in one effort we will address the dual problem of not having enough engineers and needing to use engineering creatively in addressing societal problems.

At this point, I want the reader to be excited, to feel understood, and to be ready to hear more. Because it was recommended by NCIIA that the narrative now present the historical context—and because it is wise to follow the suggested format—I am hoping that the reader wants to know about the entity that appears to get it.

Project Titles

Most government proposal applications have a space for a project title and expect you to designate one. It may seem silly to spend a lot of time on coming up with a title, but the words you use here set the stage for the proposal that's to follow. It's an opportunity to send a subliminal message to the readers, and it's an opportunity to put some punch, some pizzazz, into what may otherwise be a very serious document. A catchy title provides a quick version of your hook. You want the title to evoke emotion, to tell a story, to make the proposal memorable, and to be easy to refer to by the reviewers. In fact, it may even make the reviewers talk about your proposal more if only to wonder how you came up with that title! And if people have a little bit of fun because of that, it implants a feeling of goodwill toward your proposal.

A good title:

- Captures the essence of the project

- Is descriptive

- Is responsive to the RFP or the interests of the grantmaker

- Rolls easily off the tongue

- Is memorable

- Creates a great acronym . . . if you're lucky

Sample Titles

Frequently, especially with government proposals, the format of the title is to have two parts separated by a colon. The first part is where you have the most fun with it, where you want to evoke an image or a feeling, where you frequently use words to form clever acronyms. On the right side of the colon is the language that is more explanatory about the project. But the project will usually become known by the first part of the title. Here are some examples:

- Workforce STAT (Skills, Talent, Awareness, Training): Transforming Regional Capacity for Healthcare Education

- The Success Express: Training for College Readiness

- Drafting a Blueprint for Educating Tomorrow's Engineers Today

- VETS (Veterans Education and Training for Suicide Prevention) Program

"Workforce STAT" would be a great title even without the fact that the acronym alludes to the activities of the project, because the word *stat* evokes fast, evokes the need for action *now*, and evokes health care. Along similar lines of urgency, "The Success Express" focuses on two desired outcomes: being successful in preparing for college and doing it quickly. "Drafting a Blueprint" serves two purposes; it uses the language that you might expect of engineers, and it lets you know that the purpose of the project is planning, because you are drafting, not executing. Finally, "VETS" is an example of an acronym that describes the intended beneficiaries of the project and allows a difficult topic to be referred to without discomfort.

Technique

My staff and I find that our best titles come from a group brainstorm and that the process of doing this helps us keep our focus on what is the main point of the proposal, something that is very useful as we write it.

To arrive at our title, we work on a large whiteboard, creating columns of descriptive words for the project's goal, objectives, and actions. We talk about the intent of the funder and the buzzwords we find in the RFP. We do a free-association-style exchange, in which one person's words feed off of another's. We can take a single word and become a rapid-fire thesaurus machine.

Let me give you an example of how we arrived at a title. Our college is located in the city of Springfield, Massachusetts, on a historic site. We were working with the city government to submit a proposal under the federal Preserve America program, a program that focuses on heritage tourism. The college, the city, and local museums believed that inviting and coordinated way-finding signage would encourage both out-of-towners and the local populace to become more engaged with the city and its historic buildings and environs. We also wanted the city's citizens to be aware of the city's historical significance and to have pride in that.

As we worked to find a title, we spoke of Springfield's history and the things that made it stand out—that it is the site of Shays' Rebellion, the nation's first armory, and many manufacturing firsts, and that it is known as the City of Homes. We talked about what we hoped people would do or feel when they visited the college grounds and the accompanying National Park Service's Armory Museum. We noted that because of its location, Springfield was often viewed as a crossroads. We recognized the funder's interest in heritage tourism and our desire for getting people to the city. And during this conversation many words were jotted down to reflect the city's history and what we hoped the project would propel.

And then the volley of words began as we paired words from the lists. At one point when we were talking about going from something that was raw to something of value, we stumbled on the phrase "from raw to riches." While we liked the alliteration, there was something too raw about the word *raw*, too suggestive of other meanings. Then *raw* became *roots*, "from roots to riches." We started to get excited; we knew we were on to something at this point. One of us yelled out, "Roots, Rebellion, Riches!" Yes! That was definitely the beginning of the title; it was interesting, it was provocative, it was strong. But what would be on the other side of the colon? We worked some more. We tried "Connecting to Springfield's Heritage," but it just wasn't getting us where we wanted to go. Then we remembered that signs were the thing that monies from this grant would buy. "Connecting" became "Pointing the Way." For "heritage" we considered the words *past*, *treasures*, *legacy*. We were almost there. Then the double-meaning word *pioneering* (Springfield, MA, is located in the Pioneer Valley) got inserted, and here's the final title we developed: "Roots, Rebellion, Riches: Pointing the Way to Springfield's Pioneering Legacy." It evokes images, it remarks on our history, it raises a question that might make a reader delve into the proposal eagerly, it alludes to the signs, and its alliteration makes it memorable. Beautiful!

This whole exercise took perhaps twenty minutes, after which we had a great title, we were excited about the project, and I was jazzed about writing the proposal. It served many purposes.

Words are very powerful tools—they can explain or confuse, they can bore or excite, they can lead, they can enlighten, and they can elicit all kinds of emotions. Use them to your advantage. As you begin to write, think about what it is you hope your words will spark in the reader, and write with that image in mind.

CHAPTER 7

Overcoming Writer's Block

Even if writing is something that you enjoy and usually comes easily to you, there will be times when the words won't flow. But deadlines don't give you the option of waiting until the words come; you need to find a way to coax those words out now. Different methods will work for different people, so find the method that best corresponds to your way of thinking and learning. For example, I am a very visual person, so I do best with methods that involve writing on large sheets of paper on the wall. I'm also a very vocal person and find that saying things out loud helps me zero in on what I need to say.

Techniques

Disorderly Conduct

Nobody says you have to write your proposal in the order in which the questions are asked or in which the sections appear. Do what you are willing to do when you are willing to do it! For example, although this may not be the first or most important chapter in the book, I am writing it well before the other ones. You may be so excited about the unique approach your project is taking that you don't want to be bothered right now with writing the statement of need; you want to write about the project activities, even though that comes later in a proposal. Or maybe you are not feeling expansive enough to write elaborate project rationale but could manage working on the budget. The point is you don't have to write in chronological order.

Mind-Mapping

Mind-Mapping allows you to work outside of a chronological format. You can write as ideas occur to you, not necessarily in the order in which they'd be expected to proceed. The result will be more like a diagram or map—where one thought may be connected to many other thoughts—rather than a linear outline or chart.

Place yourself in front of a whiteboard or large easel paper taped to the wall. In the center of the board or paper write the project's goal and circle it. From there, each objective that helps realize that goal becomes a tentacle coming off the circle. And from each objective tentacle come activity threads. Throughout the process, keep asking yourself questions about what activity is going on, why does it matter, what do we hope to accomplish? I find doing all of this out loud is helpful. Look for themes. Look for relationships. As you see patterns emerge, write down the words that describe what commonalities become apparent. Then tape this up in front of your desk and try writing.

The Walk 'n' Talk

For some reason, I find that my words flow better if I get up, walk around the room, and say things out loud (using hyperactive hand gestures, of course). Sometimes when you're sitting quietly in front of your computer trying to find the right words, those words get blocked by all the chatter in your head. So the more you speak, the more those chatter words get drowned out and the easier it is for the right words to move to the forefront. Make sure when you're using this method that you have either a handheld tape recorder or a whiteboard to which you can run over and make notes as soon as the pearls pop out.

Shadowing

This is a variation of the Walk 'n' Talk. Ask a coworker to follow you around and take notes as you talk. When you review the notes, you'll be amazed at how expressive you can be.

The Cocktail Party

This technique takes two people. Pretend that you are at a cocktail party and your colleague comes up to you and asks, "What have you been working on lately?" Engage in a conversational discussion about this new project that you've designed. You'll find that when you talk about it in a colloquial way, the words come more easily. Don't think about it, just talk. Again, the listener can take notes. I've done this technique for staff, and when we get done, I hand them the notes and say, "Here, this is what's in your head. Now go write it." If you get the basic ideas down in this way, you can make it fancy later.

Cut 'n' Paste

Although computers offer us incredible efficiency and quickness in writing, they don't allow us to see the entire document at one glance. If you have written most of your proposal but find it lacking structural solidity, print it all out and tape each page in order to the wall.

At this point you can engage in a variety of techniques. For example, assign a symbol or a color to each proposal component, such as need, objective, and rationale, and march through the document, reading each paragraph and designating with your color coding what that paragraph truly addresses. You'll begin to see whether things are out of place. Then you can literally cut and paste so that like things are with like things. But before you cut up a page, be sure to mark the page number on each piece so that you can find that section when you get back to the document on the computer. Or if you forget to do that, remember the trusty "Find" function to search for specific text.

Stuck on You

This method is useful if you are having structural problems with the proposal. Write each thought on a separate sticky note, go to the wall, and place them in an order that you think makes sense. Stand back and look at it. If things seem out of order, you can easily move the sticky notes around until the ideas flow convincingly. Somewhat similar to Cut 'n' Paste, this allows you to play with broad concepts before you've written the detail.

So What?—Slight Return

Sometimes you can't write, not because you've no words but because you've lost your way. Revisit Chapter 1 and use the So what? technique on yourself. Challenge yourself out loud about why it is important that the work of your project get done. Why should someone care that your organization wants to do this? Give yourself a verbal spanking until your passion for your work triggers a flow of words. If you force yourself to defend your choices in the project's design, you will find your missing words.

Backward from the Ideal

Related to the So what? exercise is what I call working backward from the ideal. It is best done in a visual manner on a large whiteboard or easel paper in a Mind-Mapping manner. Make a statement about what you think is the ideal outcome for the problem you seek to address. Working from that statement, consider what circumstances need to be in place to achieve that outcome, and then what barriers impede that outcome. Say to yourself, "Okay, if I want that outcome to happen, what has to happen first? And what stops that from happening?" Keep working your way down until you come to precise activities. You will see linkages, you will see what you had been missing, and you will have written out an order of events.

Write On

If you can't find the words necessary to write your proposal and it is making you crazy, try writing about something that you actually enjoy or something that you know a lot about. With the former at least you'll feel happier, and with the latter at least you'll feel smarter. But mainly, you'll be writing. This activity will unclog the blockage you're experiencing.

Random Tricks

The ideas in this section need less description because once I mention them you will know what to do. Put on music that pleases or relaxes you. At deadline time, when I need to get myself pumped up, I play loud music and dance frenetically for a few minutes. A few fist pumps in the air with an exhaled "Hunh!" and I feel ready to tackle the task. Sometimes doing something physical can clear your head. I also find that a few minutes of creative play, some silliness, and some laughter can open up parts of your brain so that creative thoughts result. The point of these tricks is that you should pay attention to what unblocks *you* and do it. (And hopefully you don't work in a cubicle!)

PART TWO

But Content Is What You're Selling

As you approach this part of the book, you should have a solid footing about how to think about your project, how to find the right grantmaker, and how to find the commonalities between the two. You've thought through what will resonate with this funder and how you want to frame the presentation of your project. It's time to start writing the specific parts of your grant proposal.

You may have an eloquent writing style, but the proposal must be solid, it must have substance, and each component of it must deliver. The chapters in Part Two focus on the particular parts of a grant proposal, such as statement of need, goals and objectives, and outcomes, and will guide you to ensure that every word you write serves your purpose.

Many grantmakers indicate the order in which they want material to be presented, and that should always be your first guide. But when a preference isn't made, the chapters in Part Two—with the exception of the last two chapters—are presented in the likely order in which you will be introducing each topic in your proposal.

Chapters 15 and 16 discuss the proposal abstract and the cover letter, respectively. You may find it odd that the two things that will be on top of your proposal packet are the last chapters in this book, but that is because they are likely to be the last thing that you write. In both cases, you need the content of the proposal to be in place before they can be written. The proposal abstract is best generated from highlights of the full proposal, and the cover letter is an opportunity to augment it.

The organizational description is one component that has less of a definitive spot in the proposal. Some grantmakers prefer that this information be offered early on to introduce the potential grantee. In other instances, the organization is not as important as the work proposed to be done, but the funder wants assurance that the organization has sufficient capacity to do this work; thus, the description of it follows the description of the proposed activities.

The length of each proposal section depends on several factors:

- The overall number of pages (or words!) allowed by the grantmaker

- The nature of the grantmaker—for example, corporate proposals tend to be shorter than foundation ones

- Any indicator of how each section will be graded, by points or by discussion in the grantmaker's materials; you will allot more space to those sections given more points

At this point, I have armed you with many informed strategies so that you are ready to begin the actual writing of your letters of inquiry and proposals. Read on to learn the specifics of writing each proposal component.

CHAPTER 8

Say It Effectively

The Letter of Inquiry

A letter of inquiry is also known as a letter of intent, a query letter, a pre-proposal, or a concept paper. It is a brief summary of your project and a preliminary step to submitting a full proposal. It saves time for both the applicant and the potential funder by presenting an abbreviated version of a project.

But pay close attention to this—*abbreviated* doesn't mean shallow; a letter of inquiry is not a vague exploration of an idea. It is assumed that you have already thought through your proposed project, including a budget, and are presenting a condensed description of it. If after reading your letter of inquiry the reviewer suspects that you haven't spent sufficient time carefully designing a well-planned project, that ends it—you go no further. This is your audition for a larger role; give it the deliberation it's due.

A letter of inquiry has different uses for different types of funders. In foundation grantseeking, a letter of inquiry allows the reviewer to assess quickly whether or not there is a good match between the funder's interests and the proposer's project. If the reviewer determines that there is a good match, the organization will be invited to submit a full proposal.

Occasionally, government agencies will request a letter of intent before a full proposal is submitted. Often it does not serve the same purpose as with the foundation's letter of inquiry. Rather than being a preliminary step to whether you will be invited to submit a full proposal, more often it is just what it's called—a letter stating an organization's intent to apply for funding. Agencies needing to arrange for peer reviewers need to know how many proposals to expect.

But sometimes the letter of intent process serves as an opportunity for you to get good feedback from the agency about the quality of your proposed project. For example, if government reviewers don't think you're going in the right direction, they will give you the reasons why and suggest that you not submit a proposal. However, you are not forbidden from submitting a full proposal, so rather than being deterred by that admonition, I view that as an opportunity to revisit the project and to strengthen it using their feedback before submitting a full proposal.

You would not send a letter of inquiry to a prospective corporate funder because generally communication with corporate entities (unless it is a corporate foundation) is in a shortened form anyway and they would not use this two-step process.

Procedure

Most of the time, letters of inquiry will be sent to foundations. If background material about a foundation is not available online, your first contact with a foundation should be to request information about the foundation's mission and goals, specifically an annual report, giving guidelines, and a grants list. If, after carefully reviewing this material, you determine that this foundation is an appropriate match for your organization, your next contact will usually be a letter of inquiry. The exception to sending a letter of inquiry first is with a small family foundation, for which a full proposal as the initial request is often acceptable.

If the reviewer determines that what you propose is a good match, he or she will request a full proposal for a more complete description of the project. Sometimes when you read the words in grantseeking databases, "proposals not accepted," it does not necessarily mean that a letter of inquiry is out of order.

It may mean that the grantmaker does not want to be inundated with proposals and would like the option of determining who to invite to submit a full proposal. Letters of inquiry give the funder that option.

Technique

Consider how concise, yet engaging, you must be to keep someone's attention in conversation when there are many other people around also wanting that person's attention. And so it is with the letter of inquiry. You need to make every word count.

As when writing a proposal, write as if you were making a logical, persuasive argument based on the needs of your chosen beneficiaries and your organization's capacity to meet those needs rather than selling something. Avoid jargon, boosterism language, and flowery subjective statements that can't be supported by facts or others' words. A letter of inquiry is not written in the same style as a typical fundraising letter; it is as serious as a full proposal is.

You want to make a connection between the grantmaker's areas of interest or goals and that of your proposed work. Because a letter of inquiry seeks an invitation to submit a full proposal, there's no need to be shy about pointing out that you have vision, hopes, strategies, and intent in common.

More and more grantmakers are choosing to go the letter of inquiry route, especially with online versions. This means that you should become adept at describing your project in very succinct terms. Many of the online versions have strict word limitations and can hold you to those limitations. Mailed letters of inquiry are generally two to three pages; often the funder will indicate a page limit. Do not go over that limit!

Online Letter of Inquiry

Foundations using online application procedures will usually begin with an eligibility quiz. You will be asked a series of questions regarding the applicant and the intended use of any grant funds you seek. If you do not pass the eligibility quiz, you will not be allowed to proceed any further. You may be asked if an organization or an individual is applying; if this is a grantmaker that funds only organizations, it may ask whether you have a 501(c)(3) tax status. You may also be asked questions pertaining to the location of your organization or your project and the general focus of your work.

Many grantmakers who use online applications encourage you to read their program guidelines and to review grants made before beginning the application process. One foundation, the General Services Foundation, even poses this question as its first question in the online application, "Have you read the detailed program guidelines and reviewed our current grants lists?" I was afraid to hit yes without having done so for fear that there would be a test on the next screen! But this is a good thing for foundations to do because this way they are not likely to receive as many applications that are a poor match. It also assures the funder that you have done your homework.

Once your eligibility has been established, the online form will ask you for organizational information, which is generally identifying information, and either a mission statement or a very brief (for example, two hundred words) organizational description. This is often followed by a request for contact information.

Generally you're allowed the most space for project information, which may include some or all of the following: project title, one sentence stating the purpose of the grant, total project budget, amount of money requested, additional funding sources on hand or being sought, duration of project, main goals of the project, and project description.

Occasionally, after you have filled in all the application blocks, a grantmaker will allow you to upload attachments, such as a project budget or a traditional letter of inquiry.

Contents of a Letter of Inquiry

Because a letter of inquiry is a condensed version of a proposal, you are giving the highlights of the same information in much the same order. For example, you might use a page in a proposal to cover an executive summary, but in a letter of inquiry, you do it in a paragraph. Unless otherwise indicated by the foundation, the contents should generally follow this format:

- Opening paragraph

- Statement of need

- Project activity

- Outcomes

- Credentials

- Budget

- Closing paragraph

Further descriptions of each of these components are given in the next sections. Accompanying these descriptions, I have reproduced a single letter of inquiry and broken it up into paragraphs relevant to each component. My commentary follows each sample. If you would like to read the full letter of inquiry as a single document, see the Appendix.

Opening Paragraph

- It serves as your summary statement.

- It should be able to stand alone. If the reviewer reads nothing else, he or she should know what you want to do from reading this paragraph.

- Make it clear what you are asking the reader to do.

- Don't be afraid to put the monetary ask in the first paragraph.

- Answer the following questions:

  - Who wants to do what?
  - How much is being requested?
  - Is this a portion of a larger project cost?
  - Over what period of time is money being requested?

- State if you are responding to an RFP or make the connection between the funder's interest and your project.

- Be mindful of the funder's point of view.

- Gear the opening paragraph to your audience.

I know this seems like a lot to address, but keep this paragraph short! You will have time later for explaining the rationale for why you want to do the project, discussing your methodology, and establishing your credibility.

Groundwork Springfield—one of twenty Groundwork USA pilot communities across the United States—is an urban environmental and ecological education and employment program dedicated to change, revitalization, and transformation that will lead to a cleaner, safer, more beautiful Springfield, MA. One of Groundwork Springfield's programs is the Green Team, which focuses on the importance of both readying our youth for the green jobs of the future and preserving our earth. This project will give low-income, urban children of color the opportunity to explore a green jobs career path, contribute to the environmental betterment of their community, and obtain the leadership skills needed to take command of their own employment pursuit. With our two organizations' shared interest in both protecting the environment and creating pathways out of poverty for vulnerable youth, Groundwork Springfield believes this project will be of interest to the National Foundation and requests $100,000 over two years to support the Green Team Leadership project.

In this opening paragraph, I introduce the organization and make a point of noting that it is part of a nationwide network to increase its credibility with a nationwide funder. Not only do I use words from the funder's materials but I pointedly show where there is a shared interest. If the reviewer reads nothing else in this letter, he or she knows the basic nature of what is being proposed.

Statement of Need

(One to two paragraphs; may also be referred to as background or the issue)

- This section answers the why of the project.

- Explain what issue you are addressing.

- Explain why you have chosen to respond to this set of issues in the way that you have.

- State briefly why this matters in the area in which you will be working.

- Note who benefits. Make sure you can indicate the public good achieved.

The Issue: There are three intertwined issues that have our attention and that we believe can be addressed in the Green Team Leadership project: (1) negative environmental consequences of urban decay, (2) lack of awareness among Black and Latino populations of how these consequences affect them and their potential role in eradicating such outcomes, and (3) the need for economic security for low-income youth.

Throughout the United States, and including Springfield, communities today are faced with the devastating effects of urban decay—derelict land, abandoned brownfield sites, and toxins from decomposing trash leaching into the groundwater systems of the community. This decay leads to endemic economic, environmental, health, and social problems for all members of our community. For example, Springfield rates for asthma, lupus, asbestos, lead poisoning, and other environmental diseases are among the highest in the state, and in some cases, the nation. There are insufficient safe community green spaces, parks, and outdoor recreational facilities for children. While more likely to be affected by this, low-income, urban populations of color tend not to see their power in addressing the problems. Couple this with an exodus of businesses and jobs, a high dropout rate among youth, and widespread poverty and you have an extremely distressed community in need of interventions and few resources to provide them.

Note the use of the header, which is underlined. As you will see when you look at the full letter in the Appendix, this makes the letter look crisp and makes it easy to find information quickly. Notice that in a very concise opening paragraph in this section, you know what is needed both for the intended beneficiaries and for the community; the second paragraph expands it slightly. If you are invited to submit a full proposal, you'll have the opportunity to elaborate on this.

Project Activity
(Three to five paragraphs)

- This section answers the what and how of the project.

- Give a general overview of the activities involved. Give more detailed information if space allows.

- Highlight why your approach is novel and deserving of the special attention that funding connotes.

- Indicate if there will be collaboration with other organizations and what their roles will be. Be specific about who does what.

Project Activity: To respond to the needs stated above, we wish to revive both our city and its residents. We are particularly concerned with giving our youth—our future—the tools to engage in this personal and community revival. The primary objective of the Green Team Leadership project is to provide unemployed and under-employed children of color, aged 14–21, the opportunity to explore and become trained for green collar jobs and careers. The year-long program is a comprehensive, community-focused effort to engage youth in preserving the city's ecological and environmental assets and providing education and training for green jobs. Through this program, we not only want to provide opportunity for income security but also hope to prepare the next generation of green-thinking people in the Black and Latino communities of Springfield, MA. Our Green Team particularly targets youth who face economic, educational, or personal barriers such as deficiency in basic literacy skills, limited English, out of school, pregnancy or parenthood, or involvement in the justice system. As needed, we will provide assessment and case management, adult basic education, GED preparation, academic support, tutoring, and referrals to community resources.

Youth enrolled in our Leadership project will participate in work-readiness workshops and certification programs, relevant field trips, work experiences, and for the 18–21-year-olds, occupational skills training. Through green collar career exploration, youth will be exposed to career choices not commonly suggested to them. Each budding leader will conduct an individual research project on topics such as over-the-counter pesticides and the effects of chemicals in makeup. They will serve as group leaders in a summer program teaching younger children what they've learned from their research, passing on an inculcation of green thinking.

Although broadly stated, with these paragraphs you do get a basic understanding of who is going to do what and how. Again, you will be able to expand this section with more precise detail in a full proposal.

Outcomes

(One to two paragraphs; can go before, after, or with the project activity)

- State the specific outcomes to be achieved.

- Indicate how evaluation is part of the project—how will you know you've achieved these outcomes?

Project Outcomes and Evaluation: Green Team Leadership activities are expected to result in participants having an increased understanding of green job opportunities and the skill set required to obtain these jobs; increased work-readiness skills; increased reasoning and problem-solving skills; an increased environmental awareness and because of that a demonstration of better and healthier life choices; and increased motivation to be more active (part of our No Child Left Inside effort). The Leadership project participants will undergo a weekly performance review and will be rated on the following factors: productivity, dependability, flexibility, teamwork and leadership, safety, and conduct and appearance.

Measurable outcomes are stated, as is part of the methodology that will be used to do that measuring.

Credentials
(One to two paragraphs)

- Demonstrate why your institution or your staff is best equipped to carry out this activity.

- Put any relevant historical background about the institution here.

- Brag with substance. Indicate awards, rankings, and tangible measures that set you apart from your peers.

<u>Credentials:</u> Groundwork Springfield, a project of the nonprofit Spanish American Union, is an effort to improve the health and well-being of all Springfield residents through community-led actions. In 2007, Springfield was one of only two communities nationwide selected by Groundwork USA as a pilot community. The Groundwork USA initiative is a pilot program of the National Park Service (NPS) Rivers and Trails Program in cooperation with the Environmental Protection Agency (EPA) Brownfield Program to establish a network of independent nonprofit businesses called Groundwork Trust. Last spring, Groundwork Springfield initiated its first project, joining students, Springfield's Parks and Recreation Department, and the Springfield Housing Authority in helping to plant gardens at an elderly housing complex; more than 100 young people from the community participated.

Without going into great detail about the organization's history, size, demographics, or staff, this one paragraph immediately establishes relevant credentials to make the grantmaker feel confident about the organization's competency in and capacity for delivering on its stated goals. This information is purposefully not offered in the opening paragraph because the grantmaker is initially more interested in the proposed activity than it is in the entity doing it. Once it feels satisfied that the work is in alignment with its vision, it then needs to know that the entity proposing to do the work is capable of doing it. Therefore, your credentials paragraph needs to state your most powerful, relevant qualifications.

Budget
(One to two paragraphs)

- If appropriate, state what the total project cost will be and how much of that you will be requesting from the foundation.

- Indicate broad categories of activities to be funded.

- Include other sources of funding, both cash and in-kind. Especially indicate what your institution will contribute. Do not overlook the value of all in-kind contributions, including those of your collaborators.

Budget: Funds requested by Groundwork Springfield will be used to provide research stipends to participating youth and to provide project management to solidify the Green Team Leadership model. We are in the process of seeking additional funds to support other aspects of our Groundwork program. Recently, we hosted a community green collar jobs strategy session to discuss ways in which our city can be prepared to pursue funds from the American Recovery and Reinvestment Act. In partnership with the Pioneer Valley Planning Commission, we submitted a proposal in April to EPA's Brownfields Job Training program to train 48, and place at least 31, residents of Springfield in entry-level positions within the environmental technology industry.

A general overview of how funds would be used is provided, although no specific numbers are stated. The section also lets the funder know that the organization is not being stagnant about seeking funding for its projects.

Closing Paragraph

- Offer to give any additional information the foundation might need.

- Give a contact name and contact information for foundation follow-up. Indicate if one person is the administrative contact and another is the program contact.

- Express appreciation for the reader's attention or the opportunity to submit if it is in response to an RFP.

- Ask if you can submit a full proposal.

- Generally it is best to have the highest-ranking person available sign the letter. This indicates institutional support.

Thank you for your consideration of this request. We believe people, places, and prosperity are inextricably linked, and we work with our partners to develop projects that bring benefits to all three areas—by creating opportunities for people to learn new skills and take local action; by creating better, safer, and healthier neighborhoods; and by helping businesses and individuals fulfill their potential. We would welcome the opportunity to submit a full proposal to further describe our project. Please feel free to call me if you require any additional information about our organization, its vision, and its work.

The most important part of your closing is to state clearly what you most want: the opportunity to submit a full proposal.

Writing a Short Proposal

Some foundations and associations, particularly smaller or local ones, allow only five pages or less for a full proposal narrative, frequently only one to two pages. (With small ones like that, budget information is usually offered in additional pages.) As mentioned earlier in the chapter, more and more foundations are requesting that you submit your letter of inquiry online. For some foundations requesting smaller grant proposals, the same is true. With online submissions, you face word limitations instead of page limitations. And as a rule, proposals to corporations tend to be equally as short because brevity is the business way to communicate. Because of these limitations, you must be as concise with these full proposals as you need to be in a letter of inquiry or proposal abstract.

Therefore, much of the advice given for constructing a letter of inquiry is also useful in writing short full proposals. But if you believe that there is absolutely nothing else you can cut to make the page limitation and still be coherent, here are some other techniques you can use to meet that limitation—but remember, these are last-resort approaches!

- As long as the grantmaker allows it, the most obvious possibility is to drop down to an 11-point font, assuming you are using a 12-point font.

- Again, as long as the grantmaker allows it, extend your margins slightly.

- Rather than use a full line return between paragraphs, set the size of the white space at half the full return size.

- Put a colon after a header and start your section description on the same line rather than letting the header use up a full line on its own.

- If there are one or two words hanging on a line at the end of a paragraph, reread that paragraph and either find one or two words to cut or use a smaller word to mean the same thing as a word taking up a lot of space. This will save you a line.

Example of a Short Proposal

The following funded proposal was submitted to a community foundation that requires no more than a two-page proposal; if the proposal incites sufficient interest, the foundation then conducts a site visit. This proposal follows the topics requested by the grantmaker in the order requested. I will follow each section with remarks about what makes that section notable.

Project Plan

Our Home Sweet Home Program recruits and works with a network of community partners to build modular wheelchair ramps—at a fraction of the usual cost—for low-income people with disabilities. We have built fifty (50) ramps in the past twenty months. The people we serve are often at risk of institutionalization because they are trapped in their homes and apartments with no safe way to exit in an emergency.

The opening paragraph sets forth what the organization does and indicates who benefits from that action.

The Home Sweet Home Program uses modular ramps constructed in a two-stage process. We work with lumber companies who sell us materials at 5%–10% profit and maximize the use of volunteers. The modular design allows us to use local vocational schools and residents at Correctional Facilities run by County Sheriff's Departments in Hampshire and Hampden Counties to cut and prepare the materials needed to build the ramp sections. We then mobilize AmeriCorps, Job Corps, UMass, and other volunteers to assemble and install the modular ramps on-site. Because the ramps are pre-cut, most can be assembled and installed over a weekend. We also use volunteers and, where necessary, paid consultants who charge a reduced rate to create the site plan for the ramp and help oversee ramp installation.

Buying supplies at reduced prices and building modular ramps in a two-stage process enables us to construct ramps at one-third to one-half the usual price. Our ramps are even recyclable: they are built with screws and bolts so they can be disassembled and rebuilt in another location. In the past year a ramp we built in Southampton that was no longer needed was moved and rebuilt at a home in Amherst.

In these two paragraphs, the reader sees that this organization has mobilized several resources to meet the need of its constituency; if all these people and places are willing to help, the organization must be effective. From the description of the genuinely community-based process, the reader can feel good about supporting the organization because it makes such a creative and efficient effort to get these ramps built.

Need for Project

The lack of affordable, accessible housing still traps many people in their homes, forcing them into nursing homes and chronic care facilities—surrendering their independence and breaking up their families—when all they really need is a safe, sturdy ramp for their home or apartment. Stavros responds to this need by building low-cost modular wheelchair ramps for low-income individuals and families in partnership with community leaders, building inspectors, private businesses, vocational schools, and individual and groups who volunteer their time and skills.

More than fifty (50) individuals and families in Hampshire, Hampden, and Franklin Counties are on our waiting list. Many of these individuals have no safe way to exit in the event of fire or other emergency. Some are children with disabilities who are growing and becoming too heavy to carry up stairs. Some are people with recent or progressive disabilities who now rely on a wheelchair for mobility. Some are frail elders who can no longer climb stairs. Some are in nursing homes and want to return to their own homes. Government programs and insurance companies will not pay for ramps. We are working hard to raise funds to build ramps, and we ask you to help us with a grant of $25,000 to help us pay for ramp materials.

Need is established by using a description of why the problem exists, a statistic indicating unmet demand, and personal descriptions to make the intended recipients real.

Qualifications and Role of Personnel

Lois Brown, Home Sweet Home Program Coordinator, began working at Stavros in 1988. Since 2004 she has focused on home modifications for access, vehicle modifications and adaptive equipment. The Home Sweet Home Program addresses the numerous and growing requests Stavros has received for wheelchair ramps. As the project coordinator for Home Sweet Home, Lois has recruited donations of materials from lumber companies and volunteers from community vocational programs, college engineering departments and fraternities to help with building wheelchair ramps, and local businesses and construction companies to sponsor and support this effort. She also conducts funding resource clinics, meets consumers and assesses their access needs.

The work of the coordinator is clearly spelled out. Her longevity with the organization inspires confidence.

Number of People Impacted and How They Will Be Impacted

The number of people impacted will be determined by the number of ramps we are able to build. This will be determined by the number of people who request ramps, the material and donations received for ramp building supplies, and the number of community partners and volunteers we recruit to help us.

We currently have more than fifty (50) individuals on our waiting list for ramps. We have built forty-eight (48) ramps and installed two (2) recycled porch lifts in the past twenty (20) months and have several more ramps "in process." Every ramp built by our Home Sweet Home Program frees people with disabilities to continue living in their own homes and apartments, with family or on their own. A ramp provides a safe means of exit in an emergency. It makes it possible to take advantage of community-based services and other opportunities including school, work, volunteering, worship, and participation in community and civic activities. Our ramps enable people with a wide range of disabilities to access the world outside their door, something most of us take for granted. It allows the individuals we serve, as one person put it, "to boldly go where everyone else has gone before."

The reiteration of how many individuals are on a waiting list is a reminder of the need, and the statistics on how many ramps have been built indicate successful action. The beneficial impact of this is made clear by the descriptions of what the ramp allows. And the closing line makes one smile as it pointedly reminds those who are able-bodied of their advantage; using humor to emphasize need strongly delivers the message.

Evaluation Plan

We measure the program's success by tracking:

- Ramp requests made
- Demographics of individuals and families served
- Community partners and volunteers recruited

- Ramps built
- Communities served

- Materials and donations received

This concise evaluation plan, with no doubt as to what will be measured, is presented in a visually accessible way. Note the use of bullets in a two-column manner to save space.

Plan for Fully Funding and Sustaining Project

We are writing grants and doing a great deal of outreach to attract volunteers, local businesses, and other donors to support this program and our program staff. To date we have received grants from the XYZ Foundation, John Doe Foundation, Action Fund, Health-Related Corporate Funder, and Local Club.

We are awaiting word on proposals sent to the Local Pharmacy Foundation, the Anonymous Foundation, and the Unnamed Trust. A local builder has offered to build an accessible house in Springfield, which he will sell to us at cost so we can sell it and use the proceeds to support the Home Sweet Home Program. We are also advocating for state funding to build ramps for low-income people with disabilities.

Clearly, this organization is quite active in trying to keep its project funded, which is indicated by both the funding received and the funding sought.

Project Collaborators

The following organizations build components for the modular ramp sections we use to construct the ramps we build: Chicopee Technical School, Chicopee; Hampden County Sheriff's Department; Hampshire County Sheriff's Department; Smith Vocational School, Northampton; and Westover Job Corps.

A local building supply company, in West Hatfield and Granby, MA, provides lumber and supplies at 10% over cost with an extra 5% discount if we pay immediately. A local restaurant, in South Hadley, MA, donated facilities for two Comedy Nights to raise funds for the Home Sweet Home Program. Several local building contractors also support our efforts, including XYZ Builders, Doe Construction Service, Unnamed Builders, and Anonymous Builders.

Again, the degree to which this program has engaged the community is notable and suggests a solid, well-regarded organization. This would be of particular interest to a local community foundation.

Names of Other Organizations Carrying Out Similar Projects
We know of no other organization in Massachusetts or elsewhere that has a program to provide wheelchair ramps for low-income people with disabilities.

This statement once again points to the need for the program because no one else is offering the same service, and there is such a long waiting list.

*   *   *

Because of the need for conciseness, short proposals can be difficult to write. You are full of information about your project and the need for it, and unlike when writing a letter of inquiry, which assumes a later opportunity to expand, this is your one opportunity to say it all. If you are having difficulty writing in a condensed fashion, sometimes it is easier to write without concern for page length and then cut.

In terms of letters of inquiry, remember that just because letters of inquiry are short doesn't mean that they're less important than a full proposal. In fact, it is how well you convey what you propose to do and why the grantmaker should care that will determine whether you get to go to the next step: writing a full proposal. The next chapter starts you on your way to the full proposal.

CHAPTER 9

Say It with Substance

Organizational Description

Providing information about your organization serves a variety of purposes in a proposal:

- It introduces the organization to the reader.

- It confirms that the organization has the capacity to undertake the work that it proposes.

- It establishes the organization's knowledge base.

- It imparts strength and credibility by demonstrating knowledge and capacity.

- It describes the work of the organization and its relevance to the grant-maker's interests.

The purpose of presenting organizational or personal (if you are an individual grantseeker) information is to provide reassurance that you are the one the grantmaker can trust with its money.

Think about it: If someone asked you for money for his or her organization, you'd want to know about that organization. You might want to know how long it has been around, who is in charge there, and about its financial health. But likely you'd be especially interested in how successfully it has accomplished the work it claims to do. Just as you'd need to be reassured of these things before you gave money, so do grantmakers need to be reassured before giving money to you.

Formatting

Where in the proposal you provide information about your organization will vary, depending on the type of funder and how directive it is about proposal submissions. In many cases, this information is sprinkled throughout the proposal as it relates to each individual part. For example, in the statement of need, you are establishing your credentials through an educated presentation of the issue; in your goals and objectives, you are introducing your organization's values and beliefs.

If the grantmaker specifies that particular information be provided in particular places, follow that instruction. If there is no specific instruction, consider what it is that you want to achieve by providing the information. For example, if you want to convince the grantmaker that you can do what you propose, make statements about your organization's capacity and its history conducting similar projects just after you present the action steps to be taken.

Also consider that grantmakers place varying value on different parts of this information. For example, for some grantmakers, your organization's fiscal behavior may be of high interest. For another, it may be your experience serving a targeted population. With government proposals, you can generally determine these preferences by looking at how they allot points. With other grantmakers, you may be able to ascertain this by what questions they ask or what supporting documentation they require.

Unless otherwise requested, in addition to offering some information in your statement of need that demonstrates your topical knowledge, I recommend putting the bulk of your organizational description *after* you present your ideas about what you will do to meet that need and what will happen as a result, because what you must assert next is that your organization is exactly who can make those things happen. While a grantmaker may be impressed by your proposed project and the positive outcomes to be achieved by it, it needs the assurance that you or your organization has the ability to carry out this plan.

I've one important caution—unless asked to do so, do not automatically start your proposal with a description of your organization. Grantmaking is first about supporting a particular idea and the plan to implement that idea—*the project*. The organization proposing to do this work—albeit clearly important—is a secondary consideration. You want to first grab the reader with the excitement of what you're proposing to do and then later assure him or her that you in fact can do it. The "who" is only important once the reader accepts that this is something the grantmaker would want to fund. There are two exceptions to this proclamation:

- If you are requesting general operating support, the organization and how it operates *are* the main points.

- Those who fund academic projects place high value on the personnel who will be associated with that research or activity and will not consider the project if they don't have confidence in the personnel.

Your organization should have some standardized language already written about it, so you won't need to prepare a lot of that background from scratch. What you will have to generate is how your organization relates to the grantmaker and what the grantmaker cares about—you need to make clear that there's a connection. As you are writing your full proposal, be thinking of how you can impart a sense of strength and credibility about your organization. It may not be until you've considered the question, Who are we to undertake this work? that you find the words to solidify that image.

Introduce the Organization

Many grantmakers request organizational information; you may see this described as an organizational mission statement, an organizational overview, a brief description of the organization, and an organization's scope of work (which can include mission, focus, audience served, and geographic reach). Learning about your organization's history allows the potential grantmaker to assess your durability, your stability, and the manner in which you have conducted your business.

The things you will likely be asked about are your mission statement and basic background about your programs. One thing that is not overtly asked but is considered is the degree of commitment you display toward the people and the issue your organization purports to serve. This is something that will not be separately presented but should shine through any discussion of your organization and its work.

Mission Statement

Many grantmakers ask for your organization's mission statement as a routine part of the proposal process. The organization's mission statement should have been created when the organization was created and may have been revised over the years. If your organization does not have one, you are not in a position to be going after a grant. The ideal mission statement is concise and leaves no doubt as to what the purpose of your organization is. Brevity is also useful because online proposal forms give you limited space in which to provide your mission statement.

At some point in the proposal, you will want to demonstrate how what you are proposing to do is related to your organization's mission. This is likely to be in your statement of need or in the goals and objectives section. However, some online and government proposals may specifically ask you this question. Just as it is important for you to make a connection between your proposed project and the grantmaker's areas of interest, you must be able to make a connection between your organization's mission and the project you are proposing to do. Otherwise, the grantmaker will wonder why you want to undertake this work.

Organizational Background

Most organizations have a ready written statement about who they are that can be tweaked to fit various circumstances. This is one of the things I recommend that you have in your language library (see page 87), so that you can easily pluck it from there and insert it into a proposal when you need to.

However, if you are faced with word or page limitations, do not use up a lot of proposal space with an extensive recitation of your organization's history. Usually, what is more important than general organizational history is the organization's specific experience with the issue area in which you propose to work. Choose to talk about current problem-solving efforts related to the proposal's topic. Briefly state how your mission, history, leadership, and programs relate to the work you propose to do. Many grantmakers are particularly interested in what programs you currently have running because they'll want to see how your proposed work fits in with those.

Here are examples of the organizational information presented in two successful proposals; my commentary follows each. The first example is from a successful proposal of a local nonprofit, Stavros, submitted to a corporate funder. The combination of a corporate preference for brevity and an online submission form that limited the mission statement to 750 characters and the organization history to 500 characters (not words, *characters!*) offered a challenge.

Mission Statement

The Stavros Center for Independent Living's mission is "promoting independence and access in our communities for persons with disabilities." Stavros advocates for and helps bring into being the policies, programs, services, and supports that people of all ages with any disability or chronic illness need to continue to live independently in the community and manage their own lives and their own health care, within Western Massachusetts and throughout the United States.

Stavros' Home Sweet Home Program builds wheelchair ramps for the homes of children and adults with disabilities in low-income households and provides used medical equipment at no cost to help children and adults avoid institutionalization and remain with their families.

Organization History

Stavros was founded in 1974 by people with disabilities who envisioned a world with opportunities for growth and equal access to housing, health care, education, work, and community participation.

For thirty-four years Stavros has worked to realize their dream. Our peer counseling, skills training, advocacy, personal care assistance and other programs have helped people with disabilities of all ages and ethnicities live as active members of their communities and avoid institutionalization.

With very little space, the organization's key mission words are connected to what the wheelchair ramps would confer—independence and access. What could be more emblematic?

The next example is from a successful proposal submitted by a local non-profit, Enlace de Familias, to Hispanics in Philanthropy and was in direct response to the grantmaker's question as quoted in the extract. The total narrative was limited to eight pages; this first question used just over one page.

Provide a brief background on your organization: date created, mission, programs and constituency served.

Mission: The mission of Enlace is to promote a community where all families are given the opportunity to improve their quality of life.

Founding: Enlace de Familias was created originally in 1994 as a coalition of families and representatives of service providers and community organizations in Holyoke for the purposes of building a healthier, safer community for children. This effort was initially started by the MA Department of Social Services (DSS) because of the high number of cases of child abuse and neglect in Holyoke. As the coalition continued to envision its work, it realized that other resources and services were needed and expanded its vision and programs accordingly. Enlace is governed by a Board of Directors comprised of seven members representing community residents and area service providers. The Executive Director oversees a staff of seven and two Americorps VISTA volunteers.

Population Served: While our mission statement does not specifically target a certain demographic, Enlace serves the poorest families and individuals in Holyoke; 99% of clients receive public assistance, MassHealth, food stamps, and/or fuel assistance. Our contract with the Massachusetts Department of Social Services (DSS) requires us to serve Holyoke and Hampden County. The Massachusetts Department of Early Education and

Care (DEEC) requires that the majority of those we serve to be low-income. The majority of those served by Enlace are Latino.

<u>Programs:</u> Enlace accomplishes its mission through the work of its Family Center, Information & Referral program, parenting programs, leadership development programs, community organizing efforts, and the promotion of cooperation among community institutions.

The Family Center is housed in the middle of the downtown community where families have easy access. It is a combination of three storefronts totaling close to 9,000 sq. feet of usable space. At the Center there is a day care center licensed by the DEEC for 12 infants and toddlers. All teachers are MA EEC licensed, bi-lingual, and bi-cultural. Community-based organizations, local coalitions, local institutions, and state agencies use the multiple meeting rooms that accommodate meetings, retreats, planning sessions, etc. Within the Family Center, besides the classroom/meeting space, there are administrative offices and a warm and inviting space where families come to seek services, information and referral, and to take advantage of different trainings. Through its Information and Referral program, Enlace acts as a link among service providers in Holyoke, with the aim to better coordinate citywide services allowing more community residents to more easily receive the information and access the resources they need.

Enlace is among a very small group of agencies in Holyoke to offer family support activities, and one of few—if not the only—to create parenting programs specifically for fathers. Enlace's Family Support Services aims to help parents become more empowered mothers, fathers, and community members. Enlace offers several classes/curriculums: Parenting Journey, Nurturing Fathers, Parents Empowering Parents, Nurturing Mothers, and a new marriage and parenting ("Ma and Pa") program.

For Leadership Development we host the "Emerging Leaders Luncheons," and we provide a Leadership Development training called People Empowering People where local residents are taught the skills that allow them to have the tools they need to advocate for themselves, family members, and other parents. We assist residents in community organizing by informing, educating, and training them how to affect and maneuver the maze of existing and proposed local, state, and national laws and policy.

This proposal was for a capacity-building grant to establish a Fund Development Plan. One gets an image of an organization that is fully engaged in and connected to its community (bodes well for fundraising). It is also apparent that this organization is a full-service operation that manages multiple, ongoing activities. That suggests the ability to manage a capacity-building endeavor.

Commitment

Although commitment itself will not be a defined section of your proposal, part of telling your organizational story is conveying your organization's commitment to its mission and its work. In being assured of your organization's commitment to its work, a grantmaker is more likely to believe that your organization will be equally committed to any grant-funded work.

Longevity of the organization or leadership speaks to commitment, as does the effectiveness of your programs. Clarity of focus and keeping program work in alignment with the mission are other indicators of commitment. Keep this word in mind as you write about your organization and its work throughout the proposal.

Establish Capacity

Your primary goal when talking about your organization is to establish that it is well qualified and capable of doing the work you are proposing to do. Emphasize capacity—that's the reassurance that the grantmaker needs—that your organization has the competence to do that which you are proposing to do, that you've done something like this before, that you can deliver, and that you can do it well. Capacity can be demonstrated in a number of ways:

- Your expert knowledge of the subject area in which you propose to work

- Your history of work in the subject area and with the funder's target population

- The qualifications of your board and staff

- Your funding history

- Your financial stability

In addition to demonstrating organizational capacity to do the proposed work, you want to reassure the grantmaker that your organization has the capacity to *manage* the project if you get the grant. In addition to day-to-day management, this includes hiring appropriate staff and conducting data collection, financial accounting, required reporting, and ongoing oversight and evaluation.

Large, well-known organizations can live off of their reputations and don't need to spend as much time in making the case for their capability. If you are from a smaller organization or a lesser-known organization or if your organization is relatively new, you're going to have to work harder to prove your capacity to do the work presented in your proposal. One way to make a grantmaker feel more secure about your capacity is to partner with organizations that are more established. Another step would be to include descriptive letters of support from other organizations in your geographic area or from local governmental bodies. You could also play up what the advantage might be of working with your organization instead of a larger one—do you serve a particular population that no other organization does? Do you have a grassroots approach that engages the beneficiaries in your work? Are you able to respond more quickly to a community problem? Think about what your organization has or can do that a larger organization cannot, and build your case from there. Smaller organizations should also look to be partners of a larger organization's grant-funded project; this is sometimes referred to as a sub-award.

Knowledge

Demonstrating your knowledge of the topic in which you propose to do your work is a key way of affirming capacity. This is because if you know the subject well, the inference is that you have read a lot about it or experienced a lot, analyzed it, and arrived at the conclusions that have led to your proposed project.

Chapter 10 covers this in more detail (see page 152 in particular). Having this information in your statement of need is an example of when organizational information appears in a different section of the proposal rather than under the specific heading "Organizational Description."

Credentials/Brag with Substance

Grantmakers not only want to know that the organization they might be funding knows its subject well but also want to know that it has the experience and operative wherewithal to do what it proposes to do in that field.

So go ahead and brag, but brag with substance. If you make a claim about your organization's notoriety or abilities, do not use empty cheerleading or boosterism language; back it up with facts. If your organization or staff has notable accomplishments in the field, cite them. If you've won relevant awards, name them. Be convincing that your organization is more than qualified—that it is the best one to do what you propose to do.

People Matter

It is important that a funder or review committee believes that the people undertaking the work are not only appropriate to do so but are extremely well qualified. This is particularly important when members of a review committee hail from academia. They will carefully examine a principle investigator's curriculum vitae (CV) for indicators of relevant experience, qualifications, and competence. If you submit a person's résumé or CV, make sure that it speaks to the proposed work and demonstrates related education, research, and experience.

If a person who will be associated with your project has any star quality, be sure to make those credentials clear, as mentioned earlier. But you also want to talk about specific relevant, up-to-date training and past experience with the topic, with running a previous grant, or with basic project management.

One way to make a grantmaker feel confident in your capacity to manage a project is to present it with a well-thought-through project leadership and management plan. Specify who has what responsibilities in project oversight and management. Proposal reviewers will look at how much of the particular staff person's time is expected to be committed to a project and determine whether that amount of time seems reasonable given the project activities and expected outcomes. If what you propose is a particularly large undertaking, the grantmaker may ask you for an organizational chart.

A program officer from a large foundation focused on health care in California offered this disclosure about the role of people in his assessment of an organization:

> There are key qualities I look for in the leadership of the organization that I might recommend we fund. Those qualities are: thorough, transparent, honest, trustworthy, reputable, inquisitive, financially savvy, innovative, and thoughtful. These qualities emerge when the leadership has afforded me an opportunity to get to know him/her. So I would stress that it is not just about writing a great proposal, it is being able to pick up the phone, schedule an in-person meeting, or phone call and having a 1/2 hour conversation in which the grantseeker can bring the words in the proposal to life. Getting a grant is like getting a job . . . the good ones rarely come from just filling out a form!

Certainly this is the case with some grantmakers, but I caution you about trying this technique with all funders; larger foundations may not be so easily accessible. However, if you are not able to have a direct conversation with a program officer, try to convey those qualities listed in the quotation in your writing and presentation.

The example offered next is an excerpt from a successful proposal submitted to the U.S. Department of Labor by Springfield Technical Community College. In this example, I wanted the reviewers to have high confidence in our capacity to run a $1.65 million project that involved a total of fifteen partners in three counties. I bragged with considerable substance! The proposal narrative was twenty pages, and this section used about a page and a half.

Program Management and Organization Capacity

A Project Coordinator will be hired for the life of the grant. This person will be responsible for the daily activities of the project, partner coordination, data management, and project reporting. Michael Foss, the Dean of the School of Health and Patient Simulation, will co-manage the entire project with Dr. Patricia Hanrahan, Director of Clinical Education for the School of Health and Patient Simulation (see CVs in attachments). Both have extensive backgrounds in program management, evaluation, and patient simulation and will be responsible for overall operation and success of the project. Dean Foss and Dr. Hanrahan are currently implementing a lab upgrade for the 16 programs in the School of Health. The work is funded by a Title III grant for approximately $500,000; however, another $250,000 has been leveraged. Lab upgrade includes facility planning and management, equipment selection, purchasing, installation, training and integration into 14 of the 16 health programs. This five-year project has resulted in the creation, building, and operation of a nationally recognized patient simulation center, SIMS Medical Center (see attachment). In 2006, Laerdal Inc. recognized SIMS as a "Center of Excellence" for patient simulation. At that time, STCC was the only community college to be so recognized. SIMS Medical Center is a model for other community colleges and other institutions of higher education who wish to integrate patient simulation into their health curriculum with the intent of improved patient care. Dean Foss and Dr. Hanrahan are members of several current healthcare workforce projects, including WCTF and HCOP previously described.

College Partners: The four college partners will provide simulation facilities with a sufficient capacity and high-fidelity level to support educational experiences for the WIOC One-Day Medical Encounters and the new college credit Patient Skills course. Each college also will designate an existing counselor for advising training in health career counseling. Those counselors will be responsible for recruiting students to take the Medical Encounters experience and/or the college credit Patient Skills course. Students taking either experience will be tracked for five years to determine health program entry, attrition, graduation, and placement rates. Each of the college partners have experienced deans of health and experienced academic advisors.

Industry Partners: The four hospital partners, Baystate, Mercy, Holyoke, and Berkshire Medical, will each designate an existing employee to receive health career counseling training. The trained employees will recruit, as appropriate, current health employees to take the Patient Skills college level course with the expectation of those employees upgrading skills. All hospitals will be members of the Project Curriculum Board, responsible for development of the Medical Encounters and Patient Skills experiences. Industry input is critical since it will drive the curriculum to address skills required in today's healthcare environment. Each of the industry partners are providing current, well-experienced human resource personnel to act as contacts, members of the Project Curriculum Board, and trained counselors.

Confidence in the leadership of this effort is bolstered by notable relevant experience, previous grants management, and a significant recognition. The project managers are forward thinking and well connected. The partnership is vast and consists of several high-level organizations. Roles and responsibilities are clearly spelled out.

Getting to know your organization, the work that it does, and the people who do it should leave a potential grantmaker feeling convinced that you can successfully accomplish what your proposal presents. Remember that not all of this information will necessarily be in one place; it may be sprinkled throughout your proposal. If there's any place in the proposal where you can impress upon the grantmaker that you have strong capacity, you should do so. And any discussion of the topic you and the grantmaker share an interest in allows you to solidify the connection between you and that grantmaker. Use your words to inspire confidence and trust that your organization can meet any capacity test the grantmaker might have. The statement of need, covered in the next chapter, is where the capacity assurance begins.

CHAPTER 10

Say It with Conviction

The Statement of Need

Always follow the grantmaker's requested order of proposal contents. But if the grantmaker does not specify how it wants information to be presented, I recommend that after a brief introduction (see page 86) you start with the statement of need. Drawing from the proposal components list given in the introduction (page 11), the statement of need should answer the following questions:

- What is the issue you are addressing?

- Why does this matter?

- Why is what you propose necessary?

- Who benefits?

If you cannot establish that there is unquestionable need for the work you propose to do, then the proposal ought not to go any further. It doesn't matter how clever your approach is, how solid your methodology is, or how efficiently you propose to deliver the proposed services. If you haven't established that these things are unquestionably needed, then the reader has no reason to care about the rest.

Think about when you are asked for money as an individual, whether in person or by mail or phone; you won't give unless you're convinced of the need. Think about what it takes to persuade you that something is a good cause. You want information first, don't you? You want to know why the problem exists, what the extent of the problem is, and what else has been done to address the problem. Yes, you'll also have lots of questions about what actions will be taken by the organization or person requesting your money to address the problem, but these questions don't emerge until you're satisfied that need exists. Likewise, before considering any other factors, the proposal reviewer must first be convinced that need exists.

Clarify Your Issue

The first thing you need to do to craft your needs statement is to be clear on what the issue is that you wish to address. In the broadest sense, this will not be difficult to do. Your organization's purpose is associated with an issue; it is the reason you exist. There is a substantial issue, such as education, health, or the environment, which your organization believes needs extra attention. Your organization has a set of beliefs about what is and is not working right within that sector and seeks to make things better.

However, as is often the case with societal problems, there is not usually a singular cause and therefore not a singular solution. For example, let's say that your organization is concerned with the larger issue of education. And what you most hope to achieve is an improvement in the dropout rate of high school students in your community. Although that last statement narrowed the issue of education considerably, in itself it is still full of complexities. Do students drop out because they can't keep up with the classes? Because of problems at home? Because of substance abuse? Because they've become parents? Because they have to work? Because of a lack of motivation?

Any or all of these things could be true in addition to possibilities that I haven't mentioned. But my guess is that whatever you are proposing to do will address a particular reason or two, because your determination of the primary cause of dropping out will guide your decisions on what actions need to be taken to prevent this. Although you may believe that all these causes have significance, it is unlikely that your organization is set up to address all of them. Or if it is, your organization probably has separate programs to address the separate causes.

As discussed in Chapter 1, your project must be doable; therefore, you will need to zero in on a particular part of the larger issue in order to be credible. The narrowing of the problem you seek to ameliorate can be expressed by a particular geographic area, a particular population or subpart of that population, or a specific root cause of the problem. If you don't rein yourself in, it will be harder for you to design your program and harder for you to be successful.

When you speak to need, you must do it with precision. Remember that it will be assumed that the work you propose to do will respond to whatever problem you describe, so you want to be careful how you describe it. You might begin your discussion with an acknowledgment of the enormity of the problem in the country or in your state, but the bulk of your discussion should focus on the community in which you expect to effect change. And while you may acknowledge the multiple causes of the problem, again, the greater part of your statement of need should center on the particular aspects your actions will address.

Demonstrate Knowledge of the Field

As a reader, I must trust that your expression of need is accurate so that I can feel confident about the work you propose to do. I must believe that you know what you're talking about. For every claim that you make, I will be thinking, "How do you know that?"

In your statement of need you are offering both a compelling and a detailed snapshot of the current situation; you are providing valuable background information to lay the groundwork for the project you are proposing. It shouldn't be just descriptive; facts have power. You should be citing data, statistics, pertinent research, and an accounting of the current issues in the field. For example, you wouldn't say, "We have too many dropouts." You would say instead, "Forty-nine percent of our students drop out of high school."

Don't rely just on your passion for the topic to express its urgency. Offer the findings of a well-respected source in the field, whether it is an organization or a person. If there are a variety of sources that uphold your contentions, it will make your proposal stronger. Using well-recognized sources imbues your claims with authority. In addition, if the problem you're seeking to address is specifically local, you should refer to a locally focused report on the topic, as well.

It is also important to consult the very people that your project proposes to help. If you have arrived at your conclusions about what is needed as a result of conducting focus groups, surveys, or the like, be sure to include that information in your analysis.

Present Your Problem-Solving Approach

The bulk of the statement of need deals with why the issue matters, why it warrants attention. Once this has been established, you will present a convincing argument for why what you propose to do about it is necessary. Therefore, as you discuss the issue, you're not just making a case of need in terms of the stated problem but also laying the groundwork to make the case for your proposed solution. The details of your solution will come later in the proposal (see Chapter 11), but by narrowing your statement of need to a particular aspect of the larger problem, you are indicating the area in which you will be working.

While demonstrating your subject competency, it's important to identify who else is working in this field, what they have done, and what have been the results, especially for academic-based proposals. When describing current efforts to address the problem, also be prepared to speak to why you believe this issue hasn't been addressed sufficiently in the past.

Make connections between this research or activity and your own proposed work. Talk in broad terms about how your activities will build on others' work or how you will modify it. When speaking of deficiencies, state how your proposed work will change that. This is especially important if you are using a different approach to the problem than is the norm. Grantmakers are particularly enamored of innovation, but only if it has a basis in a thorough examination of current approaches and you can identify what is lacking.

Your problem-solving approach will be further justified if you can demonstrate that your decision making is evidence based. When discussing what you propose to do about the need you've identified, use data, research, and past experience to support your proposed problem-solving choices.

Talk About the Beneficiaries

The reader needs to be convinced not only that your chosen problem is important enough to warrant attention but also that the designated population *needs* the proposed intervention, will benefit from the intervention, and is a population that one should care about helping. Describe the geographic and demographic recipients to be served. Be precise in your descriptions, both in naming and in numbers.

Make sure your statement of need approaches the topic from the perspective of the public good to be achieved. Need is not expressed in terms of your organization and the work it does. Need is expressed in terms of what the people you seek to help need. For example, your homeless shelter doesn't need extra beds; the homeless population needs a place to sleep. Do you see the difference? It may seem like pure semantics, but the expression of human need is what is most compelling. As the reviewer, after learning of the number of people who are homeless and who seek shelter, I'd want to know how many places in the community provide this shelter and how many people these shelters can accommodate in total. If I see that that number is not sufficient compared to the number of people requesting services, and if I care about a direct service approach to the problem, I can concur that more beds in your shelter would be a solution. But I am responding to the people's need, not to your shelter's need. Nor is need expressed in terms of the existence or nonexistence of your particular project. Again, *need is expressed in terms of people*. Define things in terms of people's access to a solution.

Establish Organizational Capacity to Meet the Need

It's important to show the connection between your organization's work and the issue the grantmaker wants addressed. Not only do you have to assure the grantmaker that you have considerable knowledge of the field, but you want to leave no doubt that this is your realm; this is the subject area in which you work and seek to make change for the better.

At some point in the statement of need, the reader wants to know the answers to two questions: Why this approach? Why you or your organization? The answer to both questions is accomplished by demonstrating your competency in the field. You've shown that you are aware of the various approaches to the problem, that you have examined what works and doesn't work, that you have consulted resource materials and experts, as well as those affected by the problem, and have arrived at your proposed solution in an informed way. Perhaps you've been applying this approach for some time and have documented evidence that it is effective.

To make the case for why your organization is the one best equipped to address the problem, in addition to demonstrating competency in the field, you must convince the grantmaker that you are meeting a need that others are not. Be sure to point out your connection with the targeted population, your geographic proximity, and your history in doing similar work.

In the course of describing your objectives and accompanying activities later in the proposal, you'll be making a statement about your capacity to actually perform the proposed work. By explaining the problem and your proposed response to it in the statement of need, you'll be assuring the potential funder that you are seeing the issue in the same way it does, that you understand it fully, and that your approach makes sense.

Examples of the Statement of Need

Statement of Need to the United Way

Here is an excerpt from Enlace de Familias' ultimately funded eight-page proposal narrative submitted to the United Way. You will notice that the grantmaker calls the section "Description of Need" and asks several questions. I used underlined categories in the response to aid the reader in following along as I laid out the grave need Enlace sought to address. As you read this statement, see if you can identify places where I've met the five suggested writing strategies.

Did I clarify the issue? Did I demonstrate knowledge of the field? Did I present the organization's problem-solving approach? Did I talk about the beneficiaries? Did I establish the organization's capacity to meet the stated need?

This selection demonstrates making a case using arguments that are both factual and empathetic. For the factual argument, research is cited, demographic and educational assessment data are noted, the findings of state agencies are presented, available community and school resources are identified, and recent solutions-based efforts undertaken are enumerated. Note that the severity of the problem and the reality of the school's and community's limitations in addressing this problem are made clear just through the recitation of facts.

For the empathetic argument, I chose to tell the true story of one of the proposed project beneficiaries. Understanding that my audience was locally based and a volunteer review committee, I determined that the readers would be receptive to a human story in their community that illustrated what the facts revealed and that highlighted the complexities of the situation. I probably would not have made the same choice in presenting the case to a nationwide government program with a review committee that was held to checking off precise review criteria.

The problem-solving approach is shown to be rooted in a collaborative call for action; this wasn't just the opinion of the grantseeking agency but a desired approach of many local agencies. The very nature of the United Way is found in its name; collaboration and working together are important, so I emphasized them. Notice, too, that I used the grantmaker's language to make one of our points, demonstrating that the applicant agency is listening and understands the grantmaker's point of view.

Description of Need (What is the issue you plan to address? What is your approach? What research supports your idea? How does your strategy differ from others in the field?):

Background: The Neighborhood Elementary School is an urban elementary K–5 school serving 454 children in one of the poorest communities in the Commonwealth of Massachusetts. It has a largely transient population, 94% of the children live in poverty, 41.5% are English Language Learner (ELL) students and 18.7% are receiving special education services. Since

2003, Massachusetts Comprehensive Assessment System (MCAS) scores have remained flat or have declined in the different performance levels. For example, in 2005 only 18% of third graders and 6% of fourth graders were deemed advanced or proficient in the category of English Language Arts (ELA) and Reading. In the Mathematics category, only 9% of the fourth graders were designated as advanced or proficient.

In 2004 the Holyoke Public Schools was one of two districts statewide determined to be underperforming by the Massachusetts Office of Educational Quality and Accountability. The Massachusetts Department of Education determined that such underperforming schools should be assigned a Turn-Around Partner, and America's Choice, an affiliate of the not-for-profit National Center on Education and the Economy, was selected for the Holyoke Public Schools. Under this partnership, which began in May of 2005, Neighborhood Elementary School receives 15 days of technical assistance from America's Choice for assistance in math and ELA. Technical assistance includes on-site professional development, classroom visits, demonstration lessons, and coaching to teachers.

Overall, the goal of the Turn-Around Partnerships is to increase the number of students proficient on the MCAS and to increase the capacity of Holyoke Public Schools to deliver a college preparatory curriculum. This goal will be obtained through developing an attainable action plan, coaching, and support for the district and school levels to increase student achievement. Toward these ends, America's Choice, an organization whose mission and approach is informed by rigorous research and extensive field-testing, developed an Action Plan in 2006 for Neighborhood Elementary School.

Statement of Need: There is little argument that education is a significant ticket upwards for children of low socio-economic status. And to that end, America's Choice's Action Plan rightfully sets goals relating to academic Leadership, Management, Content, and Data Analysis. While the associated activities to meet these goals will be highly useful, there is one enormous impediment to academic success for many children at Neighborhood Elementary School. All the well-thought out action plans, curriculum innovations, and expert teaching are for naught if a child comes to school from an unstable, disruptive, and highly emotionally-charged home environment. Learning is secondary to survival. Consider the reality of 11-year-old Luis.

Luis lives at home with his mother, an older sister, an older brother and a younger brother. Luis' mother had several of her children while a teenager. The oldest, 17, is a high school dropout. Luis' parents are separated and the father lives in another part of the state and Luis has not had contact with him for some time. There is a suspected history of alcohol, drug, and physical abuse in the family.

Luis is a Spanish-speaking fourth grade special education student who has attended five schools in six years. Originally he enrolled in the Neighborhood Elementary School in 2005 from another district school, where he had been a student for several months. Prior to entering the Holyoke Public Schools, Luis attended school in Puerto Rico where he received special education services for academics. He repeated one grade, which was attributed to transience. Luis transferred to a private school; however, he reentered the Neighborhood Elementary School in the spring of 2006. His withdrawal from the private school was precipitated by continued inappropriate behavior, which he is currently demonstrating at the Neighborhood Elementary School on a daily basis.

Luis has a diagnosis of ADHD, ODD and has conflict and behavioral difficulties at school. Luis exhibits inappropriate social skills such as aggression toward others and defiance. He also exhibits impulsivity when it meets his needs. Luis refuses to work, leaves the room and building without permission, and strikes other students without apparent provocation. He uses foul language and has lack of respect for any adult supervision. He refuses to participate in any learning experience. He is unable to stay on task in the classroom. He demonstrates poor judgment and impulsive behavior. Several reward systems have been implemented and modified during the school year but have not yielded any significant change in his behavior. Aside from the damage this does to his own learning, Luis is interfering with the learning environment of the other students by his outbursts and persistent disruptions.

But Luis is not an anomaly; there are several children with similar stories. Some are living in shelters—in fact, all of the city's shelters are located in the Neighborhood Elementary School zone. Some children live in homes where domestic violence is prevalent. Some children are exposed to drug and alcohol abuse. Some children suffer from sexual abuse. Some children live with mental illness. They are often hungry, frightened, uncertain of where they'll be sleeping. Their families are broken.

While a school may recognize an under-performing child's need for counseling and provide it, addressing the root causes that underlie this need is not only a sensible thing to do, it's a humane thing to do. However, schools are intended to be the academic house; it is not their role to do social work. Yet the school is the first point of connection with a child. While we may prefer that our teachers and administrators have the room to be fully engaged in every child's learning process, the reality is that they are frequently immersed in fixing broken families instead.

Fortunately, Holyoke has many governmental programs and nonprofit organizations focused on alleviating the strains and suffering of these broken families. For example, Luis' family is receiving help from River Valley Counseling, Valley Psychiatric Services, Holyoke Health Center, Department of Social Services, Commonwealth of Massachusetts Juvenile Court, and has an educational advocate. The family is involved with the Family Stabilization Team and receives outside counseling support and training through outreach, parent training, and liaison work through the school. The family also receives housing assistance. And Luis is being seen by a therapist in a private setting.

There are many available public and private resources for families such as Luis'; the problem is connecting these families to these resources. Meeting this need is a large part of what we propose to do. As a result of the underperforming designation, the School Leadership Team of Neighborhood Elementary School has put considerable effort and thought into examining student achievement and developing instructional and administrative improvements. We want the School to be freed up and focused on implementing these needed changes, not to be using academic resources for social work purposes.

Not only are academic resources being diluted, but those resources designed to address student behavioral issues are being over-extended. At Neighborhood Elementary School, there is only one full time guidance counselor—a licensed school psychologist—for over 450 students. There is a full time Outreach Worker and a part time Parent Liaison. The Behavior Specialist comes once a week for a couple of hours and the School Resource Officer visits, but has no set times or schedule. Considering the demographics of this school cited above, these are not sufficient resources to meet the enormous need.

This is not to suggest that the Neighborhood Elementary School is not taking steps to help its underperforming students and their families. A number of safety net groups are available to give students the high intensive instruction needed to bring them up to grade-level proficiency. In 2005–2006, the school began an early morning math program targeted at struggling fourth grade students. Twice a week for an hour students came early for breakfast and received intensive instruction in problem solving strategies and open response writing. With the use of a community volunteer, the school was able to start an after-school homework clinic for students in third, fourth, and fifth grade in late spring.

Neighborhood Elementary School is also reaching out to parents and the community. It opened a Parent Center in the building in October 2005 and with the support of the Parent Liaison, has been able to offer a room filled with resources for parents to explore and use. The school has had approximately ten parents working in the school throughout the year, helping in kindergarten classes, doing breakfast duty, and coming in to eat at lunch time with their children. Over 350 family members attended Neighborhood Elementary School's Open House in October 2005—the largest attendance at an Open House in the last thirty years! Its continued relationship with River Valley Counseling and the Holyoke Public Library has allowed the school to use community services to help families utilize city services and connect them to their children's education. Through a connection with the Holyoke Adult Learning Opportunities (HALO) Center, the school began offering ELL and GED classes to Neighborhood Elementary parents in 2006–2007. Supporting parents and having them present in the school building has a positive impact on the students' motivation to learn. For highly mobile students, those who enter school October 1st or thereafter, the district has a Transient Opportunity Program (TOP) to help families stabilize and to minimize disruption to on-going classes.

However, more is needed, as United Way's priority language states, to "[e]nsure that all youth in our community have a firm foundation in life so that they may grow to become productive and successful citizens." Thus, because the mission of Enlace is to promote a community where all families are given the opportunity to improve their quality of life, working with the Neighborhood Elementary School to stabilize the lives of these broken families so their children can learn is a clearly needed and sensible collaboration.

Problem-Solving Approach: Collaboration is a key word for the work we do and the work we envision in this proposal. Making sure that effort is not duplicated, that all available resources are brought to bear on each family's problems, and that aid is offered in a synchronized, symbiotic manner is a preferred way of operating. However, the nature of public and private agencies whose staff and finances are stretched works against the holistic ideal. Instead, understandably, agencies perform just their specific functions, rather than looking at a client's needs comprehensively. While a case manager is a logical choice, too often there is not funding for such and existing staff are too overwhelmed to take on another function. At the local Community Health Network Area meeting held on May 8, 2007, there was a call for action—to find a way to have a centralized case management system for families. For each child like Luis, there is a family attached, with multiple members and multiple issues to deal with. But at this time, no one organization is able or willing to do real case management for the family as a whole. Funding from this grant would enable Enlace to fulfill a case manager function for 20 Neighborhood Elementary School student's broken families. One of Enlace's primary functions since its inception has been to provide a citywide Information & Referral point and we would build on that.

Applicable Research: Research studies dating back to the 1980s have shown a strong correlation between family involvement in children's education and increased rates of success in school. In 2002, the National Center for Family and Community Connections with Schools published an extensive review of the research in this area titled "A New Wave of Evidence: The Impact of School, Family, and Community Connections on Student Achievement." Taken as a whole, these studies found a positive and convincing relationship between family involvement and benefits for students, including improved academic achievement. This relationship holds across families of all economic, racial/ethnic, and educational backgrounds and for students of all ages. (p. 24) The research studies reviewed in this extensive article include a higher grade point average, enrollment in more academically challenging programs, passing more classes, improved attendance, better behavior, and better social skills. An interesting finding in this review of the research is that parents' communicating higher expectations, particularly in terms of college attendance, actually had a higher impact in some cases than assisting children with their homework. When their families guided them to classes that would lead to higher education, students were more likely to enroll in a higher-level program, earn credits, and score higher on tests. The connection was somewhat greater for math and science than for English, and for earning credits than scoring well on tests. Looking back from parent involvement in grades 8 through 12, Catsambis found that parents' expectations for their students to do well and attend college had the strongest effect on grade 12 test scores in all subjects. These findings held across all family backgrounds. (p. 36)

Sources

- "A New Wave of Evidence: The Impact of School, Family, and Community Connections on Student Achievement," Annual Synthesis, 2002, by Anne T. Henderson and Karen L. Mapp. Download of this article is available at www.sedl.org/pubs/catalog/items/fam33.html.
- "School, Family, and Community Partnerships: Your Handbook for Action," 2002, by Joyce L. Epstein, Mavis G. Sanders, Beth S. Simon, Karen Clark Salinas, Natalie Rodriguez Jansorn, and Frances L. Van Voorhis.

Statement of Need to a Corporate Grantmaker

Here is an excerpt from a successful proposal submitted by Springfield Technical Community College to the Future Fund of Hometown Bank. The statement of need is considerably shorter than the Enlace example because the grantmaker allowed only three pages for the complete proposal narrative. Among the many needs of the college, microscopes were chosen as the request to make for several reasons: (1) the grantmaker expressed an interest in children and education; (2) the grantmaker specifically identified a preference for projects that "include a strategy for leveraging other resources, produce measurable results . . . and are viable and sustainable"; (3) because a bank is a source of capital for businesses, we thought it would be sensitive to the need for updated equipment; and (4) we determined that a corporate grantmaker would respond positively to a tangible, long-lasting product for which the funder could be easily identified. The proposal's statement of need was written with these things in mind.

Focus on Student Success: STCC's primary goal—in its many educational activities—is student success. For many students, the decision to attend college speaks to the belief that post-secondary education will give them the knowledge and the means for a successful career path. STCC believes its job is to do everything it can to ensure that students have the necessary teaching excellence, support services, productive environment, and tools by which to learn and move toward a chosen career.

Microscopes as Important Learning Tools: In some cases the tools necessary for learning are class-specific equipment. Thus, STCC seeks to ensure the quality of all programs by maintaining facilities and equipment that reflect the most current state of practice in every professional specialization. Not only will outdated equipment not give students the relevant experience needed in the workforce, but it may dampen any enthusiasm a student might have for pursuing a particular career path.

STCC's nine science labs contend with such outdated equipment. At a time when industry is clamoring for a workforce trained in science, technology, engineering, and/or mathematics (STEM), having the necessary resources to encourage students to explore these fields is vital. At STCC, three disciplines—Biology, Anatomy & Physiology, and Microbiology—all use the science labs. Additionally, as the New England college with the most associate degree programs in the health fields, STCC is locally known for feeding the healthcare workforce pipeline, and Biology is a key course in the allied health and nursing programs. Plus, non-science students looking to fill a lab science requirement generally prefer Biology to other options. Introduction to Biology alone has nine sections in the Fall semester and six sections in the Spring semester. Easily half of STCC's students will pass through a lab at some point in their college career.

Enter the microscope, the means by which a student can first glimpse cells—the primary building blocks of all living things. It's an instrument by which a student can explore a world that is entirely new to them—a world in miniature. It is certainly possible to show students photographs, or perhaps even videos of cells, but experience has shown that what leads to true understanding is the process a student goes through when they scoop up a drop of pond water, prepare a slide, and then find for themselves a complex and beautiful organism that they never knew existed. Pre-health students go through a similar process when they look at slides of tissues and find for themselves the cells of which we are all composed. One can talk about neurons, but when students see for themselves the intricate wiring of the brain, that's what inspires them to want to know more.

Now picture labs filled with microscopes older than most of the students. With an old microscope, students are challenged to interpret images that are blurry, low in contrast, poorly lighted, and difficult to manipulate. Instead of seeing plain pond water alive with strange and active organisms, a student contends with fuzzy images. Instead of being intrigued by the complexities of neurons, a student—a potential STEM workforce member—is frustrated and put off. Outdated microscopes impede a student's full experience of the wonders of the micro-world. To be able to see what the professor is lecturing about and to have the excitement that hands-on learning can bring, a student needs a functioning microscope. By collecting the actual sample, preparing the slide, searching the slide, and finding the perfect element hidden within it, the process of search and discovery leads to understanding. Subjects move from the abstract to the understood. And when students have confidence in their ability to see what they are supposed to see, they do better in the class because they now believe they can learn the material.

Because this is such an important need, the college is committing some of its limited funds to replace microscopes in one of the labs, but three labs need full replacement. A $50,000 grant from Hometown Bank would enable STCC to fully replace all the microscopes in one lab (27) and buy new slides. And perhaps this action will encourage other funders to provide similar support to equip the third lab.

Who Will Be Served: The purchase of these microscopes and slides will not only serve those students immediately taking a lab course, it will serve thousands of students in the years to come. And microscope use extends beyond STCC students. Our microscopes are used by K–12 students during the summer camp program, on arranged class visits, and as part of a Biotechnology for Girls event, which seeks to get more young women into STEM programs. Additionally, high school and middle school teachers attending workshops, such as our BioTeach workshops, also use STCC microscopes as part of their learning.

Part of the purpose of the statement of need is to convey urgency. You want the funder to act and to act *now*. A well-crafted needs section takes into consideration what you know about the funder so that you can write something that will resonate sufficiently to encourage such action. Now that you've established that need exists, it's time to say how you will meet that need.

CHAPTER 11

Say It with *Vision* and Solutions

Goals, Objectives, Activities, and Outcomes

Goals, objectives, activities, and outcomes follow the statement of need in a proposal. This is because once you have defined the severity and extent of the problem, the question that a reader would ask next is, So, what are you going to do about it? This is the heart of the proposal and will also be the bulk of it. For proposal reviews based on a point system, this section will usually have the most points attached to it and thus should have the most pages.

This part of your proposal is about *action*. Goals are vision statements about how you will address the identified needs. Objectives are subparts of a goal and reflect your problem-solving approach. Project activities are the very precise actions you will take to achieve those objectives (and thus, ultimately, your goal). The results of those activities are the outcomes. Goals, objectives, activities, and outcomes are a linked path going from the broad to the specific.

What Is a Goal?

When you are writing a goal, you are telling the potential grantmaker what it is that you ultimately hope to achieve with the project that you are proposing.

You are making a broad statement that captures the reason you are undertaking this work. A goal is long term, a goal is a vision statement, a goal is the ends. A goal indicates purpose, announces desired change, and sets the stage for what is to come.

What Is an Objective?

An objective is an action that has to happen to achieve your goal. It answers the question *how*? Whereas a goal is the ends, an objective is the means through which a goal can be obtained. Objectives must be measurable actions that are usually defined in terms of numbers, beneficiaries, and time. Using action words, objectives describe a particular process or a particular outcome.

Goals and objectives are generally written together or in very close proximity to one another. Two examples of a goal and objective statement are offered here:

Project Goal: To improve the quality of the services Enlace provides to Holyoke children and their families through: (1) staff training, (2) increased family literacy activities, including new parent training materials, (3) new Learning Through Play equipment, and (4) community outreach.

* * *

The goal of STCC's *Workforce STAT* project is to meet regional healthcare industry needs by transforming—in an accelerated manner—large numbers of interested and willing pre-health students into a prepared, focused, well-qualified, and well-suited healthcare workforce through the following means: (1) early exposure to and awareness-building of healthcare career and coursework realities and choices, (2) hands-on simulation-based education, (3) targeted health program counseling to help students identify if healthcare work overall, and which field in particular, matches their skills, interests, and inclinations, and to foster these students so that they have the confidence and the tools to proceed quickly and strongly toward program graduation, and (4) expansion of STCC's Medical Assisting program.

In both of these examples, you learn the vision and you are introduced to how that vision will be met in general terms—the objectives. But when you read an objective such as "staff training," you don't know precisely how staff will receive training. That is what project activities describe.

What Is an Activity?

If you've brought the reader to this point, eagerly anticipating the *how* of your proposed work, you want to deliver specifics. Project activities are very precise steps that explain exactly how you will execute an objective. They may also be called implementation strategies.

What Is an Outcome?

Outcomes—also known as impacts or deliverables—are your final end point. They explain what you expect to happen as a result of all the project activity you undertook. Ideally, these outcomes will meet the need you earlier described.

Outcomes *must* be measurable—that is, quantifiable. Anything you say in your objective or project activity sections must be said in such a way that you can determine later whether it was accomplished. Of course, you won't actually know if activities indeed lead to your expected outcomes until after the project is over, but your proposal must state what you *anticipate* will happen as a result of your project's activities. These activities will be evaluated during and at the close of the grant. More information about evaluation is offered in Chapter 12.

Frequently, activities and outcomes will be presented together because one is dependent on the other; outcomes can't be described until activities are. Think of the project activity and outcome portion of your proposal as your work plan. A work plan encompasses what will be done, by whom, when, and what will result. Some grantmakers will request a work plan because they want to see if you have thought through how you're going to proceed with your project and achieve the goals and objectives you identified.

Let's return to the example of staff training. The related activities were described as:

Staff Training—The Preschool Enrichment Team (PET) of Springfield, MA, will conduct a ten-part training series designed on the Creative Curriculum for Infants and Toddlers. The focus of these trainings will be to underscore the importance of building relationships with children and families, to gain an understanding of child development theory, to explore developmentally appropriate curriculum for infants and toddlers, and to convert this knowledge to best classroom practice. The series will consist of nine trainings, one NAEYC Classroom Observation, ten planning/debriefing sessions, the administration of pre- and post-Infant/Toddler Environmental Rating Scale-Revised in two classrooms, and four one-hour ITERS-R debriefings.

You now understand exactly what training will be offered, how often, by whom, its content, and its expected outcome.

Guiding Questions

Recounting the list presented in the book's introduction, this section of the proposal answers the following questions:

Goals and Objectives

- What do you hope to achieve?

- What are the measurable and time-specific steps that must happen to reach your goal?

- Why do you choose to address the issue in the manner that you have?

Project Activities and Outcomes

- What are the specific activities involved? Who will do them? How? When?

- What specific outcomes will be achieved?

- Why is your organization the best one to do what you propose to do?

Many grantmakers will have specific questions that they want you to answer in a specific order; if that is the case, follow those instructions. But generally their questions are getting at the same pieces of information that your answers to the questions just listed would elicit. When forming a goals and objectives statement, you should be able to state why and how your vision responds to the needs earlier stated. When speaking of your project activities and outcomes, use your words to prove that you have the awareness, knowledge, and capacity to enact your vision.

Goals and Objectives Technique

When writing your goals and accompanying objectives, you are demonstrating your ability to assess the situation, to envision a solution, to determine what interventions will be most helpful and effective, and to see how these components intermesh. If you aren't as skillful in describing what you propose to do about the problem as you were eloquent in describing it, then you will lose the reader's confidence that you are the organization best suited to tackle this problem.

You are also introducing your organization's values and beliefs in your goals and objectives section. There are different opinions about what constitutes effective response and actions given a particular problem. Your goal declares what you most think needs to happen to respond to the stated need, and your objectives spell out how you think an organization must act to make that happen.

To arrive at a goal statement, use a technique similar to the So what? method described in Chapter 1. This time, the most important question you can answer is, Why? And each time you think you have arrived at exactly what the goal is, what you hope to achieve, ask yourself that question again so that you can distill to the essence of what change you want to make.

While goals can be vision statements, objectives need to be obtainable actions. When crafting objectives, be realistic; you will be evaluated on these measures. Don't set yourself up for failure just in the hopes that lofty objectives will make your proposal seem more attractive. Also, your objectives need to fit together logically; you should see linkages among them. Together they are what it takes to reach your goal.

Goals and Objectives Exercise

Let's say your organization is concerned about the environment. In particular, you believe the water quality in your community is threatened by local waste management practices. Is your goal then to address these local waste management practices? No, because if you ask yourself the question, Why address these local waste management practices? the answer will be because you are concerned about the community's water quality. Therefore, your ultimate goal—your ends—is to have clean water in your community. The focus on local waste management practices is not the goal—it is the basis of your objectives. Let's take this a step further. By asking and answering a series of questions, you will find your objectives.

Question: What is it about these waste management practices that is of concern and that you can hope to affect?

Answer: The city wants to expand the landfill over an aquifer.

Question: Why?

Answer: Because it anticipates an increased waste flow and believes the current landfill will not be able to accommodate that.

Question: What part of that can you reasonably address?

Answer: The waste flow.

Question: What can you do about waste flow?

Answer: Reduce it.

Question: How?

Answer: Waste can be reduced by the recycling and reuse of materials.

Question: How?

Answer: The many activities that you plan to undertake in your project.

So let's review:

Goal: To assure Anytown's clean water supply through the protection of the Purewater Aquifer from landfill contamination.

Objectives:

- Decrease the annual tonnage of waste deposited in the Anytown Landfill by x% in year one and y% in year two.
- Increase the amount of recycled material collected by the city x% in year one and y% in year two.
- Establish a citywide composting facility.
- Design a program to encourage the reuse of materials.
- Produce a waste reduction public awareness campaign capable of reaching all city residents.

Activities and Outcomes Technique

To determine project activities, consider the standard set of questions: Who? What? When? Where? Why? Answering these questions will essentially write the project activities section of your proposal, albeit in a somewhat different order, and subtracting one question—you've already answered why? in previous sections. But do not confuse these questions with the section names for your proposal. For example, you will not have a section titled "What?" I am using these words as a guide so that you know what it is you need to be thinking about, answering, and describing.

The proposal's activities section is when you detail, in measurable terms, the precise set of actions to be undertaken. Try to anticipate the reader's questions; every time you think you've stated things clearly, test to see if your presentation of the project activity has answered all the standard questions. Essentially all these questions add up to the larger question, How? Let that be your guide as you write project activities; you look at your objectives and ask, How? You will be writing activities for each objective; as with the objectives, be certain that project activities logically fit together. Be realistic about your organization's capacity to do the work, how much time it will take to do it, whether or not you have sufficient resources to do it, and if your expected outcomes are feasible.

Once you have established your objectives, you will further describe your project by listing under each objective specific project activities, also known as implementation strategies, which will happen to ensure that you meet that objective. For example, in the exercise about the landfill presented on page 171, to meet the objective of designing a program to encourage the reuse of materials, your activities may include setting up a trash-to-treasure hut at the landfill, publicizing Freecycle (an online free exchange community; www.freecycle.org), and working with construction contractors to encourage them to carefully extract items during a demolition and make those materials available to builders and homeowners.

Let us now examine each of the questions that are a part of arriving at your specific project activities, starting with the most substantive: What?

What?

After you have established your objectives, the next step is to determine the specific activities involved in achieving each objective. Let's dissect an example of how to do that.

If one of your objectives is to increase by 25% the number of retirees to serve as volunteer tutors in an after-school program, *what* will it take to make that happen? I see several possible steps involved:

1. You will need to identify recruitment measures, such as doing a presentation at a retirement community or developing a public service announcement.

2. You will need to have a protocol in place to handle inquiries, to sign people up, and to match them with students.

3. You may need to provide training.

4. You may wish to arrange transportation in conjunction with the retirement community.

5. You may want to plan a thank-you celebration at the end of the term to ensure that the retirees feel valued and needed and will return.

These steps are only part of your activity description; they describe the what. Once you have added information about who will do each step and when, the reader will be able to see that you have thought through what you need to do to get the desired increase in volunteers.

Sometimes the best way to arrive at the set of activities it will take to achieve your objective is to work backward from the ideal. I talk briefly about this in Chapter 7 as a means of overcoming writer's block. In this case, state your objective and ask what it would take to get there. For example, using the retiree volunteer tutor situation just described, as I was writing out the objective, I asked myself what it would take to accomplish it. My first answer was, "I need to get access to that demographic." Then I asked myself, "What are some of the ways in which I could do that?" And I came up with the two recruitment possibilities mentioned in step 1. Then I thought to myself, "Okay, so I've made contact with these people, now what?" And I answered that question in step 2. So you can see how each of those activities came up; I kept working backward. The ideal was to get more volunteers; the series of questions I asked myself led me to the activities it would take to do that.

Keep in mind what you've said in your statement of need; make sure that any barrier you say you're seeking to address has a related activity doing just that. Sometimes grantseekers raise expectations in their statement of need that they don't respond to when finally describing their project.

Who?

Of the listed project activities, who will do what and why? You will be answering these questions on two different levels: about your organization and about project staff. In essence you are defending your choices. Reassure your reader that the vision will be carried out by competent, knowledgeable people.

ESTABLISHING CREDENTIALS

Proposal reviewers may agree that what you propose to do should be done, but they will want to know why your organization is the best one to do it. You have to be convincing that your organization has the capacity to do what you are proposing to do. With your statement of need and a description of your organization's work in that arena, you have made the connection between your organization's mission and the topic you seek to address.

Now you have to satisfy the reader's need to know that this project is in good hands, not only that you know what you're doing but that you have sufficient resources to do it. If you or your organization has had experience with similar projects, be sure to talk about that. If you've handled something of complexity and delivered good results, talk about it.

Being reassuring about any project staff's credentials and capacity is equally important. Confirm that the project manager or principal investigator (PI) has the background, experience, and qualifications needed to achieve what is being proposed. Be certain that these qualifications match the subject area in which you are working.

PROJECT MANAGEMENT PLAN

For each activity, state who is linked to that activity and in what way. Clearly define each person's roles and responsibilities. If there is going to be a large project staff involved, show a staffing plan and how each player interacts with the others. A solid project management plan in which there is no doubt about who has what responsibility gives the reader confidence in your capacity to achieve your goal.

PARTNERSHIPS AND COLLABORATIONS

Increasingly, grantmakers are specifically asking for partnerships and collaborations and will sometimes give extra points for having such. Although this may add efficiency and fiscal smartness to attacking a societal problem, it adds considerable complexity to the crafting of the proposal. Because there is rarely sufficient time between the release of an RFP calling for partnerships and the proposal deadline, bringing together potential partners immediately to discuss their roles is imperative. The ideal scenario is for organizations with similar interests to explore joint activities *before* an RFP that calls for a partnership is released.

Sometimes you can anticipate where grantmakers are headed, perhaps not the specifics but the general intention, and discuss how you might work together toward that end. But if that hasn't happened, the RFP insists on a partnership, and you are faced with a short amount of time to design a project and prepare a proposal, you have a few choices: (1) limit the number of partners; (2) work with known partners with whom you've had previous experience; (3) write the proposal with general statements about how the partners will work together, and inject a partner planning period into your timeline; or (4) don't submit a proposal for this funding round, but if you think it will be repeated the following year, start working on your partnerships now.

The proposal should make clear why each partner is a part of the project, introducing the partner's work in the subject area and stating how its mission relates to the problem being tackled. Speak to what actions or resources each partner brings to the solution. Identify why each partner's participation is a benefit to the project and what that partner brings to it. Obtain letters of commitment or support from the partners confirming their involvement.

Specify each partner's roles and responsibilities and what they'll do when. The chart below offers one way in which you can show this information at a glance. You will need to explain each activity further in your proposal, but the chart clearly outlines who will do what.

ACTIVITIES	PARTNERS						
	Sleepy	Happy	Sneezy	Grumpy	Dopey	Bashful	Doc
Chop wood		x	x	x		x	
Work in the mines	x	x	x	x	x	x	x
Revive Snow White	x				x		x
Crack magic mirror				x			
Find prince		x					
Rejoice!	x	x	x		x	x	x

When and Where?

A timeline is one of the most important tools for imparting information about the project activities. Proposal reviewers will be looking to see if you have a clear understanding of what level of effort it will take to do a specific task. They'll be looking to see if you understand the sequencing of activities, how long something will take, and when it should be happening. In addition to listing each activity of the project, be sure to include evaluation and reporting activities in your timeline, too.

The fact that a timeline is visual helps communicate a lot of information easily. There are a lot of different forms that it can take depending on what you're trying to convey. In some instances it's simply a list of activities matched up to time periods. Others may indicate who is going to be doing what activities and when. More elaborate timelines may include outcomes as well.

Although questions about where something will take place may not be as important as questions about when, you still need to include that information, especially if there are many organizations involved in the implementation of the project.

The table on page 178 is an example of a timeline for a major project involving support programs for veterans attending college. A series of project activities is listed in the first column. The shaded areas indicate when each activity will take place.

Language

Your language throughout the proposal matters, but there are a couple of things worth mentioning that are particular to project activity and outcomes. The most important, yet seemingly petty, distinction I can tell you is this: When describing your activities, use the words *we will*, not "we would" or "we want to" or "we hope to" or "we wish to"—say *we will*. As in, *we will* provide fire safety training to 100 children. *We will* host free, weekly community concerts in the summer. *We will* design an art-in-the-schools program. It is a subtle statement of confidence and power.

As in all fields, in philanthropy some terms go in and out of fashion. For example, some grantmakers will ask about your methodology instead of activities. Or they'll say metrics for measurements or deliverables in place of outcomes. Pay attention to the funder's terminology and echo it; you want to use words that will be familiar to the funder.

A term that I have found to be useful when writing is *such as*. *Such as* comes in handy when you want to give a flavor of something but don't want to be held rigidly to it. Going back to our example of volunteer tutors, notice how you might frame the sentence describing recruitment: "To enlist volunteer tutors,

Timeline for VETS Program Activities

VETS Project Timeline	Fall 2009	Spring 2010	Fall 2010	Spring 2011	Fall 2011	Spring 2012
Hire veterans advocate/project coordinator	X					
Establish project advisory board	X					
Campus community survey/focus groups	X	X	X	X		X
Create comprehensive veterans service database	X					
Create persistence/completion tracking system	X					
Create counseling/disability services tracking system	X					
Create veterans website on STCC website	X					
Facilitate/advise student veterans support group	X					
Create local veterans resources list	X					
Create informational brochure for student veterans		X				
Create threat assessment/crisis management team protocols	X					
Advisory board gatekeeper training	X					
Campus police/health services gatekeeper training		X				
Veteran-specific orientation		X	X	X	X	X
Veterans services referrals		X	X	X	X	X
Monthly informational emails via veterans website	X	X	X	X	X	X
Train veteran-to-veteran mentors		X	X	X	X	X
Monitor/revise veterans website		X	X	X	X	X
Evaluate/revise veteran database		X	X	X	X	X
Modify/revise protocols as needed		X	X	X	X	X
Faculty gatekeeper training		X	X	X	X	
Student leaders/campus clubs gatekeeper training						X
Project advisory board updates/meetings		X	X	X	X	X
Final report and recommendations						X

we will undertake a variety of recruitment measures, such as doing a presentation at a retirement community or developing a public service announcement (PSA)." By using the phrase *such as*, you present two ideas of how recruitment might happen but aren't held to or limited by only those two ideas. If you are writing a proposal but are not the person who will be doing the work, you can't know all the possibilities about how a task might be accomplished, and you don't want to stifle future creativity. Nor do you want to be held to a suggestion if for good reasons it later turns out to be unwanted or unfeasible. For example, if the project manager discovered that no one responded to the PSAs, then they should be stopped and another technique tried. This is not to promote waffling; the ends—the recruitment—remains an objective for our example, but the means have some built-in leeway. The funder will be most concerned with whether the recruitment happened and was successful.

Text or Charts?

The activities and outcomes part of the proposal will require a lot of precise description about what will happen during the course of the proposal and what will happen as a result of that activity. This description can be as much as half of your proposal's length. Most of the explanations about project activity will be achieved through prose. But charts are especially useful in communicating a large amount of information at a glance and for saving space. You can use charts in lieu of prose, as long as they adequately answer any question specifically asked by the grantmaker.

Often charts are valuable because they can combine information found in different parts of the proposal and offer the reader a quick way to understand the interrelationships of various components. For instance, charts can be used to convey simple relationships, such as how the activities relate to each objective.

The chart on page 180 is excerpted from a successful proposal submitted to the U.S. Department of Labor. As you examine it, notice how it combines a lot of information in a condensed way. This information was expanded on in the proposal text, but the chart lets the reader understand how it all interrelates. In the left column is a list of the project's objectives and the related specific academic challenge(s) identified earlier in the proposal to underscore the project's need. The right column shows that the objectives were constructed with the challenges and needs squarely in mind, and indicates how the project will go about achieving each objective. The strategies were later used as the basis for presenting project outcomes.

Objective	Implementation Strategy
1. Increase the capacity of all four western Massachusetts community colleges to offer meaningful hands-on experiences to potential health students and expand the capacity of the STCC Medical Assisting Program.	**1a.** Equip and bring up-to-date simulation labs with lab assistants at four community colleges. **1b.** Provide simulation training for faculty and lab assistants and a heightened awareness of how to use simulation as a counseling tool. **1c.** Establish the geographical expansion of the Medical Assisting program through a creative use of hybrid coursework and technology-based distance learning.
2. To increase the capacity of the four partner colleges to appropriately inform and advise potential students to the variety of healthcare careers. [Responds to Academic Challenge #1]	**2a.** Increase number of K–12 Medical Encounter sessions. **2b.** Create and implement at each college the Patient Skills course. **2c.** Provide Targeted Advising Training. **2d.** Increase the number of Targeted Counselors. **2e.** Increase health careers recruitment. **2f.** Re-develop www.healthprograms.org.
3. To introduce students to the realities of healthcare careers. [Responds to Academic Challenges #1, 2]	**3a.** Provide K–12 Medical Encounter to all four college partners. **3b.** Offer the Patient Skills course.
4. To introduce students to the realities of healthcare coursework. [Responds to Academic Challenge #3]	**4a.** Provide K–12 Medical Encounter to all four college partners. **4b.** Offer the Patient Skills course. **4c.** Provide Targeted Counseling.
5. To help students identify if healthcare work overall, and which field in particular, matches their skills, interests, and inclinations. [Responds to Academic Challenges #1, 2, and 3]	**5a.** Provide K–12 Medical Encounter to all four college partners. **5b.** Offer the Patient Skills course. **5c.** Provide Targeted Counseling.

Objective	Implementation Strategy
6. To foster students in the health programs so they have the confidence and the tools to proceed quickly and strongly toward program graduation. [Responds to Academic Challenge #3]	**6a.** Provide K–12 Medical Encounter to all four partner colleges. **6b.** Offer the Patient Skills course. **6c.** Provide Targeted Counseling.
7. To rework existing Health Core to put increased emphasis on critical thinking, problem solving, teamwork, writing, language, communication, and cultural competency. [Responds to Academic Challenge #4]	**7a.** College Credit Patient Skills course. **7b.** Industry/College Review Board will provide input into curriculum changes.

In other cases, a chart may be used to convey more complex material. For example, a chart can tell a reader what activities will be done to meet a specific objective, who will do it, when it will be done, and the expected outcomes. Each of these components appears in different places in the proposal where they are described in more detail. But the chart allows the reader to easily grasp how it all fits together. The following example is a small excerpt of a larger chart that was

Objective 1: Planning and Assessment

A Partnership team will be established, and the STEM teaching needs of SPS middle schools will be defined and assessed.

Activity	Responsible Personnel	Timeline	Outcome–Deliverable
Partnership Meetings	PI, Lead Team, Staff Assistant (SA)	Fall 2008 to Fall 2010	Initial course of action outlined
Recruitment of Additional Partners for Lead Team	PI, Lead Team	Fall 2008 to Fall 2010	Partnership established
Teacher Outreach	PI, Lead Team, SA	Fall 2008 to Spring 2010	Teachers assist in targeting STEM students, topics; needs assessed
Needs Assessment	PI, Lead Team	Fall 2008 to Spring 2009	Formal evaluation of needs formulated

in a successful proposal to the National Science Foundation. Notice how many pieces of information are given in a small place—the objective, each activity that will be undertaken to meet that objective, who will take responsibility to ensure that an activity is completed, when it will happen, and what the result will be.

Most of the grant proposal will be presented in text form; however, charts are useful tools. They can take many forms; I have shown you only a few. Sometimes you use a chart when you need to save room and when you don't have a large page allowance to make your case, but primarily you use charts to display an overview of your proposal's contents. When making the decision as to how to present your information—text or chart—the final determinant should be what best answers the grantmaker's questions and what best imparts the information.

Supporting Material

Many times grantmakers will restrict your project narrative to a set number of pages, but allow for attachments. Attachments can be used to give more information about the project activity discussed in your proposal and put it into context. They can include a variety of things, such as timelines, résumés or curricula vitae (CVs), support letters, data, references, and budget and budget narratives. When determining what to put into the attachment section, your primary decision-making factor should be this: Does it add to the reader's understanding of what you're trying to do? Does it provide proof that the actions you propose are wanted and effective?

Examples of Goal, Objectives, and Activities Statements

Before and After Example

In this section, I present a before and after example of the goal and objective statement for an online submission to a corporate grantmaker who required short answers. You will notice that the content is essentially the same in both forms, but the presentation is very different and the second allows for easier access to the information. The after example was further delineated by separating objectives and activities. The funder specifically asked for goals and objectives; then activities were added to give a fuller picture.

You'll notice in the before example that there is no specific statement that has the word *goal* in it. The text consists of a descriptive set of paragraphs, but it does not tell you what the main event is. The after version presents information in a concise, orderly manner using action words. The objectives stated are measurable and further enhanced by the presentation of related activities. Not only is it more descriptive but it is more visually accessible—you can find information more quickly. These last two points are appealing to all but especially important to corporate funders.

BEFORE

Excellence in Youth Entrepreneurship (EYE) supports the principles of entrepreneurship, providing students with the knowledge and techniques needed for success. It gives students the tools needed to develop a business plan, including financial statements, market research, marketing material, presentation and business networking skills. EYE culminates in the presentation of a viable business for each student.

The EYE program uses staff outreach and partnerships with community-based organizations to recruit at-risk and underserved youth to participate in the program. Up to 100 young people each year learn about business ownership through EYE. The program features the curriculum developed by the Small Business Development Center Network, in conjunction with guest speakers and program enhancements. The material teaches entrepreneurship, information technology, and workplace literacy through business curriculum, enhancements, and a business plan creation.

AFTER

The goal of EYE is to provide high-school-aged students with the knowledge, techniques, resources, and tools needed for successful small business planning and start-up.

The goal is aligned with the following objectives:

1. Recruit 100–125 at-risk and underserved Springfield High School students to participate in the program. (Activity 1)
2. Increase at-risk students' knowledge about entrepreneurship, information technology, workplace literacy, and business ownership. (Activities 2 and 3)
3. Provide at-risk students with the skills to create a viable business plan, including financial statements, market research, marketing material, presentation, and business networking skills. (Activities 4 and 5)

The objectives will be achieved through the following activities:

1. Conduct staff outreach and form partnerships with community-based organizations, such as North End Youth Center, Futureworks Career Center, Springfield Public Schools School to Career Program, Northern Educational Services, the Urban League, Westover Job Corps Center, and area faith-based after-school programs to recruit at-risk and underserved youth to participate in the program.
2. Teach up to 100 young people each year about entrepreneurship, information technology, workplace literacy, and business ownership.
3. Provide instruction through the use of business curriculum developed by the Small Business Development Center Network, guest speakers, and program enhancements such as online resources accessed via a mobile computer lab.
4. Program participants will develop a viable business plan, including financial statements, market research, marketing material, presentation, and business networking skills.
5. At the conclusion of the course, program participants will present their full business plan to the program participants and invited family and guests.

Example of a Project Activities Section

The example in this section is from a successful proposal submitted to a state government early education and care department by a local social service nonprofit. This grantmaker allowed only four double-spaced pages, so things needed to be presented concisely; even then, it was nearly half of the allowed page amount. An example of an activities section in a longer proposal can be found in the Appendix.

Project Goal: To improve the quality of the services Enlace provides to Holyoke children and their families through: (1) staff training, (2) increased family literacy activities, including new parent training materials, (3) new Learning Through Play equipment, and (4) community outreach.

Activities: (1) *Staff Training*—The Preschool Enrichment Team (PET) of Springfield, MA, will conduct a ten-part training series designed on the Creative Curriculum for Infants and Toddlers. The focus of these trainings will be to underscore the importance of building relationships with children and families, to gain an understanding of child development theory, to explore developmentally appropriate curriculum for infants and toddlers, and to convert this knowledge to best classroom practice. The series will consist of nine trainings, one NAEYC Classroom Observation, ten planning/debriefing sessions, the administration of pre- and post-Infant/Toddler Environmental Rating Scale-Revised in two classrooms, and four one-hour ITERS-R debriefings. (2) *Family Literacy*—The parents we are targeting are young, under-educated, with under-educated parents themselves, living in a community with a school system cited by the state as underperforming. Our goal is to instill a culture of reading in these families, because literacy and a love of reading is key to achieving the very goals DEEC cites for its Quality Improvement Grant program— "to promote school readiness, school success, and positive outcomes for children." To that end, we will: (a) purchase and share Words That Cook literacy brochures, books, and a DVD series, in both Spanish and English, as well as purchase a large stock of children's books to be given to at-risk families, and (b) incorporate reading in our regularly scheduled Center activities, such as playgroup sessions, parenting programs, and special events. For example, we will have 15 mothers make a commitment to a 4-week session where they include reading to their children as part of the play activities, and at the successful completion of each 4-week session they will get one children's book. If they come for the 12 months they would have collected 12 hardcover books and additional information regarding how literacy impacts their child's life. We also will extend a similar book-earning opportunity to the men who participate in our Nurturing Fathers Program. (3) *Learning Through Play*—To coordinate with our PET staff training to heighten the teachers' knowledge of baby/toddler curricula, we will purchase baby interactive play equipment—cognitive, sensory, discovery toys. We will purchase new equipment and supplies for our gym, which is also open to homeless families. So much of our Center's activities revolve around children. Not only do we want to provide them with a safe and happy place to play and learn, but having such a place encourages their parents to come to our Center and then avail themselves of our parent-oriented programs and assistance. (4) *Community Outreach*—Enlace has successful programs that attract and help many people; now we wish to reach the hard-to-engage parents. To do this, we will purchase ads in media, such as Spanish radio and the free Spanish newspaper. Also, we will engage hospitals and clinics in publicizing our programs. We have a new brochure designed and are requesting funds to print it.

Make It Measurable: Outcomes

As you are planning your project, you will be thinking about each step that has to happen to achieve your project's goals. Part of that thinking will be about results: What will occur because you took those steps? To determine whether these results had the desired impact, you must have results—outcomes—that can be measured. And the act of measuring these outcomes is called evaluation, covered in more detail in the next chapter.

CHAPTER 12

Say It with Proof

Evaluation

The evaluation portion of your proposal usually comes right after your goals, objectives, activities, and outcomes sections because an evaluation measures how well you met those goals and objectives, how well your activities led to the desired outcomes. Nothing could be more reasonable than a grantmaker wanting to know if the money spent met the need described earlier in your proposal and produced the envisioned results.

Evaluation has become more and more important to grantmakers, both public and private, in recent years. Therefore, the evaluation section of a proposal should assure the potential funder that there is a solid way to know whether you have achieved your project goal and objectives and that you will pursue that investigation with diligence.

A grantmaker will let you know whether it wants you to conduct an evaluation of your project. If a grantmaker doesn't specifically ask you to include evaluation in your proposal, you may skip this section, although it might be impressed if you do include it in some way. For example, if you are required to file reports about your grant activity, you will at least want to acknowledge that you will track your progress for reporting purposes. Evaluations take place during the course of your project (Are things going as planned?) and at the end of your project (How well did we do in meeting our goals?).

But don't think that the only reason to engage in evaluation is to appease or please the funder; evaluation has value to your organization as well. The information gathered during the course of an evaluation can provide helpful feedback that can aid you in making decisions about your organization and its programs.

Reasons for Evaluation

There are two primary reasons to conduct an evaluation: to demonstrate accountability and to provide information. Accountability in the funding world is as important as it is in the business sector; the grantmaker needs to know that its money has been well spent. Information garnered from an evaluation can serve as an effective decision-making tool for your organization and can provide important feedback that can be useful to a variety of audiences, such as other organizations or people doing similar work to yours, researchers, and policymakers. It can provide useful data and lessons learned that may affect how others conduct their business or what policies are made.

Accountability

In accepting a grant, you are making a commitment to conduct a set of activities spelled out in your proposal in the hopes of achieving a specific goal. Accountability requires that you have both completed the work and made sincere efforts to reach your goal. The outcomes may or may not be as you had envisioned, but they do need to be reported. Almost all grantmakers require a final report and some request interim reports, especially for a multi-year grant.

Grantmakers are keen on grantees taking accountability seriously. If it is government funds being awarded as grants, the entire populace of the country has a vested interest in that money being spent productively. Certainly, the executive branch must answer to the legislative branch that it has spent monies for the purposes indicated in the accompanying legislation.

Foundations exist to do good, and they want to know that they have. But it's not enough to do good; they want to do the most good they can do with the most efficient use of funds. Keep in mind that just as the government funders have an internal accountability, so do foundation staff. In defense of the push for accountability, a foundation program officer revealed to me, "Foundations are becoming more and more accountable internally, and program officers must show grants will be effective and then measure that effectiveness."

Your first accountability on a given project is to your funder, but there are other entities who can expect to be recipients of it as well. Other donors to your organization would want to know that the work you are doing—with their or others' dollars—is done efficiently and effectively. Your board of directors has a vested interest in how the organization is managing. Executive and other staff could benefit from an assessment of project operations. And the populace your organization serves can benefit not only from your actions but from an understanding of the consequences. All of these audiences would benefit from learning the results of a project's evaluation.

When you are done describing your evaluation goals and methodologies in your proposal, you should be able to answer this question: How will you know that you did what you said you would do?

Information

Doing an evaluation for accountability purposes may seem a burden. Counteract that with doing an evaluation for information purposes and it becomes a gift. All the data, stories, and information gathered throughout the evaluation can provide you with useful insight and a constructive decision-making tool.

The data that you collect throughout the course of the project's evaluation can tell you whether the *process* you are using to undertake the project activities is effective. Are things unfolding as you thought they would? If not, with this information you can make midcourse corrections to ensure a better project outcome. At the end of the project, an evaluation tells you if particular actions do lead to desired outcomes. If you were testing a new approach, through evaluation you'd know whether this was an approach you wanted to keep. Even if things don't work out as you had originally envisioned, don't think of evaluation as punitive; it's informative, it's smart. It demonstrates a willingness to learn, a willingness to change, and a preference for that which is best for the organization and the people you serve.

Results from an evaluation are useful not only to you and the grantmaker but also to other organizations that may be doing similar work. These lessons learned can inform others of highly effective approaches or of unintended consequences to a certain method—either being very useful in determining future action. While it is unlikely that your actual evaluation will be made public, it is often expected that the results of your project activities will be made known to others through dissemination (see Chapter 13).

Evaluation Considerations

Undertaking an evaluation can be daunting, especially because you're not as likely to have the same familiarity with evaluation methodology and practice as you do with running your programs. But armed with the understanding and techniques presented in this chapter, you should be equipped to write and execute a basic evaluation plan.

Internal vs. External Evaluator

The first thing you need to determine with an evaluation is whether you should do it in-house or hire an outside evaluator. The primary factor in deciding this is the size of both the grant and the grant-funded project. If both are large, hire a professional evaluator. Grantmakers who require an evaluation generally expect to see it as a line item in your budget.

If the project is complex, with a lot of variables and a lot of distinct activities, evaluation not only will be equally as complex but will be time-consuming as well. Hire a professional evaluator; in fact, that evaluator can write the evaluation section of your proposal. For those working in academia, another resource would be to use on-campus resources to design your evaluation or to give you assessment tools.

But if your project is small and the funds you are requesting are not sufficient to pay for an evaluator, you will need to do your evaluation with in-house staff. In many cases, this will not be difficult because it will be only a matter of collecting numbers or issuing a questionnaire. But if you make the claim that you will increase client satisfaction by 20%, be prepared to measure whether that objective was reached. Evaluation techniques will be discussed in greater detail in the next few pages.

In the evaluation portion of your proposal, specify who will conduct your evaluation; it can be conducted by project personnel or outsiders or both. If you have chosen an outside evaluator, be sure to present his or her credentials. This is especially important with large-dollar government proposals.

Goal of Evaluation

An initial question you must answer when designing your evaluation is: What do you want it to accomplish? The answers to this question will determine how you proceed—the methodology you employ, the data you collect, and what you do with the data.

In the beginning of your evaluation plan, state what the goal of the project evaluation is. What do you hope to learn, prove, or demonstrate? How will the results of your evaluation be used? It may be for one or more of the following reasons:

- To determine whether your programs are working as intended

- To verify program choices

- To make changes to program activities

- To improve efficiency

- To make operations more cost effective

- To determine if something is feasible

- To determine if a specific action will have a specific consequence

- To measure the impact of specific actions

- To compare program delivery of two different projects or two different approaches

- To test if you are running the project in the way that you intended

- To demonstrate usefulness for replication

Audience of Evaluation

As you are trying to determine the goal of your evaluation, ask yourself these questions: Who needs to know what about this project? Who could use this information? To some degree the answers will affect how you will design and conduct your evaluation. The potential audience goes beyond the funder and your organization; as mentioned earlier, there are any number of people and organizations who could benefit from your findings. Think about what can be learned from your evaluation and with whom you want to share that information.

The funder may have more than one reason it wants you to carry out an evaluation. Aside from wanting reassurance that it has made a wise investment, it may be interested in testing a variety of strategies to determine where to place its resources in the future. It may need to justify its decisions to its own governing board, whether that be trustees or the legislature. It may be compiling lessons learned to share with a broader audience to influence how a particular problem will be addressed. You should be able to tell what the reason for evaluation is either directly from the grantmaker's words or from the tools, such as a website, that the grantmaker uses and promotes to share lessons learned from previous grantees.

Naturally, it will be easier to determine how your organization wants to use this information. But keep in mind that there could be a difference between what information your board of directors is interested in and what information the organization's staff needs. For example, your board may be more interested in what actions are most cost effective than in nuances of project activity or service delivery, which interests your organization's staff.

Some grantmakers will have their own evaluation questions that you are required to answer. Others may have evaluation tools that you can use, including data collection software.

Evaluation can be related to dissemination (see Chapter 13) in that you may want to share with a broader audience what you learn from having done the evaluation. Some parts of what you learn may be for internal use only, but much can be valuable to your peers. Grantmakers like to think that their grants have a life beyond the single grantee, and disseminating lessons learned can be part of ensuring that.

Formatting

Much like the goals, objectives, activities, and outcomes part of your proposal, you will often describe your evaluation plan and methodology in both text and chart format. The text portion will detail how you will go about conducting the evaluation, as described in the six itemized steps in the following section. A chart can display the relationship of activities to outcomes and demonstrate how one depends on the other. Some example charts are offered in this chapter.

Your choice about whether to use text or a chart or both will depend primarily on three factors: the grantmaker's instructions, the amount of space available, and the complexity of your project and thus your project's evaluation plan. The most important thing is that you impart what you will measure, why, and how.

Evaluation Methodology and Techniques

Your evaluation methodology consists of the procedures you will use to gather information necessary to assess your project and the procedures you will use to analyze that information. Practitioners in the evaluation field have a wide range of beliefs about the appropriate strategies, techniques, and models to use in particular situations, and I yield to their expertise. But if you do not plan to use an outside evaluator, I can give you enough information here so that, if needed, you can write the evaluation section of your proposal unaided by a professional evaluator.

Describe your evaluation methodology precisely so that the reader will understand exactly what you will do, how you will do it, and why. In the order that best fits the situation and grantmaker instructions, give the following information; these items will be further explained in the following pages:

- Clarify who will be involved in the evaluation process either as an evaluator or as a participant.

- For each project objective, state the desired outcome in measurable terms.

- Define what you will measure and what tool you will use to do that.

- Specify at what point during the project you will take these measurements.

- Explain how you will analyze that data.

- Describe what you will do with this information.

Evaluation is not something that happens only at the end of the project. Build in evaluation throughout the life of the project so that you can have good information for making midcourse corrections if necessary. For each objective, determine when you need information about that objective's progress and, therefore, at what point in the project calendar evaluation activities need to take place. Make sure that evaluation activities are listed in the main timeline of the project or that evaluation has a timeline of its own.

The Outcome Measurement Resource Network of the United Way offers many evaluation tools on its website (www.liveunited.org/outcomes). Take a look in particular at the publication "Measuring Program Outcomes: A Practical Approach" (www.liveunited.org/outcomes/resources/mpo). It provides an example of how you might present the relationship of outcomes and indicators of that outcome for your project, how you identify the data you expect to collect, and which outcome they will measure.

Tying Evaluation to Your Objectives

The most important step in the evaluation process is to make sure you have created project goals and objectives that are truly measurable; otherwise, you will not be able to design and describe an evaluation to assess them. Each project objective will need to be evaluated. To do that, form questions related to the objectives. For example, if your project goal is to increase community use of your library, and one of your project objectives is to expand the number of attendees at children's hours by 25%, your evaluation questions might be, "How many children and accompanying adults attend children's hours at the beginning of the project? How many children and accompanying adults attend children's hours at the end of the project?" Your evaluation tool in this case will be simply counting numbers of attendees. A comparison of those two figures will enable you to determine whether you have met your objective.

If your objective is not to increase the number of attendees at children's hours but to increase the level of satisfaction with that event, your evaluation questions will be different. Instead you might ask, "How many children and accompanying adults attending children's hours at the beginning of the project indicated they were satisfied or very satisfied with the event? How many children and accompanying adults attending children's hours at the end of the project indicated they were satisfied or very satisfied with the event?" Here your evaluation tool would be a survey by which you would collect this information. Again, a comparison of those figures would enable you to determine whether you had met your objective.

Operating with evaluation in mind when you are writing your objective statements will ensure that you write only objectives that are measurable. If you can't determine a means by which you will know if you've met the objective, then it isn't measurable and you need to rewrite it. Likewise, the requirement of evaluation can keep you from making promises that you can't possibly keep. Knowing that you will be graded on something later will make you pause and consider whether or not you can actually deliver it.

Formative and Summative Evaluation

The terms *formative* and *summative* are frequently used when describing evaluation. A formative evaluation is one that examines process, meaning how you are going about implementing project activities. To assess this, a formative evaluation begins when the project begins. A summative evaluation examines outcomes, the results of the project activities, and is conducted at the end of the project. A thorough project evaluation has both formative and summative components, especially if you must submit grant reports throughout the project's duration.

A formative evaluation is useful in determining if the way in which you are carrying out project activities is effective, and if you find that it is not, it allows you to make changes in how you are going about things before the end of the project. A formative evaluation focuses on process.

A summative evaluation is useful in learning whether your chosen problem-solving approach was successful in achieving the goals and objectives you had set out to do. A summative evaluation focuses on results and impact.

Types of Evaluation

Selecting the right evaluation methodology for the project will depend on (1) what you want to measure, (2) why you want to measure it, and (3) what information you expect to have as a result. Don't feel constrained by having to choose one specific method to evaluate the whole project; you can use more than one technique to perform your assessments. Also, when writing for more than one project, keep in mind that different evaluation approaches fit different situations; a single template is not likely to work for all scenarios. When choosing among the options presented in the following paragraph, consider if the method is feasible and if it is likely to provide sound data. And if you are doing an internal evaluation, be realistic about what you can do in terms of time, capacity, and resources.

There are several types of evaluation, each with a specific set of beliefs, strategies, and techniques. Some of these are Kirkpatrick, impact, objective, utilization, responsive, and logic model evaluations. It is beyond the scope of this book to provide full descriptions of each of these. Professional evaluators will be familiar with them and will know which type of evaluation to use in which circumstance.

Of these types of evaluation, the logic model is probably the one that is most useful when designing and conducting an internal evaluation without the help of a professional evaluator. The logic model is a visual expression of your project's activities and outcomes and has become popular among grantmakers.

The W. K. Kellogg Foundation brought the logic model as an evaluation tool to the forefront and offers evaluation templates—which can be used in an evaluation to any grantmaker—in its online evaluation toolkit. (Go to www. wkkf.org to access valuable evaluation guidance and resources.) In a chart form, you can present a lot of information about your project, its activities, and the expected results. Notice that in general, an evaluation chart presents information that you previously discussed in your goals, objectives, and activities section because those are the things that you are measuring and thus evaluating. In the Kellogg Foundation's basic logic model, there are five categories: resources/inputs, activities, outputs, outcomes, and impact. The chart below shows you the layout of the logic model with a brief description of the categories. You can also download this chart from the Kellogg Foundation at www.wkkf.org.

Resources	Activities	Outputs	Short- & Long-Term Outcomes	Impact
In order to accomplish our set of activities, we will need the following:	In order to address our problem or asset, we will conduct the following activities:	We expect that once completed or under way these activities will produce the following evidence of service delivery:	We expect that if completed or ongoing these activities will lead to the following changes in 1–3, then 4–6 years:	We expect that if completed these activities will lead to the following changes in 7–10 years:

This chart is reprinted with permission from the W. K. Kellogg Foundation "Logic Model Development Guide" (page 17).

If the grantmaker that you are pursuing does not have a preferred evaluation technique, the logic model, or a variation of it, is a good tool to use. For example, to create a variation of Kellogg's logic model, which makes a distinction among outputs, outcomes, and impact, you might use only the term *outcomes*. Other places have developed similar logic models that may be equally as useful to you. While the categories may be different, you'll notice that the format is the same. Using a chart form, you start at the left and build with each column. You are telling a story about what your hopes are, what you have to work with, what you intend to do, and what you hope will happen in the short term and long term. Another example for you to look at for a fuller understanding of the logic

Example from the United Way of the Bay Area, "Developing Your Logic Model"

Goals	Objectives	Major Activities	Indicators	Outcomes (specify short term and long term)
Increase the number of parents who read to their children on a daily basis and Increase the percentage of children reading at proficiency	Appropriate, high quality and convenient parent/child literacy classes are available to target population	Provide parent/child literacy classes to target population teaching parents how to read to their children and support children's literacy development	# of parents served, # of classes held, # and percentage of children who increase reading scores on pre-test and post-test	*Short term:* Based on evaluation, 90% of parents increase their knowledge about how to read to children and increase amount of time reading to children to support literacy development *Long term:* Based on evaluation, parents are consistently supporting children's literacy development and 90% of children are reading at proficiency

Reprinted with permission of the United Way of the Bay Area.

model approach is above. As an excerpt, this chart only shows one objective, but you would do this same exercise for each objective.

Evaluation Participants

Your first decision will be whether you are using an internal or external evaluator. Consider who else will be involved; project staff, other organizational staff, project partners, and project clients and beneficiaries may all need to play a role in a full project evaluation. Who is involved in an evaluation will depend on what information you are trying to collect, what you are trying to measure, and how that can be done. You will need to explain the purpose and techniques of the evaluation to participants and to be mindful of privacy issues and obtaining necessary permissions.

Data Collection and Analysis

What data do you need to collect? This is determined by what you need to measure to verify if you have met your stated objectives. Data can be collected in a variety of ways; you can mix data collection methods depending on the objective being measured. The following are some data collection instruments you can use:

- Direct measurement, such as head counts, meals delivered, or books read

- Survey

- Questionnaire

- Interview

- Focus group

- Observation

- Document review

- Review of data collected by other sources or by your organization for other purposes

The degree to which you need to describe and explain your data collection instruments will depend on the nature of the proposal reviewer. For example, if you are in academia and your proposal will be reviewed by peers, the description of your evaluation methodology will need to be quite precise and rigorous to pass muster. But for any audience, explain:

- What data you will collect

- From what source

- The data collection instruments you will use to do it

- What information you expect to result that will aid in making project decisions or refinements

- What information you expect to result that will aid in making final project assessments

Evaluations may be quantitative or qualitative or both. A quantitative evaluation refers to data that are collected and reported in numbers. A qualitative evaluation refers to data that are collected through vehicles such as interviews and surveys and reported in words. During the course of the project, your data analysis should help you understand what is and isn't working with your project's implementation and give you guidance on how to proceed. At the end of the project, your data analysis should give you information about whether your vision and approach to enacting that vision works.

If a grantmaker requires an evaluation, do not treat this part of your proposal as insignificant. Government funders especially place a heavy point value on your evaluation plan. A strong evaluation plan is one of the ways you can impart reassurance to the grantmaker about your commitment to the project and your capacity to carry it out and learn from its outcomes. And lessons learned from your project's evaluation will have value to other people. Getting the word out about your project and its outcomes is called dissemination, the subject of the next chapter.

CHAPTER 13

Say It Expansively

Project Dissemination

Project dissemination is the act of spreading the word about your project activities and outcomes. It takes place both during the project and at the close of the project. Not all grantmakers will request that this be included in a proposal, but many—particularly government agencies or large foundations—believe it is an important function of a grant-funded project and expect to see a description of how you will do it. Grantmakers want their investment to be far-reaching, and one of the ways that can happen is through the dissemination of project activities and outcomes to others.

If it is not specifically requested, it is not necessary to include it; in fact, in some types of proposals—those asking for general operating support, for example—it doesn't make sense. If you do include it, however, the dissemination section of your proposal will be one of the shorter parts. Depending on the length of the overall proposal, it could be as little as one paragraph or as much as a page or two.

As with evaluation, dissemination is a project objective of its own, with a set of specific activities integrated into the project's design and timeline. When writing the dissemination objectives and related activities, think about and address the following questions:

- What is the purpose of dissemination?

- With whom do you want to share information?

- What specifically do you hope to achieve by doing so?

Purpose and Value of Dissemination

The ultimate purpose of dissemination is to share knowledge. And the reason to share knowledge is to teach or help others. Dissemination, therefore, is about education and replication.

Writing up a dissemination plan for your proposal is not something you do just to please the grantmaker. Dissemination has usefulness for your project. Your statement about the purpose of disseminating information about your project should be specific and linked to your project goals and objectives. Think about what actions you are hoping will result. For example, you may wish to get the word out about your project to invite public participation in it. Or you might want to share project outcomes with similar organizations to encourage them to adopt your new, successful approach to serving clients. Maybe you use attention to your project as a means of attracting other funding. Presenting your findings at a conference may change the course of a particular branch of research. There are numerous ways that dissemination can affect how people think or operate. For that reason, it has enormous value.

Once you have completed writing out the project activity and outcome portion of your proposal, look at your goals and objectives through a dissemination lens. Could dissemination help you realize any of your goals and objectives? For example, if the intent of your project is to affect public policy or to change the way that government interacts with a specific populace, you would want to use dissemination to educate and get access to policymakers, the media, and the targeted populations.

Dissemination can be a useful tool for recruitment for your project. For example, say you have a project in which you want to help young fathers become better parents. You believe that engaged, nurturing fathers are more likely to moderate their behavior in other ways and are thus less likely to get into trouble.

You've found that the men who are enrolled in this project are happy about what they're learning and the changes that result in their family, yet you're having difficulty in convincing more men to participate. Consider what a TV news story could do to raise interest. That form of dissemination might bring in more project participants.

Along the same lines of raising interest, getting the word out about your project could reap you unexpected benefits. Being in the spotlight might intrigue people unfamiliar with your organization to sign on as volunteers or offer their resources or take an action that could be useful to the population you're trying to help. In the previous example, maybe a local businessman offers one of these fathers a job.

Aside from what it can accomplish for particular project goals and objectives, dissemination can serve your organization in a broader sense. It can put you in the public eye and call attention to your good works. It can give you credibility. This kind of visibility can be beneficial in fundraising.

Education

Frequently, your efforts to solve a particular problem or serve a particular populace could be enhanced if others understood the extent and nature of the problems with which you work. But they can't take the actions that you wish if they don't know what those actions are; they need to be educated. Part of dissemination is bringing attention to a particular issue, part of it is telling what you hope will happen, and part of it is telling what has happened.

Replication

Dissemination is very much related to replication. It's not enough for the grantmaker to tell everyone, "Look at what we had the good sense to fund!" The grantmaker wants its monies to go as far as possible; it wants its investment to compound.

One of the ways to do that is to pass on lessons learned. Not only does your completed project have value for your intended beneficiaries but, if it worked well, it has value to organizations seeking to achieve similar goals. Your lessons learned may offer others a new solution for addressing a shared problem. You might demonstrate more efficient use of resources, your approach might engage people other organizations had not thought to engage, or your methodology might bring together components others had not thought to combine. An innovative and successful project can offer other organizations new ways of thinking about things that may prove useful in their work.

With lessons learned, you are not only sharing information about your successes but letting others know what actions didn't have the outcomes you had anticipated and why. This is of equal importance. This helpful information could be both effort saving and money saving for organizations doing work similar to yours.

Dissemination Activities

In addition to explaining what you hope to accomplish through dissemination, this part of your proposal describes precise activities that you will undertake as part of this objective. Be varied and creative in the ways you choose to get your message out.

Education through dissemination can happen in a variety of ways; sending an article to a professional journal or doing a conference presentation are only two of many options. Consider these additional dissemination possibilities:

- Send out op-ed pieces to newspapers or articles to more popular periodicals.

- Write and issue reports or briefing papers.

- Prepare and distribute press releases.

- Create and deliver videos.

- Get newspaper coverage.

- Be interviewed on the radio.

- Make presentations to policymakers.

- Make presentations to community groups.

- List yourself on speakers' bureaus.

- Conduct community outreach activities.

- Produce a website.

- Use social networking venues.

- Convene work groups of your peers.

- Ask the grantmaker to provide an opportunity to meet with grantees doing similar work.

While spreading the word may incite others to undertake a similar project, another more certain way to encourage replication is to give other organizations the tools to do so. For example, you could create a how-to manual or a how-to DVD. You could create adaptable templates. You could establish a website on which you give substantial details about your project, including pictures. You could set up a social networking site where organizations similar to yours could share information about how they do their work. With today's technologies, all kinds of exchange venues and tools are possible.

Also, grantmakers may have a dissemination venue to which they want you to contribute your products so that they can be shared with others. For example, the U.S. Department of Labor has created a website where entities engaged in workforce development can learn about how other organizations are approaching the task of training a workforce to meet industry need.

Examples of Dissemination

The first example given in this section is taken from a successful fifteen-page proposal narrative to the National Science Foundation for a project that has partners across the country. The project's overall intent is about sharing information about teaching strategies and tools.

The National Center for Telecommunications Technologies (NCTT) will continue to disseminate nationally using traditional and emerging methods and technologies. Partner institutions will continue to be major dissemination points as they work with community colleges, four-year colleges, and high schools in their respective regions. NCTT will continue to attract an increasing number of academic and industry professionals to the semi-annual conferences and one conference per year will continue to be hosted by a Regional Partner. These conferences build regional academic and industry presence, and further disseminate content nationally. Printed textbooks and lab manuals, along with online classroom content, will continue to be developed and made available internationally. Quarterly E-Bulletins will continue to be distributed to the growing 3,500 subscriber NCTT listserv. The NCTT website will continue to be updated with information on the Center and relevant areas such as partners, curricula, students, workforce trends, ICT technology, and technical updates, and content will continue to be placed in the Open Content Portal (part of the NCTT website) for national dissemination. Through the use of new and emerging Web 2.0 based tools, NCTT will continue to introduce new methods for communication and content delivery to academic and business communities.

This next example is derived from a successful four-page proposal narrative to a public foundation. It was a project heavily focused on increasing visitation to an interactive historical website previously created with other grant funds, so dissemination is of high interest.

In order to maximize the dissemination of the website through the interactive exhibit displays, a Publicity Committee will be formed in partnership between STCC, Springfield Museums, and the Springfield Armory National Historic Site. The purpose of the Publicity Committee will be to develop marketing and outreach efforts aimed at publicizing the kiosk exhibits. This will be accomplished in the following ways:

- A total of three (3) Publicity Committee meetings will be held at four (4) month intervals throughout the twelve (12) month MFH grant cycle

- The Publicity Committee will consist of representatives from STCC and the two partners, Springfield Museums and the Springfield Armory National Historic Site
- The Publicity Committee will develop a marketing plan to be implemented by the marketing firm hired with the $1,000 in cash cost sharing provided by STCC
- As part of their Publicity Committee membership, the partners have agreed to:

  – provide links from their own websites to the Shays' Rebellion website
  – use their own existing networks for publicizing of the Shays' Rebellion website
  – provide space in their museums for bookmarks and post cards publicizing the Shays' Rebellion website

An announcement email will be sent to all museums within the National Park Service, as well as all museum organizations associated with the Springfield Museums. This email will announce the interactive exhibits at the museums, with information on visiting the museums as well as the link to the Shays' Rebellion website on the web.

This final example is just to show you that sometimes all you need to say about dissemination can be done in an objectives/activities chart. The following excerpt was taken from a successful fifteen-page proposal narrative submitted to the National Science Foundation to create an engineering education pipeline to attract and retain underrepresented populations.

Dissemination is a project activity that is win-win-win. The grantmaker is happy that word about the good works that it funded is widespread, the grantee is happy to get attention about doing the good works, and recipients of the dissemination are happy to receive valuable information about innovative approaches to solving societal and community problems. Dissemination is a way that a grantmaker's monies can reach beyond the original project.

Money is a very important consideration for both parties of the grants process and requires attentiveness to how it is requested. Continue to the next chapter for a fuller discussion of budgets, budget narratives, and sustainability.

Objective 4: Dissemination

Best practices will be distributed via NCTT, journal submissions, and conference presentations.

Activity	Responsible Personnel	Timeline	Outcome–Deliverable
Web dissemination of data	NCTT	Spring 2010	Distribution to all NCTT members
Publications	PI, Lead Team	Spring 2010	Minimum of 3 submissions
Conferences	PI, Lead Team	Spring 2010	Minimum of 2 presentations at national conferences will be conducted

CHAPTER 14

Say It Richly

Budget and Budget Narrative, Project Sustainability

Your budget is a financial representation of your proposed activities; the numbers can speak as expressively as your words. The budget demonstrates how well you have thought through all that it will take to complete your project. It also is a statement of your organization's capacity and financial sophistication. For these reasons, do not leave your budget until the last moment; it is a very important document in your proposal, so give it the time it deserves.

The proposal budget represents what you expect it will cost to undertake the proposed activities over a specified period of time. Budgets should be thorough and accurate. The less work the reviewer has to do to figure out what your revenue and expenses are, the better it is for you. To serve you best, budgets should be:

- *Transparent:* There should be no mysteries about what each activity will cost or what each figure represents.

- *Clear:* The reader should be able to find information easily and easily understand what he or she is seeing.

- *Detailed:* Apply the assume-nothing rule to budgets and budget narratives. Explain the basis for determining the cost for each line item.

- *Concise:* While you need enough detail to explain everything so as to be understood, you do not need to explain down to every last paper clip.

- *Complete:* Show all sources of income for the project and all expenditures, expressed in broad terms, for the project.

- *Reasonable:* Do not ask for money for something that is not essential to the project, but neither should you short-change yourself.

- *Realistic:* Likewise, if you underbudget, you may be seen as inexperienced—as not understanding the true costs of things or how long a task may take.

- *Documentable:* For every cost that you claim, you should be able to prove that that is the true cost.

DIRECT COSTS OR INDIRECT COSTS?

Direct costs are those expenses that can be directly attributable to the project's activities and that can be very specifically determined, such as personnel, travel, equipment, and publications.

The term *indirect* comes from the fact that there are costs that cannot be directly associated with one project activity but are incurred nonetheless by the grantee as a result of the project. Indirect costs are also referred to as overhead. Commonly, these costs would include things such as rent, utilities, miscellaneous supplies, and non-project organizational staff time—for example, for technology or accounting. These are costs that are necessary to run the organization and its projects but that can't be easily assessed to a particular activity.

Indirect costs are usually stated in the budget as a percentage of direct costs. Government grantmakers are very specific about what percentage of direct project costs is allowable to be counted as indirect costs. Generally, foundation grantmakers do not allow as high a percentage, if they allow any indirect costs to be put into the budget at all. If these percentages are not stated in the grantmaker's materials, ask if indirect or overhead costs are allowed and, if yes, if there is a set rate.

Relationship of Budget to Project Activities

Anything in the proposal should be represented in the budget, and anything in the budget should be represented in the proposal. A well-written proposal narrative can be for naught if the budget does not accurately and honestly correspond to the activities mentioned in that narrative.

For each activity that you mention in the proposal, carefully think through exactly what it will take to undertake that activity and to produce the outcomes that you are claiming. For example, if part of the project expenses includes hiring a new staff person, don't forget that that staff person will need a place to sit, a computer to work on, a telephone to talk on, and perhaps a travel budget. If you propose to purchase a piece of equipment, be sure to include in your budget any installation expenses or maintenance expenses for that equipment. Talk to the people in your organization, such as the people with information technology, human resources, or facilities responsibilities, to make sure you understand all the costs associated with equipment purchases, new hires, travel, and the like.

Walk yourself through each objective that you have stated and identify the individual steps therein. Make sure that there are sufficient funds allocated to perform each proposed activity. You don't want your project's success to be negatively affected because you did not adequately anticipate all project expenses.

How Much Money Should I Ask For?

If you are responding to a particular RFP, the grantmaker will let you know what it deems to be an appropriate amount of money to request or certainly the maximum you can request. This does not mean that you should manipulate your budget so that it reaches the maximum if that is not a true accounting of your fiscal needs. Proposal reviewers are very savvy to budget padding and will subtract points if they believe that is what you are doing.

If you are sending an unsolicited proposal to a grantmaker and its material does not suggest a range of average grants, then you must examine the dollar amounts of recent grants made to ascertain what would be an appropriate amount for which to ask. Grantseeking databases also will state the average grant size and will note the high and low grants of that particular fiscal year.

Related to this, pay attention to what is going on in the financial world, as this will affect the amount of money that the private grantmaker can or will give. By law, they must give a minimum of 5% of their assets, and if their assets are negatively affected by changes in the financial markets, then they will be giving less in total grant dollars that fiscal year. The amount available for government grants is determined through program appropriations and may also be affected by cuts.

Format

As you begin preparing your budget, first determine whether the grantmaker has a specific form to use or requires that you follow a specific format. Generally, government grant applications will have a specific budget form that you fill in. Foundations are less likely to require that you use a particular form or format. If you have any questions about the format or contents of the budget, you should clarify matters with the grantmaker's program officer.

Budgets are visual as well as numerical, so if the grantmaker does not have a budget form or format that it expects you to use, develop a budget in table or chart format. Generally, you list project expenses in the left-hand column and sources of funding across the top. Use broad categories, such as personnel, fringe, consultants, travel, equipment, supplies, contractual, and indirect costs. Specificity will come in the budget narrative. The chart on page 213 is an example of a basic budget format; you can find many examples of grant budget templates online by conducting a simple search. Some URLs are provided on page 216.

ITEM	REQUEST	IN-KIND	TOTAL
Personnel	35,000	2,500	37,500
Fringe	9,800	700	10,500
Total Personnel	44,800	3,200	48,000
Consultants	3,000		3,000
Travel	600		600
Training		2,500	2,500
Equipment	1,200	1,200	2,400
Supplies	7,200	300	7,500
Total Direct Costs	56,800	7,200	64,000
Indirect costs (10%)	5,680	720	6,400
TOTAL	62,480	7,920	70,400

Some grantmakers expect only to see expenses particular to the proposed project. Other grantmakers want to see not only project expenses but all sources of income that may relate to that project. For them, if you are receiving or requesting other grant monies, you need to create a column that will show that, and itemize the source in the budget narrative. These grantmakers want to see how their piece fits into the whole funding picture, so if there are other sources of funds for the project, those should be included in the budget presentation. Income may be expressed as both committed and requested. Your budget table might look something like the chart below.

	REQUEST	OTHER FUNDERS		IN-KIND	TOTAL
ITEM	LOYA FOUNDATION	MT FUND	TILLIGAN CORP.	YOUR ORG.	
Personnel	125,000	24,000		8,000	157,000
Training	15,000	2,500		7,000	24,500
Equipment	30,000		5,000		35,000
Supplies	5,000			150	5,150
Consultants		45,000			45,000
TOTAL	175,000	71,500	5,000	15,150	266,650

Budgets of multi-year grant requests should show each year of the grant separately and also show a cumulative total. For multi-year budgets, be sure to build in any expected annual increases in costs.

Make sure you understand what the funder's rules are regarding allowable costs. Grantmakers have very specific ideas and rules about what their monies can be used for. Honor that.

Always, always check and double-check your math in a budget. You can be sure that the proposal reviewer is doing that, and if he or she finds a mistake, it won't reflect well on your organization. As a reviewer, it would point out to me a lack of attention to detail, which would be of concern to me if I'm giving you a large sum of money to manage.

COST SHARING

Cost sharing is also referred to as matching. This means that the potential grantee will also be making an investment in the project. If cost sharing is required, the grantmaker will indicate either a percentage or a ratio that the applicant organization must contribute to the project. For example, if a grantmaker gives you a $100,000 grant and requires a 25% match, you must contribute $25,000 to the project.

These contributions can be either in cash or through in-kind means. In-kind contributions are those that do not involve the direct transfer of cash but still have monetary value. Examples are the cost of a staff person's time directed toward project activities, the use of organizational space and equipment, or donated services.

Cost sharing is viewed as an indicator of an organization's commitment to the project. If you have project partners, do not overlook the value of their in-kind contributions as well. Government grant guidelines will precisely specify what can and cannot be counted as legitimate cost sharing. Be sure to look this over carefully, as you may be surprised at what is allowable. For example, one grantmaker requiring a match of 30% allowed, as a legitimate in-kind match, the hourly value of a business' employee release time to attend training offered as a project activity. Monies raised from other funders can also count as part of your cost sharing.

If cost sharing is required, you want to make sure to show this visibly in your budget so that you get credit for your organization's contributions or for your ability to raise funds from other sources. When you create your own budget form, be sure to include a column showing cost-sharing contributions as a form of revenue. Refer to the sample budget on page 217 to see how this is done.

Government Budgets

Most government applications are now submitted online and have budget forms that you fill in online. Although they will differ from agency to agency, the forms make it clear what information the funding agency is seeking. However, work closely with the person in your organization who handles finances when filling out these forms because government grants have so many precise rules and regulations attached to them.

The websites below provide sample federal government grant budget forms. Each agency will have forms for you to use. These forms are also useful for creating your own template to use with proposals to other funders.

- U.S. Department of Education (www.ed.gov/fund/grant/apply/appforms/appforms.html)

- U.S. Department of Housing and Urban Development (www.hud.gov/offices/adm/hudclips/forms/files/424-cb.pdf)

Foundation Budgets

Foundations are less stringent about using particular budget forms; however, because many are moving toward online submissions, you will be seeing more use of a prescribed form. The Foundation Center offers on its website a free budget tutorial (http://foundationcenter.org/getstarted/tutorials/prop_budgt/index.html). One of the resources offered at the end of that tutorial is a sample budget form from the Cleveland Foundation (www.clevelandfoundation.org/Grantmaking/GranteeToolKit.html).

You can also find budget forms on websites of regional associations of grantmakers (RAG), such as the Associated Grant Makers (www.agmconnect.org/CPF). To find a RAG in your state, visit www.givingforum.org/s_forum/sec.asp?CID=575&DID=2625.

Budget Narrative

A budget narrative is also called a budget justification, which is more descriptive of the purpose of the document. Budget narratives spell out the specifics that the numbers in your budget table represent. Explaining how you arrived at the cost for each line item preempts any questions and allows for easy financial scrutiny.

Your budget narrative is an extremely important document in your full proposal packet, so make sure it thoroughly explains all project costs precisely. This will be especially important if you are requesting funds for something that might be unfamiliar to the reader, such as a piece of equipment or something that at first glance may seem to be overpriced or unnecessary. Assume nothing about the reader's understanding of the true costs of an item or the importance of a particular component to your project's success. Spell it out.

A budget narrative may be a separate document or included in the budget table. If it is a separate document, it should present information in the same order that it is presented in the budget so that the reviewer can easily follow along. It should answer any question that a reviewer might have about why a particular category requires that amount of money.

Personnel costs are often stated in terms of a percentage of a person's time that will be allocated to project activity. Your budget narrative will state each staff person's full-time salary and multiply it by the amount of time that person is expected to devote to the project. Each calculation will be itemized in the budget narrative and then totaled to arrive at a total number in the personnel column.

Example of a Budget with Budget Justification Included

	ABE Funds	Other	Total
Personnel			
Director, Returning Adult Services (20% of salary/fringe)		11,930	11,930
Transitions Coordinator (full-time)	49,501		49,501
26.2% fringe benefits	12,870	5,375	18,245
ABE Secretary (20% of salary/fringe)		8,587	8,587
Subtotal Personnel	*62,371*	*25,892*	*88,263*
Contractual Services			
ALC Instructional Staff (10 hrs x 8 wks x $24 x 4 sessions)	7,680		7,680
Subtotal Contractual Services	*7,680*		*7,680*
Supplies and Materials			
Accuplacer Re-test @ $25 x 24 students		600	600
Textbooks and Instructional Materials @ $20 x 24 students	480		480
Non-instructional supplies (presentation materials used by Transitions Coordinator)	162		162
Subtotal Supplies and Materials	*642*	*600*	*1,242*
Travel			
Coordinator travel for outreach and statewide meetings	500		500
Subtotal for Travel	*500*		*500*
Equipment			
Cost of facilities:			
Office Space for Transitions Coordinator ($7/sf x 340 sq ft)		2,380	2,380
Telephone and Internet Service ($80 x 12 months)		960	960
Classroom Lab Space ($31.50/sf x 600 sf) x 20% usage		3,780	3,780
Subtotal Equipment		*7,120*	*7,120*
Total Direct Costs:	71,193	33,612	104,805
5% Indirect Costs	3,390		
Total Project Costs	**74,583**	**33,612**	**108,195**

Project Sustainability

A project is more appealing to a potential funder if the funder believes that it can continue in some form after grant funds expire. Although this is not necessarily a realistic expectation, it is one you may have to address. Most proposal guidelines specifically ask you to address how the project will continue after the grant has run out. What is important in writing this response is that you are honest, realistic, and creative. However, if you are not specifically asked to respond to a sustainability question, there is no need to include this section in your proposal.

Unless your project has been a long-standing one, you can't know the actual project outcomes before it begins. Therefore a large part of the sustainability section of your proposal will be hypothetical. You know what you hope will happen, you know what you intend to have happen, you know what you will work hard to make happen, but you will only know the final outcome at the end of the project. You will have to offer your sustainability plan as a series of possibilities.

Your sustainability statement can be presented in terms of your project goals and objectives. In fact, you may even make project sustainability its own project goal with specific tasks, such as researching potential funders, organizing fundraising events, setting up meetings with local businesses, developing a public awareness campaign, and recruiting volunteers. More enlightened grantmakers may actually fund some of these activities in the hopes of helping sustain your project.

But the first thing to consider is that not all projects need to be continued. Is the proposed project a onetime effort, such as a particular slice of research or a capital project? If that is the case, explain in the sustainability section that once the research is completed and reported, no further actions on your organization's part are intended. Speak to how you hope this research will be used by others and be sure to carefully outline a dissemination plan (see Chapter 13). If the project is intended to have a definitive end point, reiterate the value of the final products and how you imagine they will speak to the need identified earlier in your proposal.

For capacity-building types of projects, some of the costs are start-up costs that, while the project may be ongoing after the grant has ended, will not need to be incurred again—for example, training, equipment, curriculum design, setting up a client tracking system. Therefore, point out that keeping the project running will not take the same amount of money as it took to get it started and that your organization may be able to absorb the lower costs. Or the capacity building could be directly related to sustainability, such as engaging a fundraising consultant to design a plan and teach staff how to implement it.

Another strategy for responding to questions about sustainability: If the project activity will result in some kind of fiscal efficiencies or savings for the organization, include this in your response. If this happens, then not only will the organization be in a better position to maintain the project but that very fact may make it appealing to other types of funders. For example, foundations have long been the laboratory for government programs. Foundations are in a better position to take risks, and sometimes such risks reap positive results of interest beyond the funder and grantee organization. Once government can be assured of a project's success, it may choose to absorb the project into its own programs or give it funding.

In some instances, the purpose of the grant may be for a pilot project, to test a variation on service delivery. It may be that after the course of the grant-funded project, the pilot project is found to be the preferred model. In this case, state that continuation is a matter of substituting one method of service delivery for another.

Also assert that at the project's end, you will examine whether all parts of the project need to be sustained. It may be that some activities are no longer needed or are found to be not as effective as originally hoped and thus not as much funding is needed to continue the activities.

But there will be projects that you'll want to continue and that will need to be fully funded to do so and you must speak to that. Given the variables affecting an informed answer, be clear on exactly what would be needed to continue project activity. Is it only money? Be creative; not all sustainability actions must involve funding. Could it be that donated services could be helpful? Could additional volunteers manage some part of the activity? Would collaborations with other organizations meet some of the need? Keep in mind that there are several options for continued effort, and state that you will consider them as the project unfolds.

That said, project sustainability may simply be the same actions you took to get the grant in the first place—that is, fundraising. If that is the case, say so. Itemize your fundraising plan, including other grantmakers that have been or will be approached for the same project. Assert that you will continue to look for additional support.

Finally, part of being reassuring about project sustainability is establishing that your organization conducts itself in a fiscally sound manner. State any examples of when your organization undertook a project in the past and successfully sustained it after grant funding ended.

Examples of a Sustainability Statement

Two examples of a response to a sustainability question in two successful proposals follow, one to a private grantmaker and one to a government grantmaker.

Notice in the first example that emphasis is placed on fundraising and the ability to look for income-producing activities; both actions bespeak sustainability, and both actions are ones that the capacity-building grant that eventually funded the organization was intended to cover.

> The beauty of this particular capacity-building request is that the investment is specifically targeted toward financial sustainability. By virtue of identifying new potential funders and the tools to go after them—and equipping the personnel to do it—the effort is geared to be self-sustaining. Additionally, the primary products produced—such as the Fund Development Plan and detailed foundation/corporation prospect list—will be useful tools for years. Unlike program funding, capacity-building grants target a one-time need. Not only will we have a guide, but we will have the knowledge on how to implement the Fund Development Plan. We can go after private sector monies. We can determine ways to derive income from our activities, such as day care and providing trainings to other organizations. We will know how to make income-producing use of our sizeable facility. The very thing we will be taught will be the tool for sustainability.

The second example is about workforce development, and the grant was intended to build the capacity of the organization to continue to train potential health care workers. Reference is made to a class becoming self-sustaining and institutionalizing a program—both strategies for sustainability. In addition, dissemination is woven into the section to indicate how the work will not only be sustained at the original locations but be communicated to others looking to do similar work.

The *Workforce STAT* project has built-in sustainability. The Pioneer Valley Healthcare Partnership, the newly forming, all-encompassing collaborative focused on healthcare workforce issues, will be an established regional institution. The Patient Skills course will be self-sustaining, and WIOC will institutionalize its expansion. The on-going project results and model of this project will be disseminated to all 15 community colleges in MA through the MASS Community College Deans of Health quarterly meetings. Quarterly and annual reports will be placed on our re-designed website, www.healthprograms.org. The counseling and curriculum models also will be available via the website in PDF format for easy downloading. The Project Managers will submit for presentation at the AACC conference and other conferences as deemed appropriate for the topic. Those showing an interest in the project models will be invited to one or more of the partner colleges to see the process firsthand.

CHAPTER 15

Say It Succinctly

Proposal Abstract/Executive Summary

A proposal abstract, also known as a proposal summary or executive summary, is exactly as the name implies; it takes all the descriptive detail that is found in your proposal's many narrative pages and condenses it into one small bundle. It serves to give the reader an immediate and concise understanding of your project. Not all grantmakers request an abstract or summary; when trying to decide when to use one, follow grantmaker instruction.

A proposal abstract must be a stand-alone piece; sometimes after a grant award is made, it will be used to describe your project in the grantmaker's materials. Write it as if the reader would have no other information about your proposed project, because that may actually be the case. For example, in some government review committees, when there are multiple applications, not all full proposals are read by each reviewer. Your full proposal might be read by a single reviewer, who becomes the expert in the discussion of that particular proposal; the rest of the reviewers read only the abstract of it. Consider that if your abstract is the only thing that a reviewer reads about your project, he or she must make decisions based only on that and another reviewer's impressions of your full proposal. That possibility makes your proposal abstract a crucial part of your entire grant application; give it the attention it deserves.

Technique

Even though your proposal abstract will appear on the top of your application packet, I've put the discussion of this at the end of the book because you should write the abstract after you've written everything else. You may have a very clear idea of what you are proposing to do before you begin writing the proposal narrative (in fact, I hope you do!), but details tend to uncover themselves as you write. And more evocative words will arrive in your narrative than those in your original outline. Sometimes as you are writing, a beautiful clarity descends on you that had previously been elusive. You might be visited by an exquisite Aha! moment when you see a connection or arrive at a critical analysis that adds power to your main points. These are the compelling ideas that you want to make sure are part of your abstract, and they don't tend to come at the beginning of one's writing.

But because writing the abstract comes at the end of your proposal preparation, it runs the risk of getting short shrift because either you have run out of time or you're just sick of the whole thing and want to be done with it. I encourage you to make the investment in this section because it alone may represent you. Consider these few paragraphs to be the written expression of the elevator-pitch experience—when you've got limited time to make your case to someone who could make the difference in whether you are successful. How would you use that opportunity? What would you say?

Content

By virtue of its location, a proposal abstract is the reader's first impression of your project, so you want it to be as informative as it is convincing.

You need to make clear what you are asking the grantmaker to do. In a short bit of space, you should answer the following questions, not necessarily in the order listed:

- What will be done?

- By whom?

- For what purpose?

- For how long?

- At what cost?

- What are the outcomes?

- Who will benefit?

One method you can use to condense your narrative into an abstract is to pull the highlights or topic sentence from each section of the proposal. Or if you started your communication with this grantmaker with a letter of inquiry, you can use that as the basis for writing the abstract.

If there is some part of your proposed project that is particularly novel—such as a new service delivery technique, an unusual partnership, or a clever use of technology to meet long-standing needs—you should make sure that it is presented in a highly visible way. Use it to open a paragraph, put keywords in italics or bold, or put points in bulleted form. That last suggestion may cost you space, but it helps the information stand out.

Some grantmakers will provide you with specific instructions for the content of the proposal abstract. If this is the case, be sure to present your information in the order in which it was requested.

Space Limitations

Unless otherwise directed by the funder, try to keep the proposal abstract to one page, two pages if the proposal is to be double-spaced. You may be held to even tighter constraints with online submissions, which may limit the number of words you can use. Because abstracts are page or word limited, you will have to zero in on your primary points and speak concisely about them.

Avoid getting overly detailed about any one point; this document is an overview. So if you have to make choices about what to cut, look at the questions beginning on page 223 and think about the most important thing you can say in answer to each one. For example, even the seemingly simple For how long? could draw you into an unnecessary exploration of the timeline; resist. The two questions on which you should spend the most space are: What will be done? and What are the outcomes?

Example of a Proposal Abstract

Some government agencies prefer proposals to be submitted with double-spacing, in which case the abstract is given a two-page limitation, such as the following example from a winning proposal. Here are the highlights of what makes this a good abstract:

- It follows the RFP instructions as to what should be included in the abstract:

  A one to two page abstract summarizing the proposed project and applicant profile information including: applicant name, project title, industry focus, partnership members, proposed training and capacity building activities, funding level requested, the amount of leveraged resources, the target group(s), and a project description as described in the evaluation criteria section at Section V.A of this Solicitation.

- It uses bold headers, echoing the topics listed in the instructions, to make information easy to find and to make it easy for reviewers to check off that the information requested was provided.

- It keeps to the page limitations.

- It starts off the project description with a clear and concise goal statement.

- It itemizes precise objectives to be undertaken to meet that goal.

- It enumerates training and capacity-building activities that speak to the intent of the department's RFP.

- It identifies target groups of concern to the applicant and of interest to the funder.

- It is written as a stand-alone piece sufficient to convey the intent and actions of the proposed project.

PROJECT ABSTRACT

Applicant: Springfield Technical Community College (STCC)

Project Title: Workforce STAT (Skills, Talent, Awareness, Training): Transforming Regional Capacity for Healthcare Education

Industry Focus: Health Care

Funding Requested: $1,655,957

Leveraged Resources: $1,267,866

Partnership Members: *Workforce STAT* consists of 16 partners from four western Massachusetts counties: the Regional Employment Board of Hampden County, Franklin/Hampshire Regional Employment Board, and Berkshire County Regional Employment Board; Springfield Technical, Holyoke, Greenfield, and Berkshire Community Colleges; Baystate, Berkshire, Holyoke, and Mercy Medical Centers; Springfield Public Schools; The World Is Our Classroom; Mason Square Veterans Outreach Center; MassAHEC Network (Area Health Education Centers); and the Health Careers Opportunities Project (HCOP).

Project Description: The goal of STCC's *Workforce STAT* project is to meet regional healthcare industry needs by transforming—in an accelerated manner—large numbers of interested and willing pre-health students into a prepared, focused, well-qualified, and well-suited healthcare workforce through the following means: (1) early exposure to and awareness-building of healthcare career and coursework realities and choices, (2) hands-on simulation-based education, (3) targeted health program counseling to help students identify if healthcare work overall, and which field in particular, matches their skills, interests, and inclinations, and to foster these students so that they have the confidence and the tools to proceed quickly and strongly toward program graduation, and (4) expansion of STCC's Medical Assisting program.

Proposed Training and Capacity-Building Activities:

1. Equip and bring up-to-date simulation labs with lab assistants at four community colleges.
2. Provide simulation training for faculty and lab assistants and a heightened awareness of how to use simulation in healthcare coursework.
3. Develop and deliver an industry-informed curriculum of an entry-level hands-on simulation-based Patient Skills (3) college-credit course to would-be healthcare career seekers.
4. Develop and deliver K–12 One-Day Medical Encounter learning events and teaching materials.
5. Provide advising/career counseling training to project Targeted Counselors.
6. Deliver Targeted Counseling to students in pre-health and healthcare programs.
7. Establish the geographical expansion of the Medical Assisting program through a creative use of hybrid coursework and technology-based distance learning.
8. Heighten recruitment efforts.

Target Groups: K–12 students, first-year community college students, community college students in Health programs, entry level workers who need basic skills and/or specific occupational skill training, and incumbent healthcare workers seeking new skills for jobs in demand at higher levels of the career ladder. Additionally, because of the demographics of western Massachusetts, we will be targeting potential workers who mirror the population, so as to have a more diverse skilled workforce that meets the changing population/patient diversity. Special efforts will be made to recruit and support Veterans. Working with the One Stop Career Centers, we also expect to serve dislocated workers.

When requested by the grantmaker, the proposal abstract will be the first piece of the proposal narrative, so it sets the stage for what is to come. Give it full effort, as it alone may define your project.

CHAPTER 16

Say It with Flair

The Cover Letter

The cover letter—the page that will be on top of the entire proposal packet—is discussed in the last chapter because you won't write it until all else has been written and assembled. The reason for that is that you need to determine what is missing or what needs to be highlighted. A cover letter can be used to make points that space or grantmaker-determined topics don't allow for in the proposal narrative. Cover letters are like bonuses, especially if there is a proposal page limit. If you are allowed only fifteen pages in which to make your case, think of the cover letter as the sixteenth page.

A cover letter is a more personal communication than a grant proposal. It uses a different style of writing that can speak more passionately and more emotionally than the proposal narrative can. It is an opportunity to get someone's attention, to emphasize your project's uniqueness, to make vision statements, to state how the smaller project is part of a larger whole, and to make points that the proposal application or format doesn't allow you to do. The intent of it is to evoke positive inclinations toward your proposed project.

But not all proposals can be accompanied by a cover letter. With electronic submissions, sometimes it isn't even an option. Usually you use a cover letter with foundation or association proposals submitted by mail. You can use it to add to the proposal, or to put information in that doesn't fit or that an online submission form doesn't request.

Purpose

A cover letter has several purposes; you can use it to:

- Demonstrate institutional support

- Solidify the relationship between the grantmaker and your organization

- Identify linkages between the grantmaker and your organization

- Reemphasize the main goal of the project

- Make vision statements

- Convey excitement

Demonstrate Institutional Support

A potential funder needs reassurance that an organization is truly committed to the proposed project. One of the most important ways to do that is to have your highest-ranking official sign the cover letter. You also want to reiterate in that letter whatever financial or in-kind investments your organization is making in the project.

Solidify the Relationship

You want to cite any previous interactions you may have had with the grantmaker. If you have received grants in the past, be sure to reiterate your thanks and appreciation and speak to the positive outcomes that resulted. If someone from your organization's staff has had an interaction with someone from the grantmaker's staff, mention that. As appropriate, remind grantmakers that you are not unknown to them, that they felt good enough about you in the past to give you money, and that you have a connection.

Identify Linkages

One of the most important uses of a cover letter is to irrefutably link your proposed project to the grantmaker's interests and goals. You are letting the grantmaker know that you are familiar with what it most cares about and that you share its vision of positive change in the field that it most commonly works. If you are responding to an RFP, very specifically say so and illustrate how the proposal you are submitting fits beautifully with what the grantmaker is seeking to fund.

Vision Statements

As part of making your connection with the grantmaker, you will touch on your shared vision. State how the smaller project you propose is part of a larger whole, whether it is the work of your institution, the surrounding community, or the world! The flowery, dreamy language that doesn't belong in your proposal can be used in a cover letter. It's a place where you can express things as a wish and as a hope.

Project Goal

Your proposal narrative will lay out your project goal and objectives and the activities you will undertake to meet those objectives. The cover letter is a place where you restate that goal succinctly and profoundly with the genuine emotion that leads you to pursue this work in the first place. There should be no question about the intent of the project and what you expect to happen as a result.

Convey Excitement

Although grantmakers have all kinds of precise review criteria by which they assess your proposal, they are—perhaps subconsciously—equally looking to be moved by your passion for the people you hope to serve and the topic you hope to address. Don't be shy about using language in the cover letter that will convey this. You also want to inspire the reader to think that your organization is particularly equipped to meet the challenge you both agree exists. The cheerleading or boosterism language that I caution against using in government or foundation proposals is not out of place in a cover letter.

Technique

There is not one particular way in which you should order a cover letter's material. It depends on a variety of factors, such as whether your chief executive officer knows the person to whom the letter is being addressed. But you do want your first paragraph to pop.

It is best to keep cover letters to one page. Make sure to use your organization's letterhead and have the letter signed by your organization's chief executive officer.

Under no circumstances should this letter be addressed "To whom it may concern." This is the document that's on top of the packet; you don't want the reader's first impression to be that you think so little of the potential funder that you haven't taken the time to learn who's who in the grantmaking operation. Read the grantmaker's materials carefully to identify the right person to receive your proposal. In some instances, it will be a particular program officer; in others it will be the executive director. In smaller foundations, especially those without staff, you want to address the foundation's board president.

The cover letter should also offer a contact person's name, position, phone number, address, and email address should the recipient have any questions about the project. If the person who manages the grants operation is different from the person managing the project, supply contact information for both.

Examples of Cover Letters

The following examples accompanied successful proposals.

Example 1

Dear Mr. Goode:

Enlace was delighted to receive the letter inviting us to the full proposal stage of the Community Impact initiative. It is an indicator that our two organizations are like-minded about needed interventions for children and how the social service world might best operate to meet those needs. Thus, with encouraged hopes, we submit with this letter our full proposal for Enlace's *One Family At a Time* project. We are requesting $150,000 for this project.

The *One Family At a Time* project seeks to help under-performing students at Neighborhood Elementary School improve their academic performance by positively changing the unstable home environments in which they live. By doing such, our proposed actions will address both of the Community Impact initiative's priority areas; we will not only promote successful children and youth, we will be promoting strong and sustainable communities. Our work will not only help these children and their families, it will reach out to and potentially benefit all of the parents of Neighborhood Elementary School students and many social service providers also working to aid these families.

To demonstrate further our alignment with the Community Impact initiative principles, know that all of our work will be conducted—as it always is—in collaboration with a myriad of public and private social service agencies in Holyoke. The principle of collaboration is embedded in Enlace's founding; we began as a coalition. And our current work in bringing together 38 coalitions into a Coalition of Coalitions further demonstrates our commitment to encouraging agencies to work together to solve community problems.

I very much look forward to our meeting with United Way on May 30th when we can elaborate on our vision and introduce our partners to you. Thank you for this opportunity.

Sincerely yours,
Betty Medina Lichtenstein
Executive Director

Example 2

Dear Ms. Goode:

Most of us take living at home with family or friends for granted. Sadly, a growing number of the people with disabilities we serve at Stavros Center for Independent Living are being kept in nursing homes unnecessarily, and many others, through no fault of their own, are at risk for being placed in a nursing home—all because they lack a ramp to access their home or apartment.

The Stavros Home Sweet Home Program builds ramps for people with disabilities who are trapped in their own homes or stranded in a nursing home because they can't afford a ramp.

We are asking the Jane Doe Trust to award us a $5,000 grant to help us purchase building materials in bulk at a discounted rate and build ramps at a fraction of the usual cost. In the past twenty months, we've been able to build fifty (50) ramps. That's fifty people who are able to live at home with their loved ones. But we're not done yet—Stavros has another one hundred (100) people on our waiting list with the same need. Your support will help us to get them home, to keep them home, and to keep them thriving in the communities of the Pioneer Valley.

One of the people we serve sent us a poem. We wouldn't say it about ourselves, but we'd like to share his words with you:

> *Stavros is the blood of my life,*
> *Your help keeps me going and free,*
> *Without your generous assistance,*
> *I don't know where I would be.*

Stavros is a health and welfare organization serving people with "special needs, including the blind, deaf and learning disabled, and the elderly. . . ." The Home Sweet Home Program addresses the "renovation needs and equipment" needs of low-income people with disabilities by building wheelchair ramps to make their homes or apartments accessible.

We hope you will agree that our work furthers the objectives of the Jane Doe Trust. Please join us in helping scores of people with disabilities to live in their own homes instead of in nursing homes.

Sincerely,
Jim Kruidenier
Executive Director

Proposal Samples

1. Sample Letter of Inquiry to a Major Foundation

Date

Name, Title

Program

Foundation

Address 1

Address 2

Dear Name:

Groundwork Springfield—one of twenty Groundwork USA pilot communities across the United States—is an urban environmental and ecological education and employment program dedicated to change, revitalization, and transformation that will lead to a cleaner, safer, more beautiful Springfield, MA. One of Groundwork Springfield's programs is the Green Team, which focuses on the importance of both readying our youth for the green jobs of the future and preserving our earth. This project will give low-income, urban children of color the opportunity to explore a green jobs career path, contribute to the environmental betterment of their community, and obtain the leadership skills needed to take command of their own employment pursuit. With our two organizations' shared interest in both protecting the environment and creating pathways out of poverty for vulnerable youth, Groundwork Springfield believes this project will be of interest to the National Foundation and requests $100,000 over two years to support the Green Team Leadership project.

The Issue: There are three intertwined issues that have our attention and that we believe can be addressed in the Green Team Leadership project: (1) negative environmental consequences of urban decay, (2) lack of awareness among Black and Latino populations of how these consequences affect them and their potential role in eradicating such outcomes, and (3) the need for economic security for low-income youth.

Throughout the United States, and including Springfield, communities today are faced with the devastating effects of urban decay—derelict land, abandoned brownfield sites, and toxins from decomposing trash leaching into the groundwater systems of the community. This decay leads to endemic economic, environmental, health, and social problems for all members of our community. For example, Springfield rates for asthma, lupus, asbestos, lead poisoning, and other environmental diseases are among the highest in the state, and in some cases, the nation. There are insufficient safe community green spaces, parks, and outdoor recreational facilities for children. While more likely to be affected by this, low-income, urban populations of color tend not to see their power in addressing the problems. Couple this with an exodus of businesses and jobs, a high dropout rate among youth, and widespread poverty and you have an extremely distressed community in need of interventions and few resources to provide them.

Project Activity: To respond to the needs stated above, we wish to revive both our city and its residents. We are particularly concerned with giving our youth—our future—the tools to engage in this personal and community revival. The primary objective of the Green Team Leadership project is to provide unemployed and under-employed children of color, aged 14–21, the opportunity to explore and become trained for green collar jobs and careers.

The year-long program is a comprehensive, community-focused effort to engage youth in preserving the city's ecological and environmental assets and providing education and training for green jobs. Through this program, we not only want to provide opportunity for income security but also hope to prepare the next generation of green-thinking people in the Black and Latino communities of Springfield, MA. Our Green Team particularly targets youth who face economic, educational, or personal barriers such as deficiency in basic literacy skills, limited English, out of school, pregnancy or parenthood, or involvement in the justice system. As needed, we will provide assessment and case management, adult basic education, GED preparation, academic support, tutoring, and referrals to community resources.

Youth enrolled in our Leadership project will participate in work-readiness workshops and certification programs, relevant field trips, work experiences, and for the 18–21-year-olds, occupational skills training. Through green collar career exploration, youth will be exposed to career choices not commonly suggested to them. Each budding leader will conduct an individual research project on topics such as over-the-counter pesticides and the effects of chemicals in makeup. They will serve as group leaders in a summer program teaching younger children what they've learned from their research, passing on an inculcation of green thinking.

Project Outcomes and Evaluation: Green Team Leadership activities are expected to result in participants having an increased understanding of green job opportunities and the skill set required to obtain these jobs; increased work-readiness skills; increased reasoning and problem-solving skills; an increased environmental awareness and because of that a demonstration of better and healthier life choices; and increased motivation to be more active (part of our No Child Left Inside effort). The Leadership project participants will undergo a weekly performance review and will be rated on the following factors: productivity, dependability, flexibility, teamwork and leadership, safety, and conduct and appearance.

Credentials: Groundwork Springfield, a project of the nonprofit Spanish American Union, is an effort to improve the health and well-being of all Springfield residents through community-led actions. In 2007, Springfield was one of only two communities nationwide selected by Groundwork USA as a pilot community. The Groundwork USA initiative is a pilot program of the National Park Service (NPS) Rivers and Trails Program in cooperation with the Environmental Protection Agency (EPA) Brownfield Program to establish a network of independent nonprofit businesses called Groundwork Trust. Last spring, Groundwork Springfield initiated its first project, joining students, Springfield's Parks and Recreation Department, and the Springfield Housing Authority in helping to plant gardens at an elderly housing complex; more than 100 young people from the community participated.

Budget: Funds requested by Groundwork Springfield will be used to provide research stipends to participating youth and to provide project management to solidify the Green Team Leadership model. We are in the process of seeking additional funds to support other aspects of our Groundwork program. Recently, we hosted a community green collar jobs strategy session to discuss ways in which our city can be prepared to pursue funds from the American Recovery and Reinvestment Act. In partnership with the Pioneer Valley Planning Commission, we submitted a proposal in April to EPA's Brownfields Job Training program to train 48, and place at least 31, residents of Springfield in entry-level positions within the environmental technology industry.

Thank you for your consideration of this request. We believe people, places, and prosperity are inextricably linked, and we work with our partners to develop projects that bring benefits to all three areas—by creating opportunities for people to learn new skills and take local action; by creating better, safer, and healthier neighborhoods; and by helping businesses and individuals fulfill their potential. We would welcome the opportunity to submit a full proposal to further describe our project. Please feel free to call me if you require any additional information about our organization, its vision, and its work.

Sincerely yours,
Patricia Moss, Project Manager
Groundwork Springfield

2. Sample Two-Page Proposal to a Community Foundation

INTRODUCTION: An individual who pursues Adult Basic Education (ABE) is by that act alone making a statement that he or she recognizes that higher education is a pathway to economic well-being and stability. Through the Success Express program, STCC will make it possible for more of these individuals to realize that dream. Each year, STCC offers a variety of ABE services to approximately 150 people, but demand far exceeds supply. In this past year, 600 applications for ABE services were received, but only 50 people can be served at a time. To help meet this demand and to uphold the College's core mission of educational access and opportunity, STCC proposes a new ABE service for students who lack the skills that will assure their college-readiness and wish to acquire them quickly. While access to education is vitally important, providing the tools for educational success is even more so. The goal of this intensive 36-hour "bridge" course is to position the student for college success through academic and personal development in a condensed period of time.

NEED FOR PROJECT: Springfield has an annual high school dropout rate of approximately 46%. More than half of STCC's student body does not enter college directly from high school and approximately 40% enter STCC by completing the GED requirements. The majority of these enrollees need additional math, verbal, and reading skills in order to place at college-level. More than 1,000 STCC students need developmental courses each year and many students entering STCC lack educational preparedness, college awareness, and college success skills. Research[1] and experience shows that a bridge between the attainment of a high school diploma or GED and successful management of college classes is critically needed.

---

[1] Zafft, Kallenbach, and Spohn, *Transitioning Adults to College: Adult Basic Education Program Models*, National College Transition Network, World Education Inc., Boston, MA, December 2006; and Council for the Advancement of Adult Literacy, *To Ensure America's Future: Building a National Opportunity System for Adults, Strengthening Links Between Adult Basic Education and Community Colleges*, New York, NY, February 2005.

Currently, STCC offers semester-long developmental courses to address these needs, but these courses do not count toward credits needed for graduation and many students do not see the benefit in investing that much time in such a class, especially if they have to use financial aid to do so. A recent report on transition models noted, "Identifying adult education models that help adult learners avoid cycles of remediation at the beginning of their college careers is more likely to produce students who can persist and obtain a postsecondary education credential."[2]

PROJECT PLAN: To respond to this particular problem, STCC will give these students the opportunity to gain needed skills before they even enroll. Through the Success Express, STCC will offer—for free!—four six-week intensive courses in late spring and late fall that will enable a student to be prepared for enrolling at STCC the following semester. The courses will include elements of two existing semester-long developmental classes—Review for College Writing and Pre-Algebra—and will address college readiness skills. Classes will be offered both during the day and the evening to accommodate the work schedules of students. The Director will consult with instructors and community adult learning centers in the design of this course. Topics from which the class design will draw include: the purpose of higher education and the student's role in it, study skill development, test-taking, time management, note taking, research tools, other soft skills required for college, and career planning. Writing will focus on college-level grammar, sentence structure, paragraphing, and essay development. Math lessons will likely explore: whole numbers, fractions, decimal notation, percent notation, applications and problem solving, basic statistical measures, and units of linear measurement.

This course builds on a substantial adult basic education effort at STCC. For more than 20 years, STCC has offered various developmental education programs to GED or high school graduates who need additional preparation before entering regular college credit courses. In order to meet the learning needs of an increasingly diverse population, and to provide the necessary

---

[2] Zafft, p. ix.

support for successful adjustment to the college environment, STCC has historically provided specialized college transition programs utilizing a cohort model that targets services to specific student populations with common needs. To date, such programs include: federally funded Student Support Services Program and Strengthening Institutions Program and state-funded Disadvantaged Student and College Support programs, Adult Basic Education program, ESOL Program, and Pathways to Success Program for Springfield students who did not achieve passing MCAS scores. The College's ABE Center represents a one-stop style of organization whereby all academic and student support functions are located in the same building, including STCC's nationally recognized Office of Disability Services, the Student Success Center, the Student Support Services Program (SSS), the College Counseling Center, the Career Placement Office, and the Library. All ABE services are integrated within the greater network of these student support services.

QUALIFICATIONS AND ROLE OF PERSONNEL: The Director of Returning Adult Services, Sue Soffen, has more than 20 years' experience working with returning adult students of varying backgrounds, including displaced homemakers, dislocated workers, and individuals transitioning from welfare to work. The Transitions Coordinator, Toni Maruca, has more than ten years' experience within MA Dept. of Education–funded ABE programs, and has a strong background in academic advising. Ms. Soffen and Ms. Maruca currently sit on the ABE Advisory Board of the Massachusetts Career Development Institute (MCDI) and serve on the Boards of Literacy Works of Hampden County, the Springfield Community Planning Board, and the Chicopee Community Planning Board. Ms. Soffen also sits on the Department of Transitional Assistance Advisory Board. Instructors with background and experience in the field will be selected to teach the classes. A to-be-hired part-time Coordinator/Counselor will assist Ms. Soffen and Ms. Maruca with management of this project.

NUMBER OF PEOPLE IMPACTED AND HOW THEY WILL BE IMPACTED: STCC anticipates 20 people in each of the four six-week courses, for a project total of 80 students served. An immediate benefit to these students is that they will not have to pay for this course, but will have much to gain from it. Attendance in this course will: (1) enable the student to test higher on the college placement exams, perhaps avoiding subsequent developmental classes, (2) equip the student with the skills and tools needed to manage college-level work, (3) imbue the student with an awareness of what it means to be in college, what it takes to stay in college, and how their actions will make that possible, (4) demonstrate to the student early on the support services that are available to them during their entire college career, and (5) by removing the mystery and anxiety that may be associated with going to college, instill a level of self-confidence that will serve each student throughout his or her studies.

EVALUATION PLAN: STCC will employ both formative and summative evaluation processes. Formative processes will include the evaluation of the classes by the participants (students, instructors, and staff) and allow for re-direction and corrective actions to take place on an ongoing basis. Summative evaluation will look at the planned versus actual delivery of services as measured against the objectives. To determine program efficacy, STCC will track the number of students enrolling in the Success Express program, how many complete the course, how many subsequently enroll in STCC, and how many test out of development courses. Information learned from data analysis also will be shared with instructors, so that they can better align their curriculum to address academic gaps.

PLAN FOR FULLY FUNDING AND SUSTAINING PROJECT: STCC's ABE program receives state grant funds, although recent funding cuts have been made. A grant from CFWM would allow STCC to test a modified approach to service delivery. If it proves to be successful, STCC will determine if current grant-funded programs can be adapted to incorporate this model, apply for a CFWM grant in 2009, and research and apply to additional private-sector funding sources to expand the program.

PROJECT COLLABORATORS: While this project will not have specific collaborators, the ABE staff works closely with many local organizations that share ABE and workforce development goals such as: the

Regional Employment Board of Hampden County, Future Works, Career Point, MCDI, Valley Opportunity Council Adult Learning Centers, and Springfield Public Schools.

NAMES OF OTHER ORGANIZATIONS CARRYING OUT SIMILAR PROJECTS: Holyoke Community College.

3. Sample Twenty-Page Proposal Narrative* to a Federal Agency

Introduction—*Workforce STAT: Transforming Regional Capacity for Healthcare Education*

The current healthcare workforce needs in western Massachusetts are substantial and documented (detailed below). The hospitals and healthcare providers have made it clear that existing and anticipated vacancies create a consistent demand for skilled workers. Similarly, employment data indicates a potential workforce very much in need of steady employment with living wages. Given the large numbers of pre-health students on the four western Massachusetts community college campuses, there is—without question—a large group of willing, potential workers eager to work within the healthcare fields. Thus, this is not a simple supply and demand scenario; there are sufficient numbers of interested people to meet healthcare industry demand. What is needed are interventions that will move this supply of *potential* healthcare workers more rapidly into being a supply of qualified, skilled, and *prepared* healthcare workers.

To meet this need, Springfield Technical Community College (STCC) has reviewed the data, listened to what industry says it needs, examined its current capacity, and consulted with regional partners to determine what the College and its partners can do. As a result, STCC proposes *Workforce*

---

* The narrative was accompanied by several attachments that offered additional information, including an abstract, timeline, summary of outcomes, partner descriptions, partner activity list, and letters of commitment.

STAT (Skills, Talent, Awareness, Training): Transforming Regional Capacity for Healthcare Education as part of the solution. However, to implement the *Workforce STAT* strategies for effective delivery of the needed workforce training, the four community colleges in western Massachusetts will require a capacity injection. Specifically, *Workforce STAT* proposes the following capacity-building activities: (1) to fully equip and bring up-to-date simulation labs staffed by part-time lab assistants, (2) to provide simulation train-the-trainer training for faculty and lab assistants, (3) to develop industry-informed curriculum, and (4) to explore the geographical expansion of STCC's Medical Assisting program through a creative use of hybrid coursework and technology-based distance learning.

1. Statement of Need

(a) Industry of Focus: Health Care: Hampden County, Massachusetts' largest employer—and thus, essential to the overall local economy—is the healthcare industry. To support this industry, STCC has 16 health certificate and degree programs, producing 276 graduates/year. Yet our hospitals and other health employers are suffering a critical workforce shortage. The activities presented in this proposal seek to address this need and to provide a steady stream of well-qualified, dependable, and patient-focused workers. The high need for investing in a program to produce more of these workers is made clear through data and demand—labor market data, local industry workforce projections, healthcare leaders' and strategists' recommendations, and indicators of regional economic impact.

(b) High-growth/high-demand industry in the local or regional economy: In its March 2008 Regional Labor Market Information Annual Profile for Hampden County Workforce Area, the MA Dept. of Workforce Development (MDWD) notes that "Three large sectors, Health Care and Social Assistance (17.4%), Manufacturing (11.8%), and Retail Trade (11.7%) comprise more than 40% of all jobs in Hampden County." Yet of these three sectors, only Health Care and Social Assistance generated new jobs (880) between the second quarters of 2006 and 2007. As one of the two fastest growing sectors, Health and Educational Services is projected (for the years 2004–2014) to add the most new jobs (94,450 jobs), with

Health alone accounting for nearly 64,000 of those jobs. According to the Bureau of Labor Statistics' Quarterly Census of Employment and Wages, the percentage of jobs in Health Care and Social Assistance in Hampden County (20.12%) exceeds both the percentages in MA (15.90%) and the nation (12.96%). The location quotient—a figure used to measure industry concentration in a region compared to that same industry concentration in a larger region—is 1.27 for Hampden County as compared to the whole of the U.S. This further substantiates that health care is a significant industry in Hampden County. Equally valuable in providing indications that health care is a high-growth/high-demand industry are the findings of the MDWD's Job Vacancy Survey of 4th Quarter 2007, "Demand for health care and social assistance remained high and fueled the largest number of job postings during the 4th quarter of 2007. The 20,016 open health care positions accounted for 22 percent of all jobs posted during this quarter. Over the year, the volume of open-for-hire positions in health care rose 14 percent while the job vacancy rate climbed to 4.4 percent, up from 4.0 percent a year ago." In the western Massachusetts Berkshire and Pioneer Valley regions, both the Healthcare Practitioner and Technical and Healthcare Support occupational groups exceeded the statewide vacancy rate. The four counties of western Massachusetts—Berkshire, Franklin, Hampden, and Hampshire—all have towns designated as a Medically Underserved Area and/or as a Health Professional Shortage Area. Additionally, an aging population creates demand for additional healthcare workers in two directions: (1) a large number of healthcare workers will be retiring, and (2) the number of people needing more frequent and expanded health care will be increasing.

(c) Evidence of industry demand for training: Because the healthcare industry is the state's largest employer, the MA Workforce Board Association brought together over 70 people in April 2006 for a Health Care Workforce Strategy Roundtable to develop recommendations for statewide action on health care improvement. Among those recommendations was the request to "Expand the capacity of the Commonwealth's public and private nursing education system . . . , provide upgrade training and professional development . . . , and to increase the number of individuals who can successfully fill vacancies in allied health and other critical health professions and advance through the creation of career pathways."

A two-hour healthcare industry forum was held at STCC in March 2005. The College requested guidance from leaders of the industry in identifying areas of assistance that can be provided by STCC, and in reviewing workforce requirements that can be met through the provision of quality degree, certificate, and training programs that produce well-trained and skilled graduates. Among the findings was that 83% of the respondents thought that they would not have a large enough pool of qualified, entry-level, technical skilled candidates from which to draw employees in the following 18 months.

In fact, one of our primary industry project partners, and the area's largest health employer, Baystate Health, says that to meet growth forecasts, it will need to hire approximately 10,900 FTEs, which equates to approximately 18,500 new hires over the next ten years. Baystate notes that with Connecticut having more acute shortages, there is and will be potential competition for talent from neighboring states. And if the cost of talent is not consistent with the cost of living, there's a risk of losing people to higher paying jobs in neighboring areas. Baystate and other industry members tell us that new technology and new models of care mean that new programs producing workers with a greater specialization of skills are needed. Baystate also indicates that it needs a more diverse skilled workforce to meet the changing population/patient diversity.

(d) Capacity Challenges: The U.S. Department of Labor clearly understands that community colleges are the Workforce Workhorse—that our career-based programs turn out the well-trained, qualified employees that so many industries need. But this training often requires expensive, up-to-date equipment on which faculty are fully trained in order to be of true value to industry. Being publicly funded and usually without a well-heeled alumni base, community colleges must make difficult choices about how to use limited resources, and recent statewide cuts have made this even more difficult. Without question, community colleges are facing critical capacity constraints rooted in a lack of funds.

To be highly effective in providing training that results in an increased and smoothly flowing pipeline of skilled healthcare workers, the four community colleges of western Massachusetts need: (1) upgraded, up-to-date, fully equipped simulation labs staffed by part-time lab assistants, (2) simulation training for faculty and a heightened awareness of how to use simulation in healthcare coursework, (3) curriculum development of a hands-on simulation-based patient skills course as an initial offering to would-be healthcare career seekers, (4) additional advising staff focused on students in pre-health and healthcare programs, and (5) a joint exploration of a geographical expansion of STCC's Medical Assisting program through a creative use of hybrid coursework and technology-based distance learning. Academic challenges that also cause community college capacity constraints are discussed in Training and Capacity Building Plan.

2. Linkages to Key Partners

An important element of our expected success with this project is the strong and committed pre-existing healthcare partnerships in western MA. The genuine desire of industry and education to work together, with a regional approach, to develop a qualified healthcare workforce is evident in the area's vibrant partnerships. In addition to the many one-on-one workforce efforts common between area entities (such as STCC and Baystate Health Systems), recent grant-funded partnership work includes the Pioneer Valley Allied Health Career Pipeline Project (a Health Careers Opportunity Project—HCOP), the Commonwealth of Massachusetts' Workforce Competitiveness Trust Fund Allied Health Pilot, the foundation-funded Collaborating for the Advancement of Nursing: Developing Opportunities project (CAN DO), and the Northern Tier Healthcare Training and Education Initiative (a Health Resources and Services Administration project—HRSA). Many of the *Workforce STAT* partners are also partners of these projects and as such are informed, knowledgeable, experienced, and committed to responding to the healthcare industry's needs. An effort is currently underway to solidify the Pioneer Valley Healthcare Partnership to fully coordinate the varied projects and to address workforce development issues that healthcare organizations cannot solve alone. This is a true indicator of area stakeholders' desire to work collaboratively, to avoid and reduce duplication, and to assure that efforts build on each other. The partnership for *Workforce STAT*—representing four counties—

purposefully builds on and draws from this energetic, dedicated, and substantial healthcare workforce network in western MA. The 16 *Workforce STAT* partners are:

1. <u>Three workforce investment system representatives:</u> The Regional Employment Board of Hampden County, Franklin/Hampshire Regional Employment Board, and Berkshire County Regional Employment Board
2. <u>Four community colleges:</u> STCC, Holyoke Community College (HCC), Greenfield Community College (GCC), and Berkshire Community College (BCC)
3. <u>Four health industry employers:</u> Baystate, Berkshire, Holyoke, and Mercy Medical Centers
4. <u>One K–12 public school system:</u> Springfield Public Schools
5. One local K–12 school-based nonprofit organization—The World Is Our Classroom.
6. <u>One local Veteran-serving nonprofit organization:</u> Mason Square Veterans Outreach Center
7. <u>One health career organization:</u> The MassAHEC Network (Area Health Education Centers)
8. <u>One healthcare workforce consortium:</u> Pioneer Valley Allied Health Career Pipeline Project

Each partner plays a pivotal role in this project, focused on the win-win goal of providing willing workers with a solid career opportunity and industry with a skilled and qualified workforce. The primary players are the four community colleges and the four area hospitals, which will be the core of the Project Curriculum Board (PCB)—an intentional step beyond an Advisory Board—and will play an active role in the design and delivery of our proposed work; these roles are more fully described in Sections 3 and 5. All partners will be a member of the Industry-College Review Board (ICRB), the overseeing body that will monitor and contribute advice to the project over the course of the three years. A Project Coordinator will be hired for the life of the grant and will be the first contact person for all partners. And just as the partnership preceded this proposed project, it is expected to continue long after it—the partners are that committed and the Pioneer Valley Healthcare Partnership provides the vehicle to sustain that commitment. Brief descriptions of *Workforce STAT* partners are offered in Attachment 1. Partner activities, leveraged contributions, and collaboration memberships are detailed in Attachment 2 and the attached Letters of Commitment. Total leveraged dollars exceeds $1,250,000. The chart below summarizes leveraged WIA training resources committed to supporting the project.

	WIA TITLE I WIA YOUTH FUNDS	WIA TITLE I ADULT AND DISLOCATED WORKER FUNDS
The dollar amount leveraged	$75,000 per year for 3 years	$50,000 per year for 3 years
Target audience	At-risk youth	Low income adults Veterans Dislocated workers
The workforce system partner involved	Regional Employment Board (REB) of Hampden County Inc. and its WIA Youth Providers (In-School: Pathfinder Regional Vocational Technical High School, Holyoke Public Schools and New North Citizen's Council / Out of School: MA Career Development Institute, New England Farm Workers Council, YWCA)	REB and its 2 One-Stop Career Centers, CareerPoint and FutureWorks
The role of the resources in the project	Provide assessment, eligibility, career counseling, work readiness training, case management and follow-up to 25 youth per year who will participate in the "World Is Our Classroom" and for the 10-12 youth per year to be dually enrolled in the 3-credit Patient Skills course that will also be provided with work experience in the healthcare field.	Provide assessment, eligibility, career counseling, ITA case management and follow-up to the 10 individuals per year to receive healthcare related training.
The impact of the WIA training resources	To ensure students make a more informed choice of their educational pathways through expanded awareness and exploration of these career opportunities and to enroll 25 youth into a 2-year college program in the healthcare field.	For 80% of enrollees (24 in total) to complete healthcare related training and become employed in the healthcare field.

3. Training and Capacity Building Plan

Almost 100% of the students completing our health programs who seek a job in the field can get a job in the field. The high demand for healthcare workers in the region is evidenced by the data above. What, then, impedes supply meeting demand? Several issues contribute to the fact that there are not enough credentialed applicants, produced quickly enough, for the wide variety of healthcare positions. Through intense industry consultation and self-examination, STCC has identified these contributing factors, the College's academic challenges, as delineated below. Students—and potential students—are:

1. <u>Uninformed about healthcare career opportunities:</u> There is a lack of knowledge about the breadth of healthcare positions. Too often potential students, when thinking about healthcare industry possibilities, only think of doctors and nurses. They are unaware of a variety of jobs—which do not require four year degrees—that are needed by hospitals, doctors' offices, and other healthcare facilities.

2. <u>Uninformed about healthcare career realities:</u> STCC has a large number of students who operate only with a notion, rather than the experience, of life as a healthcare worker. There is a lack of knowledge about the complexity and rigor of healthcare programs and jobs, and therefore once started, many STCC students are surprised at how demanding Health programs are and fail to complete them. Hospitals report retention problems due to the worker's inability to manage the intensity of the job. There is not an opportunity to have exposure to healthcare career realities at an early point in the college experience.

3. <u>Unprepared academically:</u> Many students arrive under-prepared for coursework and have low performance in math, science, and English. Many students linger in the General Studies Health Core program for years, not yet capable of managing the Health course requirements.

In addition, college coursework is:

4. <u>Unmatched to current industry needs:</u> In addition to the career-specific skills a healthcare worker needs, healthcare leaders have

indicated the following essential skills they seek in an employee: critical thinking, problem solving, teamwork, writing, language, communication, and cultural competency. Additionally, they want workers who are focused on and able to perform infection control, documentation, and patient safety. If industry can cite these deficiencies, then our coursework must be re-worked to emphasize the acquisition of these vital skills.

After considerable deliberation, STCC and its partners propose the following response to the above-stated capacity and academic challenges. The goal of STCC's *Workforce STAT* project is to meet regional healthcare industry needs by transforming—in an accelerated manner—large numbers of interested and willing pre-health students into a prepared, focused, well-qualified, and well-suited healthcare workforce through the following means: (1) early exposure to and awareness-building of healthcare career and coursework realities and choices, (2) hands-on simulation-based education, (3) targeted health program counseling to help students identify if healthcare work overall, and which field in particular, matches their skills, interests, and inclinations, and to foster these students so that they have the confidence and the tools to proceed quickly and strongly toward program graduation, (4) active recruitment and support of underutilized populations such as Veterans, and (5) planning for the geographic expansion of STCC's Medical Assisting program.

To assure ourselves and our readers that what we propose is novel and worthy of replication, extensive research was conducted in the Workforce Solutions Catalogue on the website (www.workforce3one.org/wfsolutions). Additionally, research was done on the Department of Labor's ETA website, the Curriki website (www.curriki.org), and Federal Resource for Educational Excellence website (www.free.ed.gov), for any programs designed to provide direct entry points into healthcare careers through simulation that targeted developmental-level students, as well as a secondary-level experiential learning component. No other programs or curricula target the population that the *Workforce STAT* project targets.

Proposed Training and Capacity-Building Activities: Members of the collaborative have created a holistic approach to addressing the issues; therefore, several of the specific activities/interventions we have designed respond to more than one objective. Objectives listed below relate to both the capacity and academic challenges cited above. Activities are described in more detail in the table to follow.

Objective	Implementation Strategy
1. To increase the capacity of all four Western Massachusetts community colleges to offer meaningful hands-on experiences to potential health students and expand the capacity of the STCC Medical Assisting Program.	**1a.** Equip and bring up-to-date simulation labs with lab assistants at four community colleges. **1b.** Provide simulation training for faculty and lab assistants and a heightened awareness of how to use simulation as a counseling tool. **1c.** Establish the geographical expansion of the Medical Assisting program through a creative use of hybrid coursework and technology-based distance learning.
2. To increase the capacity of the four partner colleges to appropriately inform and advise potential students to the variety of healthcare careers. [Responds to Academic Challenge #1]	**2a.** Increase number of K–12 Medical Encounter sessions. **2b.** Create and implement at each college the Patient Skills course. **2c.** Provide Targeted Advising Training. **2d.** Increase the number of Targeted Counselors. **2e.** Increase health careers recruitment. **2f.** Re-develop www.healthprograms.org.
3. To introduce students to the realities of healthcare careers. [Responds to Academic Challenges #1, 2]	**3a.** Provide K–12 Medical Encounter to all four college partners. **3b.** Offer the Patient Skills course.
4. To introduce students to the realities of healthcare coursework. [Responds to Academic Challenge #3]	**4a.** Provide K–12 Medical Encounter to all four college partners. **4b.** Offer the Patient Skills course. **4c.** Provide Targeted Counseling.
5. To help students identify if healthcare work overall, and which field in particular, matches their skills, interests, and inclinations. [Responds to Academic Challenges #1, 2, and 3]	**5a.** Provide K–12 Medical Encounter to all four college partners. **5b.** Offer the Patient Skills course. **5c.** Provide Targeted Counseling.

Objective	Implementation Strategy
6. To foster students in the health programs so they have the confidence and the tools to proceed quickly and strongly toward program graduation. [Responds to Academic Challenge #3]	**6a.** Provide K–12 Medical Encounter to all four partner colleges. **6b.** Offer the Patient Skills course. **6c.** Provide Targeted Counseling.
7. To rework existing Health Core to put increased emphasis on critical thinking, problem solving, teamwork, writing, language, communication, and cultural competency. [Responds to Academic Challenge #4]	**7a.** College Credit Patient Skills course. **7b.** Project Curriculum Board will provide input into curriculum changes.

Activities (presented in the order as listed under Implementation Strategies above): *Equip and Update Simulation Labs and Provide Simulation Training:* By providing simulation patients and related equipment, this project will address one of the most significant capacity challenges for the three community college partners. To learn how to fully utilize this equipment in their course delivery, STCC SIMS Medical will train three full-time faculty members from BCC, HCC, and GCC in patient simulation train-the-trainer workshops. They will then train additional faculty at each institution. Each community college partner will hire a part-time lab assistant who will be trained by STCC as a simulation specialist. To deliver the Medical Encounters effectively, at least four World Is Our Classroom faculty will be trained by STCC staff on how to use patient simulation equipment and how to develop patient-based scenarios.

Develop and Deliver K–12 One-Day Medical Encounters Learning Events and Teaching Materials: The World Is Our Classroom (WIOC), in consultation with the Project Curriculum Board, will design and deliver over the three years 150 One-Day Medical Encounters, a hands-on learning event which will be offered to approximately 1,500 K–12 students. The Medical Encounters will bring K–12 students to all community colleges' simulation labs to have a real-world experience of health care. The purpose of this activity is to: (1) stimulate interest early-on in healthcare careers, (2) expose young people to the variety of healthcare jobs available, (3) help wavering teenagers determine if this is the route they wish to pursue, and (4) demonstrate to students the real-life applicability of classroom-learned math and science. WIOC will schedule 25 Medical Encounters visits to STCC each year of the grant and will further expand its current successful programs to include BCC, GCC, and HCC (five visits each the first year, then up to ten visits each of the following two years of the grant). This expansion will be funded for three years during the life of the grant and then will be institutionalized by WIOC. Additionally, WIOC will work with the Project Curriculum Board to develop healthcare teaching materials, such as CD-ROMs and DVDs, for use by teachers in area public schools. Springfield Public Schools' School to Career program will be an active partner in engaging high school students, incorporating the same students in its own workforce development programs, and encouraging them to take the Patient Skills course through STCC's dual enrollment program, which allows high school seniors to take one course for free. The Franklin/Hampshire Regional Employment Board will provide outreach and logistical coordination for WIOC activities in its counties.

Develop and Deliver College Credit Patient Skills Course: The current General Studies Health Core curriculum contains a college credit "Health Directions Seminar" in which potential health students are introduced to a wide variety of health careers. However, this course has only lectures, with no hands-on experiences. Conversely, the proposed new college credit Patient Skills course will have significant hands-on patient-based experiences. The course will be an entry-level, simulation-based course targeted to high school seniors (under dual enrollment) and students in the General Studies Health Core program, which at STCC is a group of approximately 1,000 students who applied to but did not get accepted into any of the Health programs. Using STCC's SIMS Medical Center—a 15 bed virtual hospital, one of 15 such centers in the country and ranking among the top five—and at the newly upgraded and expanded simulation facilities at BCC, GCC, and HCC, the Patient Skills course will be a one-semester, college-credit course designed to expose students to the reality of a career in varied health fields. The four community college partners, in consultation with industry partners, will develop the curriculum for this course and the four community college partners will deliver the Patient Skills courses on their campuses, thus expanding the SIMS model beyond STCC. By updating BCC, GCC, and HCC's SIMS capacity, more students can be served. A photographic tour of SIMS Medical is available at http://health.stcc.edu.

The purpose of this course is three-fold: (1) to give students the opportunity to have hands-on healthcare experience, (2) to help students determine early on in their college career if healthcare is an appropriate and desirable field for them, and (3) to inspire students to be more engaged in their health classes as a result of seeing the immediate value of the work they will be doing. Side benefits of this class are that students will (1) get to experience multiple, small successes as they learn through doing, (2) earn points toward admission to the Health programs, and (3) even if they decide not to enroll in health programs they still have earned three general elective credits.

The class also responds to industry leaders' and workforce recruiters' concern that what classifies someone as a qualified healthcare worker goes beyond acquiring a specific skill set. As cited above, they have requested more generalized skills be acquired as well. These requested competencies—team work, communication, critical thinking, problem solving, and cultural competence—will form the core of the Patient Skills course. So that the potential health student may experience multiple "milestone successes," basic skills also will be included in the Patient Skills course, such as patient safety, infection control, documentation, and CPR.

High school students will not have to pay for the Patient Skills course under our free College Now dual enrollment program. STCC awards Veterans tuition waivers and Massachusetts National Guard tuition exemptions. After contacting the Office of Veterans' Affairs, all eligible students may apply for college enrollment in a degree-granting program and register for classes to receive V.A. benefits. For other students, there are several sources of financial aid available to cover tuition and fees, including grants, loans, student employment, and scholarships. Some students are eligible for need-based waivers for tuition and fees. STCC also provides low-interest loans, directly funded by the federal government, both subsidized and unsubsidized, depending upon financial need. Additionally, as residents of Massachusetts, students may receive State aid for tuition and fees if they meet all federal requirements.

Provide Advising Training: Targeted counselors from each of the college and hospital partner sites will receive academic advising training from the National Academic Advising Association (NACADA). The targeted counselors will learn standardized competencies for delivering career counseling in the healthcare fields and will be able to help people move through the educational system efficiently and effectively. Of equal concern is how high school counselors are advising their students about healthcare schooling and careers. STCC will continue its work with the Western Massachusetts Counselors Association, reaching out to 30-40 high school guidance counselors to engage in mini Medical Encounter experiences so they can better advise their students on what to expect in a healthcare education and career.

Deliver Targeted Counseling: There is a need for consistent and coordinated advising targeted to healthcare careers. To that end, each community college will have a targeted counselor who will be responsible for health-focused targeted counseling. These counselors will help students and employees with healthcare career goal clarification and academic advising on how best to achieve that goal. These counselors will promote the availability of the Patient Skills course class as a means to assess one's interest in and aptitude for healthcare work. Acknowledging that the ratio of available counselors to students is never what might be wished, the project partners will consider other ways to provide targeted counseling to health students. For example, the existing health programs website at STCC (and serving three other community colleges) will be further developed. The HCOP project will offer the *Workforce STAT* project a connection to its social networking activities. Other efforts to keep pre-health and health students interested, connected, and mutually supportive, such as peer-to-peer counseling, will be explored. HCOP's Teacher Advocates and *Workforce STAT* targeted counselors will work together to keep the healthcare workforce pipeline flowing.

Heighten Recruitment Efforts: Using a variety of techniques, all partners will participate in recruitment efforts to encourage students to enter the partner colleges' health programs. Many of the partners are already engaged in recruitment activities, such as Pioneer Valley AHEC's after school and summer pre-health enrichment programs for culturally diverse and disadvantaged high school students. The Masons Square Veterans Outreach Center will be encouraging its clients to consider a healthcare career and enroll in STCC's Patient Skills course as a first step. See Attachment 3 for a visual representation of the important role of recruitment and counseling.

Medical Assisting Expansion: Baystate Health Systems has over 20 out-patient clinics, all of which hire Medical Assistants. For some years now, they have requested that we expand enrollment in our program. With a predicted increasing shortage of Medical Assistants in western Massachusetts, we feel obligated to explore possible expansion. Greenfield Community College has agreed to host a satellite program should we be able to develop a viable plan. To arrive at this plan and determine the best way for coursework delivery, STCC and GCC will hold summer workshops to provide dedicated, focused time for faculty and administration from both colleges, with medical community input, to develop a proposal that meets the needs of the community, the students, and the national accreditation agency for Medical Assisting.

4. Outcomes, Benefits, and Impact

Implementation Strategy numbers are listed with each major activity area for comparison to the Objectives above.

K–12 One-Day Medical Encounter Learning Events [Strategies 2a, 3a, 4a, 5a, 6a]: Baseline is 100 for the older STCC pilot. The updated curriculum will be developed by the Project Curriculum Board and implemented by WIOC in each college partner simulation facility. A total of 1,440 students are expected to experience the Medical Encounter.

College Credit Patient Skills Course [Strategies 2b, 3b, 4b, 5b, 6b, 7a]: A one semester college level course will be developed by the Project Curriculum Board and implemented by each of the college partners in expanded high-fidelity patient-simulation facilities. Baseline is the number of students who typically enroll in the current Health Careers Seminar over one year. That figure is approximately 35 per year. We expect 25% more students will enroll in the Patient Skills course than the current number of students taking the Health Careers Seminar lecture over one year.

Advising Training [Strategy 2c]: No less than one designated employee at each college and industry partner will be trained in career counseling and tracking methods.

Targeted Counseling [Strategies 2d, 4c, 5c, 6c]: No targeted counseling exists at this time. Designated employees at each of the college and healthcare industry partners will be trained in a proven career counseling method. After training, the goal is that each attendee to the WIOC One-Day Medical Encounters will receive a follow-up contact to determine the student's perception of the experience and their needs for health career counseling. The same goal exists for the college credit Patient Skills course, but with an emphasis on assisting those students who wish to apply for a health career at one of the four college partners.

Recruitment [Strategy 2e, 2f]: The current website (www.healthprograms .org) will be re-designed to provide up-to-date information on all health programs offered in western MA. New recruitment materials will be developed for use in Targeted Counseling that includes the WIOC One-day Medical Encounters and the new Patient Skills college level course.

Engage faculty and staff in re-examining current curriculum and identify ways to incorporate industry-requested attributes [Strategy 7a, 7b]: The Project Curriculum Board will provide direct input into new curriculum development and for existing health related courses.

5. Program Management and Organization Capacity

A Project Coordinator will be hired for the life of the grant. This person will be responsible for the daily activities of the project, partner coordination, data management, and project reporting. Michael Foss, the Dean of the School of Health and Patient Simulation, will co-manage the entire project with Dr. Patricia Hanrahan, Director of Clinical Education for the School of Health and Patient Simulation (see CVs in attachments). Both have extensive backgrounds in program management, evaluation, and patient simulation and will be responsible for overall operation and success of the project. Dean Foss and Dr. Hanrahan are currently implementing a lab upgrade for the 16 programs in the School of Health. The work is funded by a Title III grant for approximately $500,000; however, another $250,000 has been leveraged. Lab upgrade includes facility planning and management, equipment selection, purchasing, installation, training and integration into 14 of the 16 health programs. This five-year project has resulted in the creation, building, and operation of a nationally recognized patient simulation center, SIMS Medical Center (see attachment). In 2006, Laerdal Inc. recognized SIMS as a "Center of Excellence" for patient simulation. At that time, STCC was the only community college to be so recognized. SIMS Medical Center is a model for other community colleges and other institutions of higher education who wish to integrate patient simulation into their health curriculum with the intent of improved patient care. Dean Foss and Dr. Hanrahan are members of several current healthcare workforce projects, including WCTF and HCOP previously described.

College Partners: The four college partners will provide simulation facilities with a sufficient capacity and high-fidelity level to support educational experiences for the WIOC One-Day Medical Encounters and the new college credit Patient Skills course. Each college also will designate an existing counselor for advising training in health career counseling. Those counselors will be responsible for recruiting students to take the Medical Encounters experience and/or the college credit Patient Skills course. Students taking either experience will be tracked for five years to determine health program entry, attrition, graduation, and placement rates. Each of the college partners have experienced deans of health and experienced academic advisors.

Industry Partners: The four hospital partners, Baystate, Mercy, Holyoke, and Berkshire Medical, will each designate an existing employee to receive health career counseling training. The trained employees will recruit, as appropriate, current health employees to take the Patient Skills college level course with the expectation of those employees upgrading skills. All hospitals will be members of the Project Curriculum Board, responsible for development of the Medical Encounters and Patient Skills experiences. Industry input is critical since it will drive the curriculum to address skills required in today's healthcare environment. Each of the industry partners are providing current, well-experienced human resource personnel to act as contacts, members of the Project Curriculum Board, and trained counselors.

Data Management: STCC will be the repository for all project data and will make use of the ETA software system offered to collect and report performance data. Each college partner has years of experience in tracking student/employee success and will do as needed for this project.

Data collected will be applied to the outcome measures as described in this and the Common Measures (see attachment) documents. Each student who attends the WIOC Medical Encounters and/or the college-level Patient Skills will be tracked through targeted counseling utilizing email, phone, and survey instruments. Data to be collected is attendance of either or both offerings, admission to a health program or pre-med track, attrition, graduation, employment, and passing rate of qualifying exam. STCC will be particularly attentive to data collection because of its participation in a new grant-funded project. It was selected to participate in the Achieving the Dream effort of the Lumina Foundation—a multi-year national initiative created to strengthen the ability of community colleges to help students of color and low-income students earn degrees and certificates by using data to close achievement gaps. The effort emphasizes the use of data to drive change, and STCC staff will have the opportunity to work with a data facilitator who provides hands-on help with the use of data.

Sustainability: The *Workforce STAT* project has built-in sustainability. The Pioneer Valley Healthcare Partnership, the newly forming, all-encompassing collaborative focused on healthcare workforce issues, will be an established regional institution. The Patient Skills course will be self-sustaining, and WIOC will institutionalize its expansion. The on-going project results and model of this project will be disseminated to all 15 community colleges in MA through the MASS Community College Deans of Health quarterly meetings. Quarterly and annual reports will be placed on our re-designed website (www.healthprograms.org). The counseling and curriculum models also will be available via the website in PDF format for easy downloading. The Project Managers will submit for presentation at the AACC conference and other conferences as deemed appropriate for the topic. Those showing an interest in the project models will be invited to one or more of the partner colleges to see the process firsthand.

6. Integration with Regional Economic and Talent Development Strategies

The *Workforce STAT* project ties in with regional economic development objectives as articulated in the Regional Employment Board of Hampden County's (REBHC) Strategic Plan: "Promote sectoral training initiatives in high growth industries, particularly in the priority clusters of healthcare and advanced precision manufacturing, which utilize a career ladder approach to provide upgraded skills, increased salary, and career advancement for new/incumbent workers." Also, STCC has a long-standing partnership with several area healthcare organizations; many serve as clinical affiliations for our health programs and they also compete heavily for our graduates as they have an excellent reputation in the healthcare community. As mentioned earlier, *Workforce STAT* will integrate its activities with those of the other regional healthcare workforce projects.

7. Partnership with Faith-Based and Community Organizations

The World Is Our Classroom nonprofit organization is a key player in the success of the Medical Encounters activities and will be interacting with all four community colleges. STCC will work with the Masons Square Veterans Outreach Center to encourage Veterans to consider healthcare careers and to explore this through the Patient Skills course at STCC. Masons Square will offer case management and support to the Veterans as they pursue this option.

INDEX

Page numbers in *italic* represent charts.

Accountability, in evaluation,
    188–89
Activism. *See also* Grassroots
    problem-solving approach
    and, 56–57
    as shrewd project activity, 56
American Cancer Society, 34
Answers. *See also* Questions
    to likely questions, in logic,
        94–95
    in project activities, 173–77
    in statement of need, 125, 150
Applications. *See also* Online
    intake form
    form, 10
    online, 7, 122
    SOA, 15
Arnold and Mabel Beckman
    Foundation, 52
Associated Grant Makers, 216
Associations. *See also*
    Foundations
    Associated Grant Makers, 216
    cover letter for, 228
    Forum of Regional
        Associations of
        Grantmakers, 89
    RAG, 89, 216
Assume nothing, 93–94
Attachments, 7, 10
Audience, 2
    communicating to, 77
    corporations as, 70–72
    determining, 6
    evaluation, 192–93
    foundations as, 67–70
    government as, 72–76
    knowing, 64–66
    operating from world of, 66–67
    for proposals, 67–76
    writing style for, 80

Backward from ideal method
    for stating project activities,
        174
    as writer's block technique,
        112
Beginners FAQ, 6–7
Beldon Fund, 42
Beliefs, of grantmakers, 37, 50
Beneficiaries, in statement of
    need, 154
Ben & Jerry's Foundation, 60–61
Brainstorming
    goals, 82
    project titles, 106–8
    proposal organization, 82
Budget justification. *See* Budget
    narrative
Budget narrative, 7, *217*
    developing, 9
    order for, 216
    role of, 216
    specificity in, 212
Budgets, 7, 9, 13, *213*
    as accurate, 209
    checking math in, 214
    clarity in, 209
    as complete, 210
    as concise, 210
    cost sharing in, 214–15
    defined, 209
    as detailed, 209
    direct/indirect costs in, 210
    as documentable, 210
    formatting, 212–14
    forms, 215–16
    foundation, 215–16
    government grants, 215
    justification, 9
    in letter of inquiry, 129
    money requested in, 211–12
    multi-year, 214

    project activities and, 211
    as realistic, 210
    as reasonable, 210
    timesavers, 88
Building-a-case writing style,
    70
Buzzwords, 8. *See also*
    Language; Words
    for grantmakers, 8
    listing, 62
    political ideology and, 58
    in RFP, 62

Capacity, 6
    credentials and, 146
    demonstrating, 144–45
    establishing, in
        organizational description,
        144–50
    examples, 147–49
    knowledge and, 145–46
    meeting, in statement of need,
        154–55
    people and, 146–48
    project activities and, 172–73
    for project management, 145
    for staffing, 175
    throughout proposal, 149
Center on Philanthropy, Indiana
    University, 41
Charts, 9
    charting rejections, 76–79,
        77
    for complex material, 181
    example, 181
    in project activities, 179–82,
        180–81
    project dissemination, *208*
    as timesavers, 88
Chronicle of Philanthropy, 41,
    65, 68

Clarity
  assume nothing, 93–95
  being understood, 92–93
  in budgets, 209
  content and, 92
  examples, 96–105
  goals of, 91
  saving space, 92
Cleveland Foundation, 216
Clips/loose pages, 84
Closing paragraph, in letter of
  inquiry, 130
Cocktail party writer's block
  technique, 111
Collaborations. *See also*
  Partnerships
  in project activities, 175–76
  in project design, 28
Commitment, in organizational
  description, 144
Communication. *See also*
  Buzzwords; Language;
  Writing
  to audience, 77
  cover letter as personal, 228
Community foundations, 69
Compton Foundation Inc., 54–55
Concept paper, 119
Conciseness, in writing style, 72
Content. *See also* Table of
  contents
  clarity and, 92
  formatting, 231
  for letter of inquiry, 7, 122–30
  for proposal abstract, 223–24
Continuation
  demonstrated in project
  design, 28
  funding, 13
Corporations, 6
  as audience, 70–72
  foundations of, 70–71
  letter of inquiry for, 120
  motivation for giving, 70
  writing style for, 71–72
Cost sharing
  in budget, 214–15
  defined, 14
  as required, 215
Cover letter, 10, 117
  for associations, 228
  conveying excitement, 230–31
  demonstrating support, 229
  examples, 232–34
  formatting, 231
  for foundations, 228, 231
  goals in, 230
  for government grants, 231
  identifying linkages, 230
  length, 231

objectives in, 230
as personal communication, 228
purpose of, 229–31
role of, 228–29
solidifying relationship,
  229–30
technique for, 231
vision statements in, 230
when written, 228
Credentials
  capacity and, 146
  in letter of inquiry, 128–29
  project activities establishing,
  174–75
Curriculum vitae (CV), 75, 146.
  See also Résumés
Cut 'n' paste writer's block
  technique, 111
CVs. *See* Curriculum vitae

Data collection/analysis, in
  evaluation, 199–200
Deadlines, 44
Decision makers, 5, 31, 45
Deliverables, 168. *See also*
  Impacts; Outcomes
Department of Education, U.S.,
  215
Department of Housing and Urban
  Development, U.S., 215
Department of Labor, U.S., 147,
  179, 205
Direct costs, in budget, 210
Direct service
  defined, 51
  problem-solving approach
  and, 49, 51–52
Disorderly conduct writer's
  block technique, 109–10
Documents, 10

Economic downturn,
  grantseeking and, 3–4
Editing, 10, 85. *See also*
  Formatting; Readability
Education
  in problem-solving approach,
  55–56
  in project dissemination, 203
Eligibility
  for fund matching, 34–35
  preselection and, 35
  quiz, 121–22
Ends vs. means, 22
Evaluation, 12
  accountability in, 188–89
  audience, 192–93
  considerations, 190–93
  data collection/analysis,
  199–200

formative, 195–96
formatting, 193
goal of, 191–92
impact, 196
information in, 189–90
internal vs. external
  evaluator, 190–91
Kirkpatrick, 196
logic model, 196–98
methodology, 78, 193–200
objectives and, 194–95
participants, 198
placement of, 187
quantitative/qualitative, 200
reasons for, 188–90
as required, 200
responsive, 196
role of, 187–88
summative, 195–96
types of, 196–98
utilization, 196
Evaluators
  external, 9, 190–91
  internal, 9, 190–91
  outside, 9
Examples
  capacity, 147–49
  charts, 181
  clarity, 96–105
  cover letters, 232–34
  formatting, 232–34
  goals, 182–84
  logic, 96–105
  objectives, 167–68, 182–84
  organizational description,
  141–44
  outcomes, 169
  passion, 96–105
  project activities, 169, 184–86
  project dissemination, 205–8
  project sustainability, 220–21
  proposal abstract, 225–27
  short proposals, 131–36
  statement of need, 155–65
Excitement, in cover letter,
  230–31
Executive summary, 10, 222.
  See also Proposal abstract;
  Proposal summary
External evaluator, 9, 190–91

Family foundations, 70
Footers, 84
Formative evaluation, 195–96
Formatting
  budget, 212–14
  clips/loose pages, 84
  content, 231
  cover letters, 231
  evaluation, 193

examples, 232–34
footers, 84
headings, 85, 86
letter of inquiry, 123
organizational description,
 138–39
proposal abstract, 225
proposals, 83–84
section tabs, 86
short proposals, 131
table of contents, 86
Forms, 9
 application, 10
 budget, 215–16
 common, 88–89
 990-PF, 32
 online intake, 8, 70
Forum of Regional Associations
 of Grantmakers, 89
Foundation Center, 3, 38, 41,
 68, 215
 Cooperating Collection, 31
Foundation Directory Online,
 32
Foundations, 3, 6
 Arnold and Mabel Beckman
  Foundation, 52
 as audience, 67–70
 Ben & Jerry's Foundation,
  60–61
 budgets for, 215–16
 Cleveland Foundation, 216
 community, 69
 Compton Foundation Inc.,
  54–55
 considerations, 42–45, 44
 of corporations, 70–71
 cover letter for, 228, 231
 deadlines, 44
 evolution and, 43
 family, 70
 funding cycles, 44
 General Services Foundation,
  122
 grantmaking and, 43
 Hewlett Foundation, 79
 history of, 42–43
 ideology of, 40
 information sources on, 32
 Jessie Smith Noyes
  Foundation, 56–57
 JM Foundation, 61–62
 letter of inquiry for, 119
 Lynde and Harry Bradley
  Foundation, The, 59–60
 motivation for giving, 67
 NSF, 83, 96, 182, 205–6, 208
 officers, 42–43
 public, 206–7
 review committees, 68–69

Smith Richardson
 Foundation, 53
societal problems and, 36–37
staffing, 42–43, 67–68
types, 43
W. K. Kellogg Foundation, 197
writing style for, 69–70
Z. Smith Reynolds
 Foundation Inc., 55–56
Fundable projects, 6
 beginning/middle/end of, 27
 fund matching and, 21
 ideas vs., 27
 inclusive, 28
 project doable, 27
 questions for, 23–24
 so what method for, 24–25
 who benefits, 26
Funders, 2, 4, 6
 fund matching and, 5, 31, 34
 nature of, 48
Funding
 benefit many people in, 28
 collaborations, 28
 continuation, 13
 foundation cycles, 44
 fundraising, 4
Fund matching
 criteria for, 34–40
 eligibility for, 34–35
 fundable projects and, 21
 funders and, 5, 31, 34
 geographic area for, 34, 36
 grant size for, 38–39
 problem-solving approach
  for, 40
 RFP and, 38
 subject matter for, 36–37
Future Fund of Hometown
 Bank, 163–65

General Services Foundation, 122
Geographic area
 fundmaking to confined, 36
 for fund matching, 34, 36
 political ideology and, 58
 preferred, 36
Giving USA, 41
Goals, 6, 12, 117. See also
 Objectives
 achieving, 25–26
 brainstorming, 82
 clarity of, 91
 in cover letter, 230
 defined, 166
 of evaluation, 191–92
 examples, 182–84
 exercise, 171–72
 in grantwriting, 90
 guiding questions, 169

identifying, 22–25
objectives written with, 167
project activities vs., 22–23
so what method, for stating,
 170
technique for, 170–71
as vision statements, 166–67
written with objectives, 167
Google search engine, 68
Government, 6
 as audience, 72–76
 Department of Education,
  U.S., 215
 Department of Housing and
  Urban Development, U.S.,
  215
 Department of Labor, U.S.,
  147, 179, 205
 motivation for giving, 72
 technical assistance from, 76
 writing style for, 75
Government grants, 4, 38, 57, 76
 budgets, 215
 cover letter, 231
 letter of inquiry for, 119–20
 mind-set for, 40
 review committees, 72–74
 review criteria for, 74–75
 RFP, 72
 writing style for, 75
Grant(s), 1, 3. See also
  Government grants
 defined, 6
 reviewing those made, 32, 34
 size, for fund matching, 38–39
Grantmakers, 2–3, 4. See also
  Foundations
 applying language of, 63
 background work/research,
  19–20, 31–32
 beliefs of, 37, 50
 buzzwords for, 8
 calling, 6
 larger issues and, 22
 materials of, 63
 personalities, 47
 point of contact for, 8
 point of view, 8, 45
 political ideology, 57–59
 preferences of, 34, 117
 preferred problem-solving
  approach, 48–50
 priorities of, 37
 project dissemination venue,
  205
 questions of, 9
 RAG, 89, 216
 staffing, 229
 trends of, 40–41
 understanding, 30–31

Grantmaking
    foundations and, 43
    political ideology in, 58
Grant proposals. *See* Proposals
Grantseeking, 1, 4
    beginning process, 6
    economic downturn and,
        3–4
Grantwriters
    beginning, 4
    experienced, 4
Grantwriting, 2. *See also*
        Writing; Writing style
    approaching, 13
    goal in, 90
    persuasive, 46
    preparation, 19–20
    principles of, 3
    strategy, 4
    timesavers, 87–89
    writing and, 19
Grassroots, 57
GuideStar, 32

Headings
    formatting, 85, 86
    in proposal abstract, 225
Head Start, 67
Hewlett Foundation, 79
Hook, 5
    defined, 46
    finding, 46–47

Ideology, 40. *See also* Political
        ideology
Impact evaluation, 196
Impacts. *See also* Deliverables;
        Outcomes
    as end point, 168
    evaluation, 196
Inclusive project design, 28
Independent Sector, 41
Indirect costs
    in budget, 210
    defined, 14
Information
    in evaluation, 189–90
    finding in proposals, 86
    sources on foundations, 32
In-kind, 14
Internal evaluator, 9, 190–91
Introduction, 11
    in organizational description,
        139–44
    for project focus, 87
    in proposals, 86–87
Investment, 28
Invitation to submit, 10. *See
        also* Request for proposals

Jessie Smith Noyes Foundation,
        56–57
JM Foundation, 61–62

Kirkpatrick evaluation, 196
Knowledge
    capacity and, 145–46
    of field, statement of need
        demonstrating, 152–53

Language. *See also* Buzzwords;
        Voice; Words; Writing style
    applying grantmakers', 63
    for organizational
        description, 139
    in project activities, 177, 179
    "such as," 177, 179
    technical/nontechnical, in
        writing style, 80
Language library, 87–88, 140
Length
    cover letter, 231
    letter of inquiry, 7, 121
    project dissemination, 201
    proposal abstract, 223–24
    proposals, 7, 118
Letter of inquiry, 8, 10, 35. *See
        also* Concept paper; Letter
        of intent; Pre-proposal;
        Query letter; Short
        proposals
    budget, 129
    closing paragraph, 130
    content, 7, 122–30
    for corporations, 120
    credentials, 128–29
    defined, 7, 14
    formatting, 123
    for foundations, 119
    for government grants,
        119–20
    length, 7, 121
    online, 121–22
    opening paragraphs, 123–24
    outcomes in, 127–28
    presenting abbreviated
        project, 119–20
    procedure for, 120–21
    project activities in, 126–27
    proposal vs., 7
    statement of need in, 125–26
    technique for, 121
Letter of intent, 119–20
Leverage, 28
Linkages, 230
Listening, 65
Logic, 94
    answering likely questions,
        94–95

examples, 96–105
    in objectives, 171
    in project activities, 172–73
    rationale vs. method, 95
Logic model evaluation, 1
        96–98
Lynde and Harry Bradley
        Foundation, The, 59–60

Marquis, 65
Matching. *See* Cost sharing
Means vs. ends, 22
Measurable objectives, 26
"Measurement Program
        Outcomes: A Practical
        Approach," 194
Methodology
    evaluation, 78, 193–200
    replicability in, 29
Methods
    backward from ideal, 112, 174
    rationale vs., 95
    so what, 24–25, 112, 170
Milbank Jeremiah, 61
Mind-mapping writer's block
        technique, 110
Mission
    affirming, 23
    stating, 6
Mission statement
    defined, 15
    in organizational description,
        140
Money, in budget, 211–12
Motivation for giving
    corporations, 70
    foundations, 67
    government, 72
Multi-year budgets, 214

National Collegiate Inventors
        and Innovators Alliance
        (NCIIA), 102–5
National Institute of Health
        (NIH), 83
National Science Foundation
        (NSF), 83, 96, 182, 205–6,
        208
NCIIA. *See* National Collegiate
        Inventors and Innovators
        Alliance
NIH. *See* National Institute of
        Health
990-PF form, 32
Nonprofit organizations, 3,
        35, 51
Novel project design, 28–29
NSF. *See* National Science
        Foundation

Objective evaluation, 196
Objectives, 9, 12, 117. *See also*
  Goals
  in cover letter, 230
  defined, 14–15, 166, 167
  evaluation and, 194–95
  examples, 167–68, 182–84
  exercise, 171–72
  guiding questions, 169
  logic in, 171
  measurable, 26
  project dissemination as, 201
  project sustainability and, 218
  technique for, 170–71
  written with goals, 167
Online intake form, 8, 70
Opening pages
  assessment of, 101–2
  in proposals, 97–102
Opening paragraphs
  assessment of, 97, 103–5
  letter of inquiry, 123–24
  in proposals, 96–97, 102–5
Organizational background,
  140–41
Organizational description,
  10–11, 118
  caution about, 139
  commitment in, 144
  establishing capacity in, 144–50
  examples, 141–44
  formatting, 138–39
  introduction in, 139–44
  language for, 139
  mission statement, 140
  organizational background,
    140–41
  placement of, 138
  purposes in, 137–38
Organizations, 1, 6, 139–44
  nonprofit, 3, 35, 51
  role of people in assessment,
    147
Outcome Measurement
  Resource Network, United
  Way, 194
Outcomes, 9, 12, 117. *See also*
  Deliverables; Impacts
  defined, 14–15, 166, 168
  examples, 169
  guiding questions, 169–70
  in letter of inquiry, 127–28
  as measurable, 168
  presented with project
    activities, 168
  technique for determining,
    172–82
Outside evaluator, 9
Over-the-transom proposals, 15

Partnerships, 78, *176. See also*
  Collaborations
  engaging, 9
  in project activities, 175–76
Passion
  examples, 96–105
  expressing, 95–96
People. *See also* Beneficiaries;
  Staffing
  benefit many, in funding, 28
  capacity and, 146–48
  role in organization
    assessment, 147
Persuasion, in grantwriting, 46
Philanthropy News Digest, 38,
  65, 68
PI. *See* Principal investigator
Point of contact, for
  grantmakers, 8
Point of view, 5, 24. *See also*
  Voice
  determining, 47–48
  of grantmakers, 8, 45
  parts of, 45
Policy implications, 24
Political ideology
  buzzwords and, 58
  definitive, 58
  geographic area and, 58
  of grantmakers, 57–59
  in grantmaking, 58
  identifying, 59–62
  problems and, 57
Population, 26
Power
  responsibility and, 6
  of words, 108
Preparation, grantwriting, 19–20
Pre-proposal, 119
Preselection, eligibility and, 35
Principal investigator (PI), 15,
  75, 146, 175
Private grant sources, 4
Problem-solving approach
  activism and, 56–57
  determining best, 40
  direct service and, 49, 51–52
  education in, 55–56
  elements of, 49–50
  for fund matching, 40
  grantmakers' preferred, 48–50
  research and, 52–53
  research for activism
    purposes and, 54–55
  research for policy purposes
    and, 53–54
  statement of need presenting,
    153–54
  variety of, 49

Project activities, 9, 12
  activism as, 56
  asking/answering what,
    173–74
  asking/answering when/
    where, 176–77
  asking/answering who,
    174–76
  backward from ideal method,
    for stating, 174
  budget and, 211
  capacity and, 172–73
  charts, 179–82, *180–81*
  collaborations in, 175–76
  credentials established in,
    174–75
  defined, 166, 168
  examples, 169, 184–86
  goals vs., 22–23
  guiding questions, 169–70
  language in, 177, 179
  in letter of inquiry, 126–27
  logic in, 172–73
  measurable, 26
  partnerships in, 175–76
  presented with outcomes,
    168
  project management in, 175
  supporting material, 182
  technique for determining,
    172–82
  timeline for, 176–77, *178*
Project design
  benefiting many, 28
  collaboration in, 28
  continuation demonstrated
    in, 28
  elevating appeal, 27
  as inclusive, 28
  leverage and, 28
  as novel, 28–29
  replicability in, 27
  showing investment, 28
Project dissemination, 13
  activities, 204–5
  chart, *208*
  defined, 201
  education in, 203
  examples, 205–8
  grantmaker's venue for,
    205
  length, 201
  as objective, 201
  purpose, 202–4
  questions for, 201–2
  recruitment and, 202
  replication and, 203–4
  value of, 202–4
  as win-win-win, 208

Project management
  capacity for, 145
  in project activities, 175
Project managers, 75
Projects. *See* Fundable projects
Project sustainability
  actions, 220
  examples, 220–21
  as hypothetical, 218
  objectives and, 218
  past projects and, 220
  requests for, 218
  strategies, 219–20
Project titles
  brainstorming for, 106–8
  opportunity created with, 105
  samples, 106
  technique for selecting,
    106–8
Proposal(s), 1–2, 4. *See also*
    Short proposals
  audience for, 67–76
  basic components, 10–13
  capacity throughout, 149
  defined, 6–7
  editing, 10, 85
  feedback, 79
  finding information in, 86
  formatting, 83–84
  full, 8
  heart of, 166
  inspiring to action, 91
  introduction, 86–87
  length, 7, 118
  letter of inquiry vs., 7
  making easy to follow, 85
  opening pages, 97–102
  opening paragraphs, 96–97,
    102–5
  over-the-transom, 15
  packet, 9–10
  parts of, 7
  readability of, 84–85
  requirements, 8
  reviewing, 10
  unsolicited, 35
  visually/factually accessible,
    81–82
  winning, 3, 5
  writing steps for, 8–10
Proposal abstract, 7, 10, 11,
    117. *See also* Executive
    summary; Proposal
    summary
  condensing, 223
  content, 223–24
  defined, 222
  example, 225–27
  formatting, 225

headings, 225
length, 223–24
placement of, 223, 227
questions for, 223–24
requirements for, 223
space limitations, 223–24
as stand-alone piece, 222
technique for, 223–25
Proposal mapping, 82–83, *83*
Proposal narrative, 9, 10
  defined, 7
Proposal organization
  brainstorming, 82
  proposal mapping, 82–83, *83*
  structure and, 81–82
Proposal summary, 11, 222. *See
  also* Executive summary;
  Proposal abstract
Public foundations, 206–7
Public grant sources, 4
Public policy, 24, 57. *See also*
  Political ideology

Qualitative evaluation, 200
Quantitative evaluation, 200
Query letter, 119
Questions. *See also* Answers
  answering, in statement of
    need, 125, 150
  for fundable projects, 23–24
  for goals, 169
  of grantmakers, 9
  logic answering, 94–95
  for objectives, 169
  for outcomes, 169–70
  for project activities, 169–70
  for project dissemination,
    201–2
  for proposal abstract, 223–24

RAG. *See* Regional Association
    of Grantmakers
Random tricks writer's block
    technique, 113
Rationale vs. method, 95
Readability, 84–85. *See also*
    Editing; Formatting
Reader, 5
Recruitment, project
    dissemination and, 202
Regional Association of
    Grantmakers (RAG), 89,
    216
Rejections, 6, 31
  asking why, 79
  charting, 76–79, *77*
  learning from, 76–79
Relationships, cover letter
    solidifying, 229–30

Replicability
  in methodology, 29
  in project design, 29
  project dissemination and,
    203–4
Request for proposals (RFP), 8,
    69, 75, 124, 130, 175, 211,
    225, 230
  buzzwords in, 62
  defined, 15
  fund matching and, 38
  government grants, 72
Research
  for activism purposes, 54–55
  grantmakers, 19–20, 31–32
  for policy purposes, 53–54
  problem-solving approach
    and, 52–53
  roadmap, *33*
Responsibility, 6
Responsive evaluation, 196
Résumés, 75, 146. *See also*
    Curricula vitae
Review committees, 66
  foundations, 68–69
  government grants, 72–74
  writing style for, 73–74
Review criteria, 9
  defined, 15
  for government grants,
    74–75
  writing style for, 75
Reviewers, 5. *See also*
    Evaluators
  appreciating, 79
  comments by, 78
Reviewing
  grants made, 32, 34
  proposals, 10
RFP. *See* Request for proposals

Section tabs, 86
Shadowing writer's block
    technique, 111
Short proposals
  difficulties with, 136
  example, 131–36
  formatting, 131
  writing, 130–31
Smith Richardson Foundation,
    53
SOA. *See* Solicitation of
    applications
Societal problems, 36–37
Solicitation of applications
    (SOA), 15
So what method
  for fundable projects, 24–25
  for goal statement, 170

as writer's block technique, 112

Specificity, in budget narrative, 212

Staffing. *See also* People
capacity for, 175
of foundations, 42–43, 67–68
of grantmaker's, 229

Statement of need, 11, 117
answering why of project, 125
beneficiaries in, 154
capacity met in, 154–55
conveying urgency, 165
demonstrating knowledge of field, 152–53
examples, 155–65
issues clarified with, 151–52
in letter of inquiry, 125–26
placement of, 150
problem-solving approach presented in, 153–54
questions to answer, 125, 150

Strategies
grantwriting, 4
project sustainability, 219–20

Stuck on you writer's block technique, 112

Subject matter
categories, 37
for fund matching, 36–37
other, in writer's block techniques, 113
in writing, 113

"Such as," 177, 179

Summative evaluation, 195–96

Support, in cover letter, 229

Table of contents, 86

Tax code designation, 35

Techniques. *See also* Writer's block techniques
cover letters, 231
determining outcomes, 172–82
determining project activities, 172–82
goals, 170–71
letter of inquiry, 121
objectives, 170–71
proposal abstract, 223–25
selecting project titles, 106–8

Templates, 88

Timeline, 9
for project activities, 176–77, *178*
as timesaver, 88

Timesavers
budgets, 88
common forms, 88–89
language library, 87–88
templates, 88
timelines/charts, 88

Trends
of grantmakers, 40–41
identifying, 41

"2009 Foundation Giving Forecast," 3

United Way, 155–62, 198
Outcome Measurement Resource Network, 194

Utilization evaluation, 196

Vision statements, 230

Voice, 2. *See also* Language; Writing style

W. K. Kellogg Foundation, 197

Walk 'n' talk writer's block technique, 110

Websites
Associated Grant Makers, 216
Center on Philanthropy, Indiana University, 41
Chronicle of Philanthropy, 41, 65, 68
Department Education, U.S., 215
Department of Housing and Urban Development, U.S., 215
Department of Labor, U.S., 205
Foundation Center, 3, 31, 38, 41, 68, 215
Foundation Directory Online, 32
Giving USA, 41
Google search engine, 68
GuideStar, 32
Independent Sector, 41
JM Foundation, 61
Marquis, 65
NCIIA, 104

Philanthropy News Digest, 38, 65, 68
RAG forum, 89, 216
United Way, 194
W. K. Kellogg Foundation, 197

Words. *See also* Buzzwords
choice of, 2
conveying voice, 2
effective, 1–2
power of, 108

Work continued, 29

Writer's block techniques
backward from ideal, 112
cocktail party, 111
cut 'n' paste, 111
disorderly conduct, 109–10
mind-mapping, 110
random tricks, 113
shadowing, 111
so what method, 112
stuck on you, 112
walk 'n' talk, 110
writing on other subject matter, 113

Writing. *See also* Grantwriters; Grantwriting; Writer's block techniques
academic, 93
as if talking to friend, 90–91
short proposals, 130–31
skills, 13
steps for proposals, 8–10
subject matter in, 113

Writing style
for audience, 80
building-a-case, 70
conciseness in, 72
for corporations, 71–72
for foundations, 69–70
for government grants, 75
overall advice for, 79–80
for review committees, 73–74
for review criteria, 75
technical/nontechnical language in, 80

YMCA, 34

Z. Smith Reynolds Foundation Inc., 55–56

ABOUT THE AUTHOR

No child has ever said, "I want to be a grantwriter when I grow up!" and **Deborah S. Koch** was no exception. Yet she has raised millions of dollars for higher education and community nonprofits, and has developed a unique approach to grantseeking—a career she came to through a series of unintended stepping-stones, beginning with a five-year stint as the Grants and Projects staffperson in a West Virginia congressman's office. After receiving an MPA from the John F. Kennedy School of Government at Harvard University, Ms. Koch advanced to foundation fundraising from a research and public policy background.

Ms. Koch has published several works, including *Mission Possible: 202 Ways to Strengthen the Nonprofit Sector's Infrastructure* and *The Nonprofit Policy Agenda*. She has conducted numerous grantseeking workshops around the country and has consulted for groups such as the Council on Foundations, the National Council of Nonprofit Associations, the Foundation Center, and the Kellogg Foundation. She has worked as a research and writing consultant, and served as director of foundation relations at a large university. Currently working as director of grants for Springfield Technical Community College, Ms. Koch lives in Northampton, Massachusetts, with her husband, Charlie, in a little house with a big view.

T17.0410